Praise for *Navigating the Future*

"You will be brilliantly coached how to move from your fractured perceptions and personal confusion into a more evolved and manageable personal vision."

—STEVE KORNICIJK
VICE PRESIDENT OF CREATIVE AFFAIRS,
NEIMAN MARCUS

"Reading these pages lifted my spirit. For once someone has captured the power, passion and pleasure of what lies before us. *Navigating the Future* is highly readable, urgently compelling and unfailingly accessible."

—ISSIARA BEY
DIRECTOR OF CORPORATE AFFAIRS,
SONY MUSIC ENTERTAINMENT GROUP

"The authors tell us we are getting smarter. Indeed, *Navigating the Future* stimulates a fresh response and our natural creativity in a succinct and graceful text."

—MARILYN FERGUSON
AUTHOR OF *AQUARIAN CONSPIRACY*

"Drawing on their many years of facilitating personal growth, the Tarlows have provided us with a powerful and practical guide for transformation and optimal health in the 21st century."

—ROBERT S. IVKER, D.O.
PRESIDENT OF THE AMERICAN HOLISTIC MEDICAL ASSOCIATION
AND AUTHOR OF THE BEST-SELLING *SINUS SURVIVAL*

"The Tarlows have tapped into one of the keyholes to another set of possibilities that will make life workable in our entirely new future environment."

—DIANA NALL BROWNE
VICE PRESIDENT,
SYSTEMS DEVELOPMENT INFORMATION SYSTEMS,
PARAMOUNT PICTURES

A
&

Personal
&

Guide to
&

Achieving
&

Success
&

in the

Navigating
THE
FUTURE

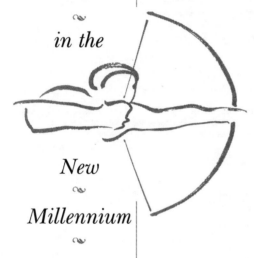

New
&

Millennium
&

Mikela Tarlow, *M.A., M.Ed.*
With Philip Tarlow

McGRAW-HILL
New York   San Francisco   Washington, D.C.   Auckland   Bogotá
Caracas   Lisbon   London   Madrid   Mexico City   Milan
Montreal   New Delhi   San Juan   Singapore
Sydney   Tokyo   Toronto

Library of Congress Cataloging-in-Publication Data

Tarlow, Mikela.
     Navigating the future : a personal guide to achieving success in
the next millennium / Mikela Tarlow with Philip Tarlow.
        p.   cm.
     ISBN 0-07-063364-9 (alk. paper)
     1. Change (Psychology)   2. Future life—Psychological aspects.
I. Tarlow, Philip. II. Title.
BF637.C4T37   1999
158—dc21   98-23201
                                            CIP

McGraw-Hill

*A Division of The **McGraw·Hill** Companies*

1 2 3 4 5 6 7 8 9 0   DOC/DOC   9 0 3 2 1 0 9 8

ISBN 0-07-063364-9

Printed and bound by R.R. Donnelley & Sons Company.

McGraw-Hill books are available at special quantity discounts to use as premiums and sales promotions, or for use in corporate training programs. For more information, please write to the Director of Special Sales, McGraw-Hill, 11 West 19th
Street, New York, NY 10011. Or contact your local bookstore.

Contents

PART 3 WHAT WILL WE FIND?
The Other Side of the Portal

Preface

This "journey in words" arises out of my own close encounter with the future. And although I am the one putting the words to paper, my husband, Philip, is a co-author in the sense that we traveled the journey together and the core ideas arose out of a shared personal search.

It's been more than six years now since we decided to take a few months off without working. We had been traveling more than half the year, leading seminars all over the world, and keeping an equally intense schedule while at home. At the same time we took a break from our workaholic lifestyle, we also decided to move from south Florida to the Bay area, a dramatic change in our social world. These far-reaching life changes unleashed an avalanche of feelings. The few months "sabbatical" we had planned soon stretched to almost 15.

Everyone thinks they would love a year off to do nothing. But it can be far more soul-wrenching than you might imagine! I can only describe this period as a deconstruction of our identity; all the external cues that had given our lives form had suddenly vanished. What had been driving us for so many years suddenly seemed so much less important. Then we reached a point in this journey, seemingly to nowhere, where we realized we could never go back. We could no longer do things the way we once did.

It was only out of our eventual willingness to throw out *everything* that glimmers of a new direction appeared. Out of the emptiness of this space, we began to discover a new more natural relationship to our bodies, our feelings, our stories about ourselves, and our entire approach to taking action. These experiments were the seeds for the material you'll find in this book.

I don't believe what we went through was just "burnout" or midlife crisis. The shifts we discovered came out of a need to create a much more dynamic and creative relationship to our future.

We began sharing these ideas in our seminars and discovered that although not many people have taken a year off as we did, quite a few have begun their own versions of the journey we're on, or at least have begun to ask many of the same questions. Most people can relate to the need to radically deconstruct their present way of doing things, to break from an unsatisfying momentum in their lives, to discover a new order of perception and action that is far more meaningful and closer to their hearts.

Most people can relate to the loss of direction that an accelerating culture provokes. Once-predictable events have taken a course of their own. Real issues are masked by smoke and mirrors. New possibilities stare us in the face, often forcing an encounter whether we like it or not. Rapid change is provoking long submerged and unchartered feelings. And now with the future barreling at us like an F-16 coming down the runway, there's nowhere to run. We have no choice but to face what is coming. And that is the purpose of this book, to help you face what is coming.

The main discovery we made during our period of reexamination is that the future is in fact accessible to us now, *if you know where to look.* Even modern physics supports our personal insight and suggests that there may be as many as nine more dimensions curled up inside of what we currently see, much like the petals of a flower not yet opened.

I offer the Zen archer as a metaphor for how we can begin to think about the future. It is said an accomplished Zen archer can hit a bull's eye even if he is blindfolded. He is able to do this not because he has a keener eye or a steadier hand. He internalizes the target; *the bull's eye is accomplished within himself.* Releasing the bow is merely a reflection of a more perfect internal state. He touches his desired future by carving out new possibilities within himself. Typically, we relate to the future as a faraway event, an imaginary target representing our unrealized dreams.

> *Throughout this book I define the future not as something that exists out there in time but as the moment you transcend habitual patterns and touch something that is truly beyond what you already know.*

The future will not be reached by the mere progression of time or expansion of technological opportunities, it will be reached only by delving into our own hearts and minds. It is at this personal edge that the true shape of the future will be forged.

Our journey into the hyperspeed, digitalized, holographic world of the new millennium will be guided by the same principles travelers have used since the beginnings of time. We will be guided by the equivalent of a polestar—centerpoints within our psyches; still places within our own nature that can most accurately sense where we must go.

Reaching a desirable future does not rely on the magnitude of choices we are handed. It depends on our ability to navigate, to chart a viable personal course no matter how perilous or seductive the cultural terrain. The ability to navigate rests on a growing internal complexity, a new kind of intelligence that is slowly making its way into the heart and mind of each and every one of us.

In the coming pages, I merely put into words experiences you are already feeling. I provide a road map for a journey *you are already on.*

MIKELA TARLOW

Acknowledgments

I want to first thank all the people who have taken our seminars and who helped us develop the threads of these ideas. I cannot begin to acknowledge all the people who encouraged us through the years to write this book and who believed in our work. There are really too many to name. So I will limit myself to people who directly influenced the content of the book, sometimes without knowing it. Thank you Fred for your inspiration for the title and your ever brilliant way of describing what is; Joan for the Emotions of Change and your poetry of feelings; Kevin for Mythmaking and a lot of other stuff; Nancye for Shadow Dancing and for your unshakable faith in us; Lorraine and David for the Sweat chapter; Marvin, believe it or not, for the Relationship chapter; Meredith for Accelerating Results and all your incredible questions about this topic. I also must thank Parmananda, Rita, David, Zia, Wendy, Charles, Diana, Mark, Jay, Lisa, Isisara, Ann, and Stephen for your friendship over the years. To Ron and Kimberly, thank you for *always* asking about this book. To everyone at Gremillion, your love of the arts and artists helps make this world a saner place.

I am deeply grateful for having met our agent, Howard Yoon. You made it easy from the very first time we talked. Your patience, persistence, and intelligence were invaluable, especially in those days when our ideas were in their infancy. And thank you for giving us the phrase, "Psychological Futurism."

Thanks to our editor Mary Glenn for always believing in what we wanted to say. Thank you for "getting it," right from the start. On quite a few occasions, you saw things more clearly than we did. It has been a pleasure working with you and all the McGraw-Hill staff every step of the way.

I also want to thank the people of this wonderful town we live in. There is something about the wacky spirit of this place that has allowed me to feel like I have a home for the first time in my life. And I thank the magnificent mountains and powerful land for its magical inspiration.

Finally, I want to thank Philip's family: Roy, Mary, Liz, Ken, Gail, Tracy, David, Mort, Doris, Arthur, Marina, and Philip's son Dimitri. None of my immediate family is alive, so for the last 15 years you have been my family. If I sometimes miss the mark on the "family thing," please know that I am truly grateful that each and every one of you are in my life. Thank you Liz, Mary, and Roy for your support, and especially Mary for your very valuable comments on the text.

More than anything, it means so much to me that at 87, Philip's father, Roy, has his first book being published, *The Seed of Creation*. Roy, I felt your strength and commitment as we both wrote together over the last few years. It is an extraordinary gift to have shared with you. I am also so thrilled that you have already started your second book. When we walk along the streets of New York, it's a challenge and a delight just trying to keep up with your pace, literally and figuratively. The way you are flowing into the future inspires me to believe that life mainly wants us to keep getting fuller, richer, more vital, more creative, and more productive with every passing day.

A Note to the Reader

The soul thinks, understands, and communicates in images. Each chapter, therefore, begins with a story, or an image, the purpose of which is to convey the essence of the chapter. The soul *remembers* images, and the rhythms of movement. Even if you forget the details of a chapter, the story allows you to remember the spirit of what was said and to continue to explore the energy framework that underlies the ideas.

Every chapter is written so that the key ideas are easily discovered. I have constructed the book to serve an effective reading style: Try skimming this book first and then going back to read in more depth. With the use of boldface emphasis, topic headings, and illustrations, I have made it easy to quickly find core ideas. If you find that some material does not interest you at first, you can skim without losing meaning until you get to a part that piques your interest again.

Knowledge is best grounded in action. We learn best when we have to do something. Therefore, each of the eight navigational tools which comprise the heart of the book is followed by a practice section, practical ideas and processes that you can perform on your own.

I am a big believer in the power of groups to move each individual along faster, and most of the seminar work Philip and I do is through small groups. Learning is more fun with other people. At the close of the book is a reader's guide which offers ideas for reading this book in a group. It gives points of discussion and ideas for small group exploration.

Introduction: The Stargate Dilemma

You are on an archeological dig somewhere in the Middle East. It's hot, dusty, and tedious. Day after day the sun beats down on you as you remove a few more shovels full of sand and find nothing but an occasional pottery shard here and there.

Then one day you strike what seems to be pure stone. With growing anticipation, you shovel and sweep away more sand, revealing a massive doorway coded with unintelligible characters. After some investigation you surmise that it was not built by ancient people, but rather is a portal left behind by an alien race. This is the opening premise of the movie *Stargate*.

Relentless futurist that I am, naturally I was first in line, popcorn in hand and ready for action, when *Stargate* came out.

> The team of archeologists stumbles upon this door. They assume the writing is code which, if understood, could unlock the secrets of the future. Years later, with great fanfare, they break the code. When they turn the final key, the door opens and reveals an interdimensional path into space and time, fully equipped, of course, with fabulous special effects! A team of explorers then gathers to take the journey through time to undiscovered galaxies. They cross a threshold into what promises to be a world of entirely new possibilities.
>
> When they reach the other side, they encounter the people who left this Stargate. The masses, it turns out, are fearful, bereft of hope, and possess almost no power in their society. The leader is a despicable character, greedy and cruel, who uses powerful weapons to keep his people enslaved. Predictably, the explorers are left with no choice but to overthrow the leader and free the masses.

After seeing this movie with a friend, her only comment was, "Here they go all that way, light years into the future, across untold galaxies, at great personal risk, into realms of power we have only imagined, and all the film makers can envision is someone with a bigger gun. Why bother? We might as well have stayed home!"

This is exactly the kind of problem we are up against. We can modify our genes, split and rejoin atoms, send probes to the far reaches of the solar system, make almost any product computer smart, play with nanotechnology, construct robotlike devices that can move around in submicroscopic realms where we can play God and begin to rearrange the very structure of matter, **but we just can't escape our feelings.**

We have opened a door into the future, hoping that free markets, unbridled capitalism, and new technologies will usher in an era of abundance, leisure, and peace. Yet much of our current news coverage points to a future that might not be so rosy. The sinister side of what lies ahead reveals itself in tales of global sweat shops, child prostitution, terrorism on the rise, stolen nuclear weapons, heightening cultural tensions, ruthless multinationals, social decay of our cities, corrupt governments, horrifying new diseases, environmental degradation, the same old greed and corruption. Our world has become increasingly fractured, and we as individuals have become more isolated, fatigued, and anxious. With every year a growing number of us suffer clinical depression, panic disorders, chronic fatigue, stress-related diseases, a growing inability to make our relationships last, disillusionment with our careers, and an extraordinary phenomenon called "time sickness," the sensation of moving so fast that you can no longer correctly sense the passage of time. It's no wonder we would sometimes rather just stay home under the covers.

The more ominous the future appears, the more we shut down.

If it's that out of control, who wants to think about what lies ahead; we want to just carve out a shelter from the storm for ourselves and our families. When problems seem too challenging, it's natural to try to forget. We cope by focusing on an ever narrower pursuit of self-interest. We stay away from the tough questions, yearning to have it simple again. The only problem with this quite natural response is that all lasting motivation arises from a faith in the future. Without faith, without motivation, we all give up.

This book tries to make the future feel a little more manageable, somewhat more hopeful, and a lot more motivating. **More than anything, I want to rekindle your passion for the future.**

Where Is the Future?

Although this book is about our future, there's little talk about technological advances. "Tomorrow" depends less on the direction of technology than on the direction of our own psyches.

> ➤ How often have you enthusiastically thrown yourself into a new project, only to find the same nagging emptiness on the other side?
>
> ➤ How often have you participated in a promising new business solution, only to find that in the end, the same problems popped up again in different form?
>
> ➤ How often have you begun working with a new client or colleague or entered a new relationship, with great anticipation, only to encounter the same patterns and the same disappointments as in the past?
>
> ➤ Maybe you or your company has ventured into new digital art forms or new information solutions, yet you find no discernible increase in your efficiency or expansion of your creativity.

Growth is *always* compromised by personal resistance and habits. Despite technological progress, most of us have more stress, less time, and function within ever-shrinking creative windows. The promise of a communication renaissance becomes irrelevant if you burn out along the way. A world of unlimited possibilities is pointless if you are not healthy enough to be in it. This is the dilemma posed by Stargate: **How can you discover a future that is truly beyond what you already have?**

Of course, our future will be shaped in part by an unfolding information economy and a digital culture that transcends geographic boundaries. It will also be shaped by the quality of public discourse and how we construct our social myths. Another dimension will take shape through new organizational styles and innovative business solutions. Still other domains will be shaped by artists and the creative directions they pioneer. Even so, common to every one of these determinants of the future is the individual and the very personal ways each of us devises to handle stress, perceive change, construct purpose, and evolve relationships. Tomorrow will always be driven by practical, everyday, personal creative breakthroughs.

new artistic directions
emerging organizational styles and business solutions
Ultimately it is our personal psychology that will drive the future.
changing social myths and the quality of public discourse
an uncharted information economy and a digital culture

A Psychological Futurism

A great deal has been written about the kinds of business structures that will be most suited to the turbulence that lies ahead, yet little has been written about the kinds of people who will be best suited to this ride. This is why I choose to focus on the part of the future locked in our own very personal response, the small shifts in how we transform our perceptions, ideas, and actions.

This new focus for exploration I call **psychological futurism,** an examination of how the individual can evolve more effectively in fast-moving and turbulent systems. It is an understanding based on the common patterns of how we develop responses to new cultural demands.

In the rush to capitalize on technological breakthroughs we tend to ignore the impact of continuous sweeping change on the individual psyche. This is probably because both the human psyche and the future are far messier, fuzzier, and more complex than any technical problem ever is. But the shape of technological progress ultimately hinges on the people who use it. Therefore, a business owner dealing with transforming markets needs *new perceptual skills.* When old values and traditions disappear almost overnight, we need *new emotional paths* for dealing with the instability that results. Businesses will meet the requirement for *new relationship skills,* or they will be faced with an ever more dissatisfied work force. It is issues like these and thousands more that call for psychological futurism, as a way of coming to grips with the new demands.

> When I compare how much money has been invested in technology
> versus that spent on understanding social dynamics—
> how behavior evolves in these environments—it's a hugely baffling imbalance.
> And yet so much hinges on understanding the latter.
>
> John Hagel, coauthor of *Net Gain* [1]

With the right keys, every individual, business, and community has the opportunity to enter a world of unprecedented renewal. Yet it is all pointless unless we understand the nature of the journey we are undertaking and rewrite the close of the story. Otherwise, we could have an ending that would undermine any vision we might have of the future. The 12 chapters of this book take you through the three stages essential to rewriting the "Stargate dilemma."

Part 1: Finding the Portal

It's human nature to look to the future. We have always studied the skies for clues about what lies ahead. Wise leaders would observe the tides of restlessness sweeping the tribe and devise proclamations that would stay one step ahead of the group. Our hunter/gatherer forebears honed an invisible sense of where to find the best game and the finest berries. Divination and prophecy were legitimate and revered skills in ancient times. A few correct hits assured the ancient futurist a favored place very close to the king. **In fact, knowing the future has always been one of the quickest routes to power.**

Now millennium fever is making futurism highly fashionable. Sometimes it seems as if almost everyone has a take on where we are heading. Yet the most important thing about all the scenario building and future tripping is that it opens the door for each of us to begin tuning into our own personal sense of what lies ahead.

Awakening our ability to see unfolding patterns may be the most important psychological skill we can cultivate.

The first part of this book is designed to awaken your sense of what's to come. In it, I describe a series of thresholds that lie ahead in the hope of provoking your own "memories" of the future.

The future exists in that subtle zone where what we already know magically dissolves into something yet to be imagined. Unless we find this "edge" in our personal and professional lives, we will not progress. Unless we identify this threshold in a very meaningful way, we will continue to conduct business as usual and thereby miss a very important portal. *Going somewhere new always requires finding an entrance never before taken.*

Part 2: Eight Navigational Tools

The next task is to get through the door. This is the fun part. Remember, it's the part of the journey that comes with great special effects. An accelerating culture brings with it information glut, uncharted moral decisions, unprecedented stress, transient relationships, confusion of purpose, and a sea of emotional challenges. In fact, our current culture may have already advanced beyond our psychological capabilities.

Since we can't turn back the clock, we need skills for catching up. This does not mean developing more intricate plans and visions. Catching up to the unique rhythm of the time means experiencing our present-time actions from a new perspective. It means learning to feel, sense, and think in entirely new patterns.

If we persist in our current habits and opinions, the shape of tomorrow will already have been cast. Only if we can change our perspectives and patterns through everyday action can the "future" even exist. Section 2 explores the eight ways to shift and expand your current patterns of behavior.

Part 3: The Other Side of the Portal

Although the behavioral shifts I outline in the second section are often subtle, their impact can be huge. If a rocket alters direction even a fraction of a percent, it's destination can change to an entirely different galaxy. In the same way, we can discover entirely new destinations for ourselves just by making small shifts in our ordinary activities.

In his great play *Pygmalion*, George Bernard Shaw says if you expect great things from someone, then that person will tend to step into the shoes you provide. Educators even refer to this as the "Pygmalion effect;" what a teacher is told in advance about a student can significantly affect the teacher's expectation and the student's subsequent success. There is now a powerful body of research to confirm this thesis. Optimists really do tend to have better things happen for them. Those who have expanded models of the world tend to have more peak experiences. It follows that if our expectation of the future is designed with greater wisdom and creativity, it may affect how our collective story turns out.

With a heightened future sense, we may actually shift the course of our collective destiny.

One of the most profound problems facing our culture is that we don't have transitional stories. Other than a very skimpy image that our politicians have suggested about building a bridge to the twenty-first century, we don't have many road maps. Despite an abundance of options, we often don't really know where we want to go. Unless we can powerfully picture the other side of the doorway, our present will come to a standstill. We won't want to move ahead.

A final assumption shaping this book is that our *collective* future hinges on how we each manage our very *personal* vision of what lies ahead.

Philip and I work with people from all walks of life: heads of corporations, managers, artists, entrepreneurs, the self-employed, and people between careers. We have begun to notice that whatever the outward circumstances of their lives, *people are getting smarter.*

People are always shocked to hear this. With so much written about the "dumbing" of America and the decline of public discourse, with so many individuals feeling burned out and disconnected, with so much of what we see and hear seeming to be in decline, it's hard to imagine we are getting smarter.

When I look around, I see a culture becoming aware of itself. People are being stirred to connect with a more sustainable future. They are becoming more real about the issues that confront them. People are taking extraordinarily selfless and courageous actions. The part of us that is getting smarter is the part of us that is beginning to circle closer to what is really important, our personal strengths and our innermost hopes. We are becoming smarter in ways that are starting to echo each other. There are common paths we will each take for moving through a culture that is being fractured and fused into a wild sea of choices. My purpose is to make these common threads understandable, useful, and practical in everyday life.

PART 1

WHERE ARE WE HEADED?

Finding the Portal

A villager in a remote Brazilian town accompanied a visiting anthro-pologist to the capital city. Having never ventured beyond the rain for-est, the villager had no idea what to expect. When he reached the city, he gasped in disbelief at what he saw. When he returned to his village, he could not stop talking about his adventure.

"There was something called a wheelbarrow, I saw it with my own eyes!" he said. "Do you realize how many bananas I could carry? More than I could ever possibly need at one time!"

He didn't even mention the skyscrapers, automobiles, or computers he had seen. He never even registered them. They were so far removed from his life in the rain forest that there was no way he could make sense of them. He went to the city and saw only a wheelbarrow.

There is a little bit of this villager in all of us. We look at our world and register only what is familiar. We wake up each day and, since it appears to look almost like yesterday, we assume nothing very important has changed. Although many of us have already begun building our huts in the global village, we still persist in seeing events through the same filters we have always used.

I invite you to take a journey into the future; a journey beyond your famil-iar perceptual world. I will hold a mirror to the waves of social change that are reconfiguring our world and reveal an image of unprecedented per-sonal transformation. I will disclose an interior landscape, currents that are sweeping our psyches just beneath the surface of our ordinary awareness. I will uncover a part of our personal experience that is inseparable from larger cultural forces. I will introduce you to the **spirit of our time**.

CHAPTER 1

The Spirit of Our Time

To begin the journey takes an understanding of what makes this particular time unique. The historian Arnold Toynbee felt there were always overarching psychic forces that are the true shapers of history. Every era possesses clear emotional dynamics that its "collective soul" is trying to understand. Out of the seemingly divergent directions a culture may take, a voice of vision is always struggling to be heard. The Germans called this the *zeitgeist,* the spirit of the time.

So, how does the zeitgeist operate? If you look at a TV show or school book from the fifties, it is as if a different language is being spoken. The images appear so antiquated. How did we ever fall for this stuff? Even a TV show or magazine article from just 10 years ago seems hopelessly dated. Yet at the time, not only did these images make sense, they seemed cutting edge.

The spirit of a time is the invisible filter that organizes the disparate events into a *gestalt,* or unified perception. That is why these images made sense back then and they don't now; our filter has changed.

When the spirit of the time shifts, past interpretations no longer hold water.

It is easy to describe the spirit of past decades. In hindsight, the tempo of the time looks much more coherent than when it is being lived.

➤ Imagine Sandra Dee singing in the background; sit back and relax as you ease into the denial of the fifties. Race, pain, and rebellion were not yet issues in this "apple pie" world. Plastic, the creative highlight of the day, became a driving metaphor for the decade. Lucy was on TV, endlessly trying to break out of her housewife role, always knowing that Ricky would be there to save her from her failed attempts. Conformity reigned, adolescence was not yet such a difficult experience, and *father still knew best.*

➤ Now switch to the sixties and Donovan singing "Hurdy Gurdy Man" or Joni Mitchell wistfully telling us that "we've paved paradise." As the first man landed on the moon, we "transcended" into a psychedelic haze that began to blow our minds and caused us to question the very appearance of reality. At the same time strong seeds of cynicism were being sown as we saw that our world was not what it appeared. Shamanic teachings and eastern thought crossed the borders and often seemed more relevant than what our leaders were offering us.

➤ The assassinations of Martin Luther King and John and Robert Kennedy, race riots, and the spiritual devastation of the Vietnam War took such a toll we had to escape. War protesters turned into Wall Street brokers and our rage was channeled into the rampant greed of the eighties. Disco and pop numbed our souls. Psychedelics gave way to alcohol and downers. No one was "home" when the country was sold to the highest bidder. Only the voice of the hood beginning to trickle into rappers' songs and a few lonely ecologists suggested that perhaps not all was right in this Reagan-inspired fantasy world.

➤ Gen-X inherited a culture without direction. Anything goes, nothing matters. All our familiar paths had washed out. Everything became darker: the songs, the crimes, the scandals, the denial. Terrorism became the weapon of choice for a system that fosters powerlessness. Then came the Net, the perfect drug and the key to a revolution. Sadly, this creative revolution often was consumed by the insatiable appetite of the marketplace.

As these brief scenarios show, a very, very different energy drives each era. The images, the songs, the advertising, the news are all seen through the filter of the current zeitgeist. **The spirit of the time shapes the dreams we dream, the questions we ask, the possibilities we entertain, even our definitions of creativity.**

So what is the spirit shaping the beginning of the new millennium? What are the invisible forces modifying the course of world events? Can we discover a gestalt that will allow this emerging era to make sense?

A wave of modern day prophets have appeared with visions of how the next few decades will unfold. Every month *Wired* magazine offers a column in which experts in various fields offer odds and a date for when a particular future development is likely to occur. We are inundated with professional opinions about which trends are likely and new versions of the *real* reason our culture is in trouble.

My purpose is not to debate the relative merits of these views or even to offer my own version of what trends are most likely to emerge. My purpose is to shed light on a spirit that is underlying our interpretation of all these diverse events, a larger gestalt that is weaving together a maze of differing directions.

A Second Curve World

If you examine the futurist literature, there is a key visual and conceptual image that keeps showing up. The Tofflers describe a third wave, an information wave sweeping through society and overtaking the assumptions of the second wave, industrial world. Others describe a postindustrial world, a cultural breakpoint that will finally still our rampant consumption and usher in a new domain of motivations. Still others define a new paradigm of thought that is repatterning all manner of human activity. In each case, the underlying image is comparable and unfolds in a four-part model that looks like this:

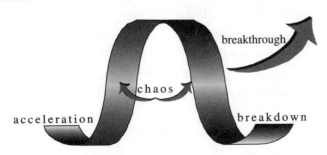

This image is a template of sorts. Often when we look out at events, they appear unrelated. If you could somehow magically look beneath these appearances, you would see a network of patterns that are linking together everything from political events to very personal experiences. There is an energetic integrity, much like the anatomy of the body, that is giving shape to all our social forms. The image shown above represents a pulse that is beginning to beat so loud, we are all moving to the new rhythm. It is a cognitive pattern that is infiltrating every domain of behavior. This image of one curve dissolving into another is beginning to leave it's stamp everywhere we turn.

For now, I will spell out each of these four phases in more detail. Even if you are already familiar with this image of acceleration leading to breakdown, chaos, and subsequent breakthrough, you will find it of interest to see how much of the popular business and personal advice fits into this model, and more important, how much of what you experience on a daily basis can be explained by this cycle.

1. Surfs Up!

In the last three decades, we have gained an average of five extra hours per week of leisure time, yet you would be hard pressed to find anyone who actually feels that they have more time. The acceleration we all feel is far more complex than having too much to do. It is more a result of a complexity or density of information and experience that we must integrate. The shortening of our attention spans makes it seem as if things are moving faster, as we process more and more bits per hour. Traditional boundaries have collapsed so we move into new situations much faster. Layers of meaning and layers of tasks are placed one on top of the other, so nothing is simple and sequential any more.

We all feel strangely compelled to keep moving faster. Unconsciously, we begin to crave the intensity of experience. Subliminal messages everywhere are telling us that acceleration is in fact a form of power.

The waves are coming in faster and bigger than at any time in history, a degree of change greater than the industrial revolution, in one-tenth the time.

In a geometric curve like the one on the following page, the volume doubles in ever shorter time intervals. It is best known perhaps as the pop-

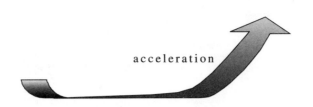

acceleration

ulation curve, showing that the population once took 1000 years to double, then 200 years, then 50, then 10, and so forth. This same type of curve can now be used to represent expansion or acceleration in almost every area of human experience: the extinction of species, increases in computing capacity, scientific developments, loss of topsoil, demands on water supplies, use of wind generators, growth of the World Wide Web, individuals reporting paranormal phenomena, and on and on. Every area of human activity, positive and negative, seems to be escalating exponentially, and the pressure is driving business, relationships, and our own psyches.

Relentless acceleration infiltrates all that we do. It shapes the choices we make and the values we serve.

The unrelenting acceleration of events leads to the fear of being left behind. In just the past few years, we've been subjected to a wave of advice that says only those who can turn on a dime will thrive in the years ahead. Ample evidence is given of corporate "dinosaurs" who saw their market share evaporate almost overnight because they did not adapt to the new business climate. Individuals come out of nowhere to become cultural idols and just as quickly become forgotten. Even serious magazines feel it their duty to offer lists of who and what's hot and what's not.

In response, corporate reengineering became the rage, a theoretical framework and justification for getting rid of organizational fat. Just-in-time delivery, products arriving moments before they are needed, meant information needed to be highly tuned to market forces. We were exhorted to become "one minute managers," able to make faster, more intuitive decisions. Even individuals felt the need to "reengineer" by releasing unproductive directions. Terrified to lose the wave, we all run a little faster. Everyone is striving to become nimble and lean, unencumbered by conceptual baggage. Any delay could be fatal; time was more than money, it was survival!

> Every morning the gazelle wakes up and knows
> that he must run faster than the tiger or he will be eaten.
> Every morning the tiger wakes up and knows
> he must run faster than the gazelle or he will starve.
> It doesn't matter if you are a tiger or a gazelle, you better start running.
>
> attributed to the CEO of Home Depot

With success increasingly defined as the ability to inspire and deliver acceleration, hardly anyone has time to question what speed has done to our lives.

Information-based companies need to operate at an even faster pace dictated by "net time." For them, long-range planning is completely irrelevant, a quaint vestige of the past. These companies can't predict days into the future, let alone years. In fact, any fixed corporate or personal agenda might cause you to miss your next clue.

In finance, as institutional stockholders increase their power over corporate boards, the quarterly report is all that matters. The focus shifts to one-hit wonders, killer applications, and fast-profit products. No one has time for long-term strategy or developing talent or culturing a market. Decision making and visioning take place in ever decreasing time frames. Madison Avenue accurately captured the tone in its "just do it" campaign for Nike—don't analyze, don't plan, don't wonder, don't talk, *just do it.*

This relentless acceleration can't help but affect you on a personal level.

➤ You constantly feel the anguish of playing catch-up, as if you've been left at the starting gate while everyone else is already far down the track.

➤ You find yourself discarding ideas you once held dear in favor of an easier sell.

➤ Perhaps the buzz of acceleration has become so addictive you no longer want to unplug; adrenaline has become your new drug.

➤ Or maybe you're beginning to feel it's been a very long time since you stopped to smell the roses, that maybe you have paid too great a price for your new-found speed.

➤ Or you may feel so overwhelmed you just retreat. You spend every free moment "wombing in" just to muster enough energy to survive the next day.

Although the feelings differ in each case, it's speed that is defining what you feel. This context of acceleration is reshaping your values and driving your ideas, the way you communicate, and how you make decisions. *The speed of the market, the speed of the digital world, the speed of financial realities has also become the speed of your very own psyche.*

2. Breaking the Form

The next phase of change carries a very different and distinctive emotional tone. The curious thing about a geometrically accelerating curve is that at some point the speed begins to rattle the stability of the existing system, stressing it to the breaking point. A critical point is reached where no more speed is possible, and existing forms, beliefs, and ideas are no longer adequate to handle the increasing tension.

breakdown

Rapid acceleration inevitably ushers in an era of breakdown and collapse, the second phase of the curve. Whether it is a business experiencing a rise in tension and increased mistakes because it has expanded too quickly or individuals getting fed up because they are overloaded with demands, the process is the same. You begin to question the rules that you have unconsciously accepted and many of the values which have insidiously redesigned your life. Doubt, cynicism, and challenging everything you see are signs that breakdown has begun. In this stage, although you try harder, it brings diminishing returns. More becomes less. Whether it is a failing relationship or a job that no longer interests you, it takes more and more effort just to stay even.

For instance, in business, the craze for downsizing got redesignated as "dumbsizing." Experts began to point out that few gains would be realized by further cutting labor. Many companies were as lean and efficient as they could be. Even with ultrafast communications and flattened hierarchies, productivity often stagnated. There's considerable evidence that the rampant proliferation of information is, in fact, *slowing* our conceptual progress, contributing to a decline in our attention span, oversimplifying public debate, and diluting the impact of any dialogue.[1] Other emerging research suggests that coping with digital-age speed may be tough on our bodies, our imaginations, and our perceptual capabilities.[2] Parents note an inability among children to get excited unless presented with ever bigger and more extraordinary experiences and wonder if this has forever dulled their children's ability to appreciate the simple things in life.

In response, some companies began to ban in-house mail except for limited hours, finding that it created more work, not less, and diminished the quality of employee relations. A new direction of advice emerged telling us to disconnect from the constant buzz if we expect to maintain our sanity. Pundits introduced the new term "downteching" to define a new trend in which individuals and businesses actually power down, simplify their technical solutions, and sometimes even go back to outdated, simpler programs and methods that everyone already knows. Many of the most profitable companies, it turned out, were those that took their time making decisions and hung in with products even though they didn't achieve instant success. In the breakdown phase, it pays to march to a different drummer.

In other words, nimbleness and speed are not the only solutions to new cultural demands. One is to return to fundamentals, old-time business truths and personal values that have nothing to do with what's trendy. "Voluntary simplicity," declaring that enough is enough; "cashing out," leaving behind high overhead lifestyles; and "unplugging," turning off the endless bombardment are all important and growing consumer trends.

When existing assumptions, beliefs, and patterns of action prove inadequate for the volume and variety of exchange that an organization, relationship, or individual must handle, breakdown begins.

A few consultants took the next logical step, advising that if it's not broken yet, break it. We begin to actively search out belief systems to smash. The new economic climate requires that we shake up outmoded features of the corporate culture, our own entrenched habits, and the biases that keep us from catching new trends. The focus of breakdown is to clear away unexamined assumptions, to be less concerned about shortening the learning curve and more focused on shortening the *forgetting curve,* the ability of an individual or business to let go of what they already know.

Everyone wants to go to heaven, but no one wants to die.[3]

James Hillman

According to the business and personal advice of the breakdown phase, the worst insult is to be accused of operating from the dreaded "old paradigm." We now begin thinking outside the box, finding solutions by letting go of our known directions. The new music, often a barometer for the culture, began to worship dissolution and even death. A hip cosmetics company called Urban Decay swept the market with colors named Gash and Uzi. Madison Avenue uses seemingly drugged out, androgynous models in shabby settings to advertise the latest expensive fashions. Benetton created a sensation with ads depicting violence, blood and gore, never once showing one of their brightly colored, yuppie sweaters.

Image-breaking is not only what sells, but curiously it brings some relief from the suffocating acceleration. Twenty-year-olds suddenly emerge as consultants to entertainment and high-tech industries, since experience is now viewed as a liability. Decision makers say they need fresh eyes and naive thinking in order to decide where to go next. Both individuals and companies now must function in a climate of constant redefinition of who they are and even of what their skills, products, or services are. For everyone, dissolution is the new constant.

In this phase of the curve, leadership becomes the ability to break down existing forms and to provoke others to do the same. Scott Adams' immensely successful Dilbert cartoons and books are filled with what might be called "breakdown humor." Irrelevant procedures, forms that have no meaning, and bosses who spout mindless jargon provide abundant fuel for Dilbert, who is constantly subjected to absurd demands. This is not escapist humor. Adams bases Dilbert on real-life stories offered by managers from all over the country. It seems to have hit a vein that was desperately seeking expression.

But despite Dilbert's humorous support, the breakdown phase of change is frequently not as much fun as the acceleration phase, especially on a personal level:

> You may find that your familiar surroundings are beginning to annoy you.

> You mistrust people's motives and doubt ideas that you once accepted as givens.

> Actions that were once meaningful and exciting suddenly feel pointless. Your get up and go has got up and gone. Fantasies of winning the lottery preoccupy your thoughts.

> No one seems to be getting it right or giving you what you want. You feel increasingly ineffectual, frustrated, or disconnected from those around you.

> You want to break from anything that looks familiar. You follow with great interest the stories of corporate executives who chuck it all to write the great American novel or take up farming. Companies like Ben and Jerry's with their "fun days" and CEOs like Richard Branson who parachutes from an airplane to create visibility for the Virgin Empire, seem to be the best models of cutting-edge leadership.

Breakdown is a time of cleaning out, changing priorities, and giving up control. It's a time to confront sacred cows and to realize that a lot of emperors have no clothes.

3. Chaos Rules

Breakdown eventually gives way to the next phase where you have no idea what you're doing and neither does anyone else. When old forms have broken down and new ones are not yet in place, anything goes. We enter a time without rules, a phase when identity begins to unravel. Knowledge is dismantled and invisible forces seem to reign.

The next wave of advisors told us that if we *think* we know what's coming, if we think we've figured things out, if we're still giving everything a name and a description, then we are really in trouble, because we have not embraced the magic of chaos. Leaping into the void is the way to tap into one's deepest levels of creativity. Unless you can let go of conceptual and emotional assumptions, you can never allow anything bigger to enter.

Descriptions of the X generation would suggest it's already well equipped for an era of chaos—fluid identity, unattached to outcomes, the ability to dismiss persuasion, a distrust of appearances, and little need for commitment. These descriptors, however, have less to do with an age group than a mindset for coping with a culture without form.

The world was made from nothing and the nothing keeps showing through.[4]

Briggs and Peat

In response, many software companies adopted a style of product development in which the product is purposely delivered before it is fully finished. Their customers then work out the bugs and the product is modified on the fly. This is particularly efficient for software, since legions of computer whizzes stand ever-ready to descend on a new product to patch the holes. It is an effective way of riding chaos: Don't figure it out; allow market forces to go where they want and complete the task. In fact, some analysts think that Japan's commitment to quality that worked so well for cars translated poorly into the software arena. Trying to work out the bugs in advance kept them hopelessly behind the curve. Chaotic markets don't respond to attempts at perfection because unseen forces are always more of a factor than you can ever imagine. Fast punches and quick reaction time are far more appropriate skills.

In times of chaos, edges blur and normal definitions erode.

Ads masquerade as education. Market research is done under the guise of customer service. We are told the invasion of privacy is necessary for technological progress. Censorship is allowed because it is necessary for peace. Nothing is what it seems. Past notions of gender, age, race, nation, and community dissolve. Anything can become anything. The best "futurists" are often those who don't even try to identify trends but rather focus on the skills that will let events, markets, and the public inform them where they want to go.

Chaotic markets led to organizations with moving lines of authority, shifting work groups, and fluid job descriptions. W. L. Gore, the maker of Gore-Tex, is often cited as a model of a flexible, moving organization, reputedly instructing new employees to, *Look around and find something to do.* The chaos consultants, Margaret Wheatley among them, tell us that companies like Gore are right on track. Organizations are composed of intangible, moving fields of influence that become less productive if defined too closely.[5] The greatest creativity is unleashed when organizations pay attention to these subtle energies and people have the freedom to follow their seemingly aimless meanderings. Managing chaos rests on the ability to juggle paradox, think in shades of gray, and delay fixed solutions. From chaos theory, we learn that very small micromovements in a system can have totally unpredictable implications, like the proverbial butterfly which by flapping its wings in Japan eventually causes tornadoes in the midwest.

Chaos is upon us.
Every single power relationship is going to be called into question by cyberspace.[6]

John Pierre Barlow, Electronic Frontier Foundation

Virtual companies, existing almost exclusively in net time, take this chaotic model a step further. They're like spider webs, moving in and out of markets. Stability is nonexistent; products, services, players, and organizational structures all are designed for change at a moment's notice. In two years, Netscape accrued 40 million customers to become the fastest growing company ever, and then saw a significant percentage of its market erode in an equally dramatic timeframe. It is a kind of volatility that has never before existed. Business has become less about form and structure than about energy and social forces.

In parallel developments, we learn that the body is deeply affected by the mind and in fact may be less "physical" than we think, composed instead of layers of interrelated fields of intelligence.[7] The ancient Chinese practice of Feng Shui, using principles of energy to design physical spaces, has become one of the hottest things going. It's all part of the same trend. Health, business, design, and even leadership seem to rest on harnessing unseen and invisible forces.

Chaotic times require a new way of thinking, sometimes called "fuzzy logic." Fuzzy logic operates like a thermostat, kicking in only when a critical level is reached. You move toward goals in a zig-zag fashion because straight-line cause-and-effect solutions do not exist in a chaotic world. The best chaos riders are those who listen more than they act, are comfortable with long pauses, can handle periods of having no clear direction, and see no problem with contradictory statements. They can handle multiple tasks at once because they see them all as related. They prefer to function without job titles since what they do is never really definable. Power no longer lives in physical resources, but in the world of ideas and imagination. In this phase, dreamers and story tellers often hold the reins.

Out of this creative soup, a new breed of companies emerge that certainly don't have mission statements and may not even have a fixed product! They scan the landscape for spaces between existing systems that they can fill. Individuals, called "ho-bos," design their employment paths the same way others are building companies. They no longer think in terms of a job or even a career, but merely stop-offs on their creative journey through time and space. We are all coached to think loose and easy like these ho-bos.

The marketing missionaries tell us that society has become so fractured that we can only hope to catch ever smaller marketing niches as the population gets categorized into ever narrower slots. The only way to rise above the fray of our cultural noise and the splintering of the market is to make people feel that somehow you are speaking directly to them. Experts predict the fracturing of markets will become so extreme that ultimately, the more highly complex organizations will begin to cater to market units of one, and the era of mass marketing will come to an end.

The capacity for consumers to individualize and shape products is being called *demassification*. It changes everything, requiring a new relationship to product development, delivery, corporate organization, advertising, quality control, innovation, personal creativity, everything.

Moving boundaries, lack of form and shifts in power relationships may not damage the bottom line (they may, in fact, help at times) but as with the breakdown phase, they're tough on the psyche. Madison Avenue presaged both the dilemma and the solution in an ad for a new perfume named *Chaos* telling us to, "Find the center within." The personal and business advisors agree:

> ➤ They *coach* us on paths for finding our centers, so we can keep our heads while all around us people are losing theirs.

> ➤ They promote "principled" leadership, civility, and love to allow us to find arenas of personal commitment that provide stability and focus and help deal with turbulent systems.

> ➤ Poets and gurus are enlisted to help us heal the holes in our souls. Purpose becomes the hottest new pursuit, allowing us to find personal vision in the midst of a sea of chaos.

When external guideposts disappear, internal compasses are all that remain. *The individual and each person's world of preferences and values become the new beacons in times of chaos, personal vision the only way of finding direction, and images the only way to think in a world without form. Imagination is how the new forms of power will be unearthed.*

4. A New Order Emerges

Just before water is about to boil, the molecules collide at a faster and faster rate. Their speed increases to such a degree that a liquid state cannot handle any more energy. It must turn into steam. A new level of organization is the only solution to the tension in the system. Breakdown and chaos release huge quantities of energy from what was once a stable system. This free-floating energy eventually seeks out a new level of order, a new stability.

Nobel award winning biologist Ilya Prygione called this a dissipative structure. All systems follow a similar evolutionary path. Increasing stress leads to collapse of the old organizational model. When a system breaks from its existing momentum and finds a new level of organization is the moment of dissipative structure. It is a critical juncture, a *qualitative* break from the past, offering an entirely new world of possibilities.

 breakthrough

Many names are put forward for what is essentially a dissipative structure: breakpoint, new world order, crisis of meaning, axial point, turning point, breakthrough society, phase transition, the rapture. These names come from diverse sources—politicians, historians, sociologists, and theologians, yet they all speak to a similar feeling, the relief that arises when a new order of solution emerges—the creative "aha." The key feature of this phase is, of course, that the endpoint is unknown. If the end could be predicted or even envisioned, then it would not be new.

Obvious solutions and knowable endpoints seem to be retreating from grasp. We are operating without known structures, making it a time of heightened sensitivity.

It's like the intuitive space that occurs when the curtain comes down on a project; like a predator, you become attuned to even the slightest indication of a direction.

The study of how new order arises from chaos is called complexity theory. Greater complexity, or you might say new intelligence, only seems to occur when unpredictable possibilities arrive in a way that brings not just new information, but an ability to entirely rewrite our perceptions of what lies ahead.

The corollary wave of business advice tells us that patching things up will not work. We are coached not to dwell on solutions, but to discern new paradigms, shifts in *how* we look at a problem. Out of this thrust, the learning, adaptive, or relational organization is born, a place where the group becomes wiser as it goes along. It is based on the premise that the health of any business or relationship requires a commitment to deepening intelligence.

Some companies have indeed been able to see themselves at a deeper level and reinvent themselves in a way that allows them not just to expand but to respond to entirely new dimensions of the market. Entire fields, such as auto sales, accounting, and travel booking, have had their normal services to erode almost overnight and have had to instantly create new frontiers, hence the term second-curve businesses sometimes used to describe them.

An even more intuitive understanding of how order arises from chaos, is demonstrated by a handful of savvy entrepreneurs who create entire companies they know will endure for only a year or two because of the short life span of their product. These new visionaries seem to have a third eye, able to see things from new angles. They see a market moment and grab it fast. And they pull out millions from these guerrilla companies.

New realms of order show themselves in emergent social forms as well. The census bureau has been forced to add a new category of biracial, because so many individuals see themselves as belonging to more than one group. The growing number of children with parents from two religions are forging new paths for creating religious identity.

A leader in this phase is committed to intelligence, not just getting results. One of the main skills you need is an ability to allow individuals, groups, and organizations to become *aware of themselves*. A leader committed to fostering greater intelligence offers creative mirrors rather than solutions. Another key skill is being able to draw attention to new islands of focus, to help people see connections and influences that were previously invisible. The new leaders are like anthropologists observing a foreign culture. They look for deep structures and hidden patterns that underlie the obvious evidence.

On a personal level, you know you are in this stage of the creative cycle when:

➤ You find yourself discussing things and using words that, although unfamiliar, somehow are exciting and motivating.

➤ Confusion or disorder of the past suddenly reconfigures in a positive direction you have never seen before.

> You feel a sense of being compelled, pulled, attracted by ideas that lie ahead, rather than trying to make things happen.

> You sense that a natural motivation has taken place that makes your actions feel much wiser. It changes not just specific issues or projects of concern to you, but everything. It brings all you do to a higher level.

Breakthrough is a time of creativity. Your sense of self, your relationships, and your projects or work become keener and more fulfilling than you have previously known. There is a quality of surrender as if a greater intelligence is setting your direction.

Channel Surfing

Three blind men were asked to describe an elephant.
One felt the trunk and said, "Oh, it's like a snake."
One felt his skin and said, "Oh, it's like sandpaper."
One felt his foot and said, "Oh, it's big and round like a turtle."

How you perceive and describe what is happening in our culture depends entirely on your angle of view.

> Some have built their theories by focusing on the unprecedented speed of our culture and the need for hyper-accelerated systems and faster responses.

> Some are the harbingers of breakdown, warning us that things can't continue the way they are and that fundamental assumptions need to be reexamined.

> Some are the chaos riders, advocating a world without rules, without geographic borders, and beyond fixed identities.

> Still others speak to the clues that entirely new and almost indescribable directions are emerging just beyond the edge of our ordinary awareness. They speak to the need not so much for faster, but for more imaginative responses.

The perspective that is most relevant depends entirely on which issues of the curve are most dominant in a given moment. In others words, all the popular advice is right, at least some of the time.

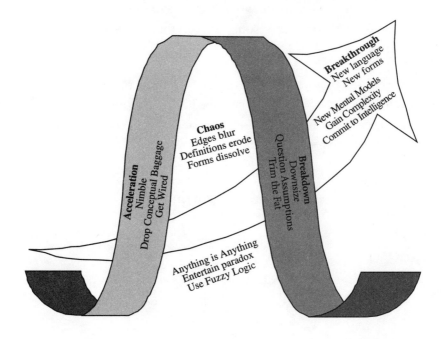

Although the chronicles of each phase offer vital insights, these contributions lose impact if taken to the extreme. For example, if you only address acceleration, you ignore a lot of factors that also speak to a slowing and deepening. If you only focus on chaos, you miss evidence that reveals a new level of stability. To understand the true psychological impact of our culture, we must view this evolutionary cycle integrally and holistically.

This entire cycle of metamorphosis—acceleration, breakdown, chaos, and breakthrough—can manifest itself in a single day's occurrences. You may start the morning with a project that seems better than chocolate cake and by the end of the day throw it in the garbage. Another idea only casually mentioned may become a number one priority, causing you to refocus so you can be hot on the trail. A person you thought was a stumbling block may unexpectedly save your neck and hold the key to a breakthrough, while your best ally flakes out. You may do everything according to plan and a project falls apart; then your worst mistake becomes your biggest money maker. *One decision makes you smaller, another makes you larger, often without any relation to thought given, effort invested, or expectation.*

At any given moment, you are juggling the need to speed up, break down, surf chaos, and walk into new possibilities—simultaneously. The spirit of our time does not rest on any one phase, but on our ability to negotiate the entire cycle over and over again. It requires becoming adept at detecting the subtle shifts that indicate a new set of criteria are beginning to operate. We need to know when to mobilize speed, provoke dissolution, ride with formlessness, or discern breakthrough, each at the precise moment that creates maximum effect.

> *These four "modes"—faster, slower, anywhere/nowhere, and someplace new—will play on our psyches until they gradually carve out entirely new psychological paths and rhythms.*

You will soon operate as if you have a remote control in your hands and are flipping between channels. Your power to diagnose, switch, and combine modes will begin to inform your relationships, projects, and business simultaneously. Suddenly acceleration, breakdown, chaos, and the unknown become one event. By mastering the dynamics of each discrete phase, a new emotional gestalt begins to form that encompasses the entire cycle and allows you to effortlessly blend one stage into the next.

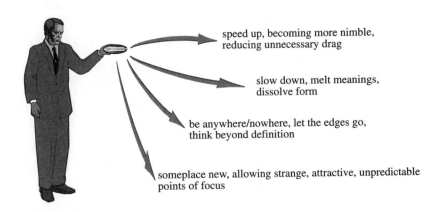

speed up, becoming more nimble, reducing unnecessary drag

slow down, melt meanings, dissolve form

be anywhere/nowhere, let the edges go, think beyond definition

someplace new, allowing strange, attractive, unpredictable points of focus

The notion of an endless evolutionary cycle is now resonating through every corporation, every mom and pop business, in government, and in our personal lives, leaving it's imprint wherever we turn. Some individuals get downsized and never quite recover; others resell their services to the same company, making more money and enjoying greater freedom than before. Some companies hit a wall which threatens their survival and fall, while others rise from the ashes expanded entities. Some relationships reach an impasse and part, while others rebound to build new dimensions of intimacy. The difference between a rewarding outcome and a painful one rests entirely on how effectively you ride the wave.

Of course these kinds of creative transitions have always been a part of life. But what makes now so different from any other time in history is that these cycles are occurring faster, from more directions, with greater frequency, and on more levels, *simultaneously.* They are demanding new levels of adaptive ability.

Our ordinary faculties for change are no longer adequate for the dimensions of transformation that we all must integrate. Success rests in one's ability to negotiate this birth-death cycle without getting stuck in any one dimension. The power that comes from mastering "continuous discontinuities" differs from the power that arises from the strong analytic skills that were once so effective. The capacity for quantum leaps calls on very different faculties than the sequential, cause and effect brand of change—having a vision, developing a plan, and reaping the harvest.

The new order of continuous discontinuity is better described in terms of energy and forces than structures and form. It is defined by instinct and intuition more than plan and theory. It is a world of mystery and awe and subtle rhythms rather than certainty, control, and easily observable rules. It is like the computer programs which allow you to blend or "morph" one image with another so that the transition is seamless, no one point where one image ends and the other begins and no one point where one image dominates.

Speed may be attained not by accelerating, but by looking sideways or stopping completely. *Since the chemistry of progression now obeys different laws, people will know that unseen forces affect any system, making perception one of the most effective forms of power.* More people will begin to understand how deeply we all can shape reality. The question is not how to enter the so called "second curve," but how to "become" third, fourth, and subsequent curves.

The spirit of our time rests on how powerfully we learn to design each of these transformative junctures:

- ➤ How much or what we let accelerate
- ➤ How powerfully we break down or disintegrate what is no longer working
- ➤ How far and how effectively we ride the void
- ➤ And how great we allow the leaps to be

Toward a Unity of Transformation

The promise of continual transformation *is* the spirit guiding our time. It is the gestalt that gives sense to the diverse directions of our culture. It is an image that is emerging simultaneously from all points on the globe, from all disciplines of thought. It's in the air.

We are about to experience probably the most powerful zeitgeist in the history of humankind. As our global culture appropriates images and transmits them into the heart of every small village, more of us will share the same experiences and the same visual language. Never before will the spirit of a time have crossed so many borders and been viewed by so many people simultaneously.

Wired magazine carried an interesting interview with the CEO of Mattel Toys. When asked what kids of today want in their toys, he said it in a word, "transformation." Contemporary music has already woven the transformation theme into lyrics that ride the airwaves 24 hours a day. The movie industry and the mass media have begun to organize around this spirit and drive it home. In the not-too-distant future, we can anticipate a global awareness of and subscription to the spirit of transformation:

- ➤ People will talk about their relationships not so much in terms of compatibility or past wounds they are healing, but whether the relationship is dynamic enough to usher each individual into a new level of self expression.

➤ Educators will know that our schools have been rendered irrelevant and must be redesigned from the ground up so the new spirit of transformation is recognized and at the core of any educational design.

➤ Entrepreneurs will know that the future rests not in horizontal expansion but in imagining new dimensions of the market based on a finely tuned vertical vision which entertains factors far beyond the traditional scope of business.

➤ When a company has been sized-down and demand-upped, the human resource people will know that motivation must be sourced from some new belief system not yet in place, maybe not yet even discovered.

➤ Our public commentators will begin to look through the eyes of this morphing spirit and describe the shadows and tensions of contemporary cultures as the birth pangs of new sociological worlds emerging.

We will soon begin to view all events through this lens of metamorphosis. This underlying pattern of deepening dissolution and reemergence will increasingly dominate our vision and drive our emotional ryhthms.

The spirit of our time is an emerging sense that all concepts are transient and all forms are changeable. Stability is merely a function of fixed meanings. When meanings dissolve and redefine themselves, then how we perceive the world is forever altered. This parallels themes from quantum physics, Buddhism, shamanic practices, and the intuitive knowledge held by artists. What is so striking is that business realities and the impact of our cultural messages are leading us all to function in this way. It becomes not just a philosophy but a new emotional reality.

The spirit of our time is demanding that we each become truly creative, not just about a particular project, but as an everyday way of being. If the spirit of our time is a "morpher," then so are we. This is the new sense of self, the new emotional, cognitive rhythm that is beginning to take hold.

Here is an old Sufi story, altered a bit.

> *Amal is cleaning his house for some visiting friends. In the frenzy of cleaning up, his precious ring rolls under the couch and he is unable to find it.*
>
> *When his friends arrive, they see Amal outside looking around in the grass.*

"What are you doing?" THEY ASK.

"I am looking for my ring." HE REPLIES.

"Oh let us help you. Where did you lose it?" HIS FRIENDS SAY.

"I lost it in the house." AMAL REPLIES.

"Then why are you looking out here?" HIS FRIENDS SAY.

"Because this is where the light is." AMAL REPLIES.

It's seductive to focus on the glitz of an exploding economy and evermore multifaceted culture. But if what we seek is personal and internal, we must look inside ourselves to find it. If we have the courage to do this, we will find a strange emotional process underway, a process I call **global alchemy**.

CHAPTER 2

Global Alchemy

The morphing spirit of our time is rattling the forms we hold dear and toying with our cherished beliefs. More importantly, it is slowly reshaping our sense of self. And that is what this chapter is about.

In the middle ages, alchemists sought to make gold from ordinary elements such as lead. This was code for the transformation of consciousness, since such practices had to be kept secret at the time. The hidden message of these early alchemists was to use ordinary experiences as the medium for personal transformation. Our challenge as modern day alchemists is to not merely adapt to the social transformations that surround us, but to use these events as the keys for personal transformation.

Global alchemy refers to the idea that cultural trends can transform our everyday lives in often invisible ways. It refers to that part of our psyche that is inseparable from the larger culture, that feels its birth pangs as our own.

Participation Mystique

Each of us has an inherent capacity to read the social pulse. No matter how you may try to ignore what's happening around you, you can't escape it. It permeates every image in your perceptual field. It emanates from every product you touch. Mysterious feelings grab hold of you that can't be fully explained by the events in your life.

The term *participation mystique* refers to our ability to absorb and inherit the tensions and anxieties of the earth. The Germans call the same idea *weltshmertz*, meaning "world pain." Both terms revolve around the point where our personal boundaries soften and we feel the emotions of the planet as our own. *Thus much of what we claim as our personal feelings may in fact be linked to the ebbs and flows of our larger social world.*

The eastern concept of the *hara* or *ki* takes this idea a step further. The area two inches below the navel is believed to be the point where our personal energy is centered. I once saw a man six-five and over three hundred pounds be lifted off the ground and effortlessly flipped into the air by a slightly built Akido teacher who was only five-two. The teacher was able to do this not through physical strength, but because he was centered in his hara. I was fascinated to later discover that the real translation of the hara is "internalized nature," the part of us that is one with the world. When we locate this place of inner unity, our own personal power becomes enhanced. We tap into a force and creativity far beyond our own.

If we indeed absorb and inherit the emotions of the world around us, and if this connection leads us to greater power, then consciously opening our capacity to intuitively connect with social forces is a vital key. It allows us to become more attuned to the flow of the future.

A Brief History of the Near Future

The intent of the next section is to support you in opening to this connection, not to provide an in-depth understanding of the cultural references I will use, but to give a face and complexion to feelings that are already sweeping your awareness.

Often we ignore these kind of feelings because the impact of world events seems so overwhelming, our challenges so daunting. A doorway into the future can only be discovered if we allow ourselves to emotionally connect with the unique chemistry of this time and access a strength that is beyond our own. As you read the next section, try to focus on how it makes you feel. Focus on the emotions that are stirred by the events I describe. Pay attention to your hara; it is already one with the following social transformations.

The First Wave

The workplace and the surrounding economic terrain are growing more volatile and unstable with every passing day. Walking on this unpredictable ground requires a greater emotional fluidity.

One out of every four people has seriously thought of leaving their job in the last year. More than one in ten have either downscaled, cashing out of high-overhead lifestyles to live simpler lives, or have found lower-paying jobs that offer more personal satisfaction. Stress-related diseases and fatigue are the number one problem in industrial countries. An extraordinary one in four will experience clinical symptoms of anxiety in this next year or become clinically depressed at some point in life. No matter what your age, you probably have seriously thought about bailing out of the race. Why are so many of us tired, disconnected, and unenthusiastic about what we do?

1. Every business is undergoing a series of shifts that will continually redefine not only what they do but how they do it.

Eighty-six percent of small companies, which employ the majority of the U.S. work force, say they will make a *significant change* in the way they do business in the coming year, and almost every large company is restructuring so it, too can gain this level of nimbleness. Whether you work for a large corporation, a small business, or are self-employed, you are probably in the midst of sorting through all or some of the following themes:

> *New markets and new dimensions of the market.*

> *New kinds of products and services.*

> *New delivery options/new forms of dissemination.*

> *More innovative and dramatic promotion in order to be noticed.*

> *New technology/new skills.*

> *New kinds of customers* with more specialized needs, holding new levels of information, and able to be directly involved in the design of your product.

> *New management and new notions of leadership.*

➤ *New business models* based on dissolving boundaries between customers, suppliers, shippers, research, advertising, etc. It is in these kinds of *social innovations* that many feel lie the *real* new horizons of business.

➤ *New employee issues* because of increasing pressure for companies to include a growing list of concerns in the corporate agenda, such as day care and human relations training.

➤ *New social forces* arising from a growing consumer militancy and demands for heightened corporate responsibility.

New demands arise from every one of the above factors.

No wonder we all feel a little crazed. You may be hired or start your business with one set of assumptions, yet face an entirely different set of pressures not far down the road. An identity crisis of sorts is filtering through every level of business.

2. These rapidly transforming business practices are in turn conducted within a workplace that is even more volatile.

Even with employment levels at historic highs, job uncertainty has never been greater. Waves of downsizing continue, even as record profits are reported. As more companies move their operations overseas for cheaper labor and less regulation, they become less committed to the individual worker. Contract labor and outsourcing allow businesses to sidestep union restrictions, save on benefits, and further avoid responsibilities to the individual. Factors such as these contribute to a phenomenon called *de-jobbing,* the permanent erasure of a job from the corporate books and the growing ability for corporations to expand and contract according to their own needs.

Windows of opportunity are shorter, so you must make your mark much faster. The question is not what you know, but what have you done lately. "You, Inc." is one solution being touted, at least for white collar workers. Don't think about benefits or security. Don't look to your employer for direction. You run your own company and the product is *You.* This self reliance can bring heightened opportunity to chart directions that are very personalized. On the other hand it may leave many feeling increasingly disconnected to the environment in which they work.

As this new work environment takes root, we will be forced to modify fundamental assumptions about the role of work in society. This means following the rules and expecting rewards for hard work are no longer primary, and entirely new values have been set in motion. *In this new economic world of less loyalty, there will be a great premium on generating the increased motivation so necessary for innovation and which is the lifeblood of any business.*

3. Surrounding a workplace in flux, an economy of increasing disparities is being fostered, leaving more uncertainty in it's wake.

The United States currently has the greatest income disparity of any industrialized nation: 20 percent of the population controls 80 percent of the resources, and 1 percent holds the lion's share of 67 percent. Studies suggest that a majority of the U.S. population is just one paycheck away from homelessness. Europe is rapidly catching up to the United States and reaching a level of income disparity not seen since the 1920s, just before fascism took hold. Michael Dertouzos, Director of the MIT Lab for Computer Science, counters much of the popular wisdom. He says the information marketplace will *not* level the playing field, but rather will exacerbate the growing gap between the rich and the poor.[1]

We are effectively creating a permanent underclass destined to work at a minimum wage that every year offers less buying power. Twenty-five percent of the United States is now functionally illiterate, astonishing compared to a level of 4.3 percent in 1930. In an era where manufacturing is easily moved to other countries, most well-paying jobs will be found in high tech fields requiring more skills than ever before. These jobs will be mostly unavailable to those who are coming of working age. Some sociologists contend that the United States and most industrialized nations are creating the equivalent of third world countries within their very own borders.

History shows us that social unrest is a predictable outcome whenever economic disparities like this are allowed to rise too far. Another danger is that at some point the larger economy will also topple if too few are able to afford what is being offered. *We are rapidly approaching a threshold where the fundamental assumptions of our consumer-driven economy will have to be reexamined.*

4. The larger international financial market may also be a house of cards completely untested by economic realities.

This is a paraphrase of a statement issued by Alexandre Lamfalussy, one of the industrial world's top bankers. Our financial system is based less on production and more on the flow of capital. A parallel financial universe is being created in cyberspace, featuring derivatives and other exotic investment instruments and manipulated by an elite club who have incredible influence on currencies and interest rates, often more than governments themselves. This money is not attached to anything real. It is a highly volatile, unregulated universe extremely vulnerable to fluctuations. Much of the world economy has, in effect, become a financial video game.

5. One world, ready or not.

William Greider suggests that global capitalism threatens to devour all cultures as we now know them. The nation-state is almost gone and the marketplace is the "new closet dictator."[2] The information wave has led to a centralization of economic control that dwarfs that of the industrial era. Because of buy-outs and mergers, fourteen media giants now control the vast majority of everything we see, hear, and read. Most major cities are one-newspaper towns, so there is no battling of opinions any more. We have been subtly sold the idea that anything but a totally unfettered market is somehow a violation of the Constitution, that protecting the common good is antidemocratic.

Government serves no purpose except to preserve the commons; our shared resources of forests, rivers, security, education, and the like. Unless the belief in a commons is restored, nations as we now know them will cease to exist. To quote international financier George Soros,

> "I cannot see this system surviving. Political instability and financial instability are going to feed off themselves in a self-reinforcing fashion. In my opinion, we have entered a period of global disintegration, only we are not yet aware of it."[3]

The final straw in our current economic equation is that in many ways capitalism, as it has evolved, may be a flawed myth. For the most part, it has not evolved in a way that supports the health of the planet as a whole.

*No wonder it is hard to feel secure, motivated, and committed to what
we do. We are asked to deliver more, often within a company that is less loyal
and offers fewer rewards, within a system that is increasingly unjust, while we
watch the surplus siphoned off for what is essentially gambling, all in service
of an ideology that may be going bankrupt. Even if you are not directly
impacted by these economic trends, you can't help but feel the ripples that
emanate from this more volatile economic landscape, for it is slowly creeping
into every arena of activity.*

*Of course, many companies are more civil and many people love what
they do. For some, this new volatility is opening many creative economic
opportunities. These are also many who would offer a far different vision;
who feel the economy is not only on the right track, but on the threshold of
unprecedented global prosperity. Even if this is your perspective, it's harder
than ever to ignore the shadow cast by the growing number who feel and live
in the other scenario. And few would argue that there aren't at least some
huge pockets of economic quicksand up ahead.*

The Second Wave

Our personal lives may be crazier than our professional lives.

A recent study revealed that an extraordinary 40 percent of working
women consider their jobs more relaxing than going home. Therefore,
they stay at work longer than they need to![4] Since half of all fathers live
somewhere else, they're not home either. Domestic violence is at an all
time high, so home is often not a refuge. One in four children live in
poverty and one in four will grow up without knowing how to read and
write. Studies estimate that the average parent spends fewer than eight
minutes a day talking to their kids. Sure, we are stressed by a workplace
in flux, but it would appear that home is often just as challenging! For
many, *home* has become *work*.

1. Changes in the family have ushered in a new psychological
world.

Sixty percent of minority children and 40 percent of all children will have
only one parent involved in their lives. Seventy-five percent of all children

will experience a change at some point in who functions as their parent. Half of all marriages end in divorce, and according to some accounts 40 percent of those who are married have affairs.

The idea of the nuclear family is a phenomenon of only the last generation or two. Throughout history, grandparents and extended families always helped in raising, supporting, and nurturing children. The social safety net was provided by the larger village or tribe. Much of the reason the nuclear family is in trouble is because extended family and community no longer exist. It is unrealistic to expect one or two adults to have the range of experience, time, and energy to fulfill the entire parenting role a child requires. It *does* take a village to raise a child!

As a result of these challenges, never have family members spent so little time together. Not only is the average parent-child interaction less than eight minutes a day, much of that time is spent on logistics: negotiating chores, transportation, and so on. Children who grow up in these linguistically impoverished homes enter school with less dense language patterns and less sophisticated thoughts, a handicap which has been proven very difficult to overcome.

In the movie *True Lies,* Arnold Schwarzeneggar gets upset when his daughter totally ignores something he says. His sidekick, Tom Arnold, chides him, "Don't you know you're not her parent anymore. Madonna is her mother and Axl Rose is her father." If the average child watches six hours of TV a day, then who is the parent? The media has taken over and is shaping the minds of an entire generation.

Furthermore, the nuclear family is ill-equipped to convey a sense of history. History is intergenerational. When grandparents fall out of the loop, the roots are gone. *In just a few generations we have created a social milieu in which individuals are raised untethered to the past, the community, and often, even their own parents.*

2. The age wave is about to hit, bringing a host of new tensions.

In the industrialized world, the median age now rises with every year. Almost half the U.S. population is now over 40, and in a few years almost one in six will be over 65. Throughout the industrialized world, a smaller percentage of individuals will have to support their aging populations, and education, infrastructure, and child care will pay the price. It threatens to pit young against old in the coming political debate. Age may replace race as the new nexus of social tension.

Optimists take heart in believing that a population of wise elders will come to power at precisely the moment that our social challenges are greatest. Pessimists counter this, saying the boomers have been programmed to stay perpetually young and conditioned to avoid tough questions. Wise or foolish, the needs and values of the boomers will soon dominate America's response to this grand dissipative structure, in the same way the WW II generation has dominated the past 40 years. Ten trillion dollars in assets is about to be placed in boomer hands as their parents leave them the largest inheritance ever! For better or worse, the "Woodstock kids" will be holding the financial reins when the new paradigm really starts rolling in, and their values will be a deciding force in how this scenario unfolds.

3. The community we live in is either decaying or going virtual.

Studies show when cops start walking the beat, neighbors get out of their houses and start meeting each other, and mom and pop stores move back in. Crime goes down, schools get better, and the quality of life goes up. This is not rocket science. Separation breeds decay; involvement creates health. Yet the economic forces tearing apart what little is left of our communities show no signs of letting up.

Corporate giving to the community is down, and it won't return because CEOs are more interested in protecting their stock price from raiders and in pocketing big profits themselves. In states where health insurance is least available, bankruptcy and homelessness are dramatically higher. When casinos open, any banker will tell you savings rates really do go down. When factories shut down, crime goes up. The reliance on private schools tears away those with greater means to help the public schools. Factors such as these are chipping away at what little is left of community life.

Can the newly emerging virtual communities step in and restore what we have lost? While some extraordinary grass roots efforts have been fostered in cyberspace, virtual communities are no replacement for face-to-face interaction. They will never match the vitality of a neighborhood. The bonding in virtual communities is often weak; it requires only shared interests, not shared lives. In fact, it may even prevent some individuals who could have been involved from participating, by creating the illusion that they are.

Without community, there is no sense of place. We have become social nomads, capable of picking up at a moment's notice, rarely forging bonds that would tie us down. We easily adapt to new settings, since superficial relationships are not only acceptable, they are efficient and encouraged by a swiftly moving social world.

Nearly 20 percent of the industrial world lives alone, mostly in neighborhoods where they don't know anyone. We are so busy that those who do live together barely talk. It's more frightening to go out, and there's more entertainment at home anyway. Increasingly, we are "wombing in," carving out a secure haven filled with technological toys as we pioneer new ways to indulge our personal preferences and ease the pain of the family and community life we have lost. The real trend in both our families and communities is toward a social fabric that breeds isolation.

The Third Wave

The stress of our worklives and this growing personal isolation are in turn being exacerbated by a very provocative cultural milieu.

Work is tough. Home and community are virtually nonexistent. So where do you go? We all participate in an intangible environment known as culture. Like everything else, culture has been ripped from tradition. For example, Disney's version of Hercules bears little relationship to the original Greek myth, and in a few more years, no one will even know the first version existed. Culture resides on TV, the media, and the Web. It is created moment to moment. Since most forms of the media are being programmed by market interests, the intent is persuasion rather than informative depth. Even though the social milieu that surrounds us is often closer to "culture lite" the impact is as profound.

1. As family and community collapse, we are developing a culture that is more homogenous, one-dimensional, and easily manipulated.

Since the advent of TV, children are growing up with aesthetic sensibilities largely based on shared experiences. They listen to the same music and visit global chat rooms. Kids from fundamentalist islamic countries, nomadic African tribes, and the suburbs of Chicago are tapping their feet to the same beat and mouthing the same lyrics. Any shifts in our collective direction can easily be disseminated and absorbed since we don't have to wait for ideas to filter through slow-moving, stubborn cultural barriers. We have started to become one mind, wanting the same stuff, moving in unison to an emerging global beat.

2. Randomization of power; centralization and decentralization

No one's in charge; everyone's in charge. Alvin Toffler calls it a "powershift," a redefinition of what constitutes power.[5] As power shifts from the arena of tangible resources to the realm of ideas, information, and imagination, it becomes simultaneously more accessible and fluid, and more centralized and vulnerable.

In the Middle East, individuals on the West Bank began their own peace initiative, forging new dialogues with e-mail and then meeting for coffee. A relatively small environmental group, Rainforest Action Network, has been waging an effective war on the Internet against one of the largest multinationals, Mitsubishi, attacking them for their relentless destruction of the world's forests. The web has extraordinary potential to feed individual empowerment.

At the same time, this access brings greater vulnerability. Army experts now think that the wars of the future will be techno-wars, a form of information terrorism. Recently, a teenage hacker entered computer systems owned by the Pentagon, Navy, utility companies, airports, major corporations, credit companies, and others. When asked if he had encountered a system he couldn't crack, he reflected only briefly before replying, "No." The most frightening part of his story is that technically this kid wasn't even that good. Many have the skills to do what he did. Since the United States is more wired than any other nation, it is by far the most vulnerable target. Several military leaders have stated publicly that a technological Pearl Harbor may be just around the corner.

Guardians of privacy and intellectual freedom on the Web feel that this alarmist position is a ploy to invade personal privacy and keep control of the digital world. It's an interesting feedback loop: Increased personal access leads to increased vulnerability, which leads to increased willingness to monitor and control, which in turn leads to decreased personal freedom and privacy. There is no simple answer, but it adds fuel to the fire that culture, once a source of direction and stability, has become as difficult to negotiate as everything else.

3. As if this is not enough, an entirely new conceptual and social framework is being built on this new digital landscape.

TV is a "push" medium; it pushes a stream of images at us. Newspapers are a "pull" medium; they let us pull out what we want. Yet we seldom talk about them in that way. It follows that one of the most powerful features of cyberspace is not so much what computers can do for us, but how they make us think, talk, and interact.

A computer becomes a window to a world of pulses and flows, patterns and vortices. "Cyber-sociologists" speak with awe about the democratization of information." They chart the evolutionary life of an idea as dialogue creates each next permutation, rendering ownership impossible.

One outcome of this is a new social universe. In cyberspace, the self no longer dwells in your personality, or even your gender; these become masks that can be put on and taken off at will. It is not so much the quality of chat rooms that is so appealing; it is the fascination of being able to play with our sense of identity. Of course, a rare individual spins out of control, becomes addicted to his fantasy of himself, and is increasingly unable to face the realities of a nondigital life. But potentially, a wise user, learning the impermanence of personality, could actually become more self-realized.

This new world of information is seductive, intrusive, and demands more and more of our attention. Although in the last 20 years we have gained a few more leisure hours per week, it has all been eaten up by increased TV watching. There is a dark side to this new information environment more insidious than our continued loss of privacy or techno-terrorism. The volume of input we all receive makes it hard to hear our own thoughts. The provocative array of choices robs us of self-direction. *Preferences take the place of true individuality, making us more passive and open to suggestion.*

4. On the other hand, as our global conversation progresses, a more complex dialogue may eventually emerge.

In many ways, the Net is merely one big group process event. Leaderless, without obvious rules, its main task seems to be to observe itself. Even commercial enterprises with clear financial goals can hardly make sense out of the free-for-all. The Web will be shaped by our attention to the world of energy underlying our words. New software, browsers, and languages are merely the result of some astute programmer who listens for a direction that is bubbling beneath the surface and offers a way to technically support it.

The World Wide Web is coming to approximate a global nervous system. The smallest unit of discourse can be swept to the heart of the world power centers. Browsers and push technology work just like neural nets, filtering and organizing packets of information. The Web gives voice to individuals and ideas that normally would have been edited. The more universal access is achieved, the more it will provide a vivid reflection of global tensions and resolutions. It will be like peering into a huge planetary brain to see which thoughts are swirling around and which ones are coalescing into denser and more permanent concepts.

Modern culture has become a crazy quilt of blended ideologies: the ancient and the new, east and west, science and art. The esoteric and once closely held teachings of every world religion are now available for general consumption. As the body of world knowledge becomes instantly accessible, it will bring us ever closer to touching the collective conscious and unconscious of all of human history. *Conceptually, we now dwell at the center of the universe, able to reach into any culture and time for the information we need.*

5. Ultimately, it is the fragility of our environment, not economics, cyberspace, or new conceptual domains, that will provide the context for unity and the framework for a global village.

Ecology is the ultimate nexus of global thought. All separation dissolves around this issue. Clearly, banning chlorofluorocarbons in the industrial world is irrelevant if China allows it. If Russia continues to dump live radioactive waste into the North Sea, how long before fishing fleets throughout the world reap the harvest? If the rain forest contributes much of the planet's oxygen, how much longer can it be cut before we all get a little breathless? Along every dimension—water, air, soil, extinction of species, loss of habitats—environmental stress is reaching a critical threshold. Resolution will require the cooperation of every nation. After all, biologically, we have always been one world.

So our home away from home is also not so relaxing. It is homogenizing diversity, playing with our sense of self, and toying with our capacity to think independently. Our global culture is at the same time more dominating and more vulnerable than at any time in history. It is bringing us together at an unprecedented level, at the same time that it is raising the potential for us to fear each other in ways we never could have dreamed. It is challenging us to more complex dialogues, provoking us to wake up, and asking us to act as if the planet mattered. Culture once was womblike, a source of comfort, definition, stability, protection. Now it is as confrontational and provocative as what we are seeking to escape.

A Wave within a Wave within a Wave

If we could render these three waves visually, it would look like those nesting Russian dolls, one wave encapsulating the next. The wave of economic transformation is echoed in the transfiguration of our families and communities and ripples inexorably through the cultural images we all share.

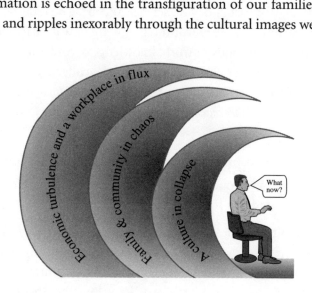

And inside this turbulent, trembling, morphing environment is where you sit. How do you feel? Overwhelmed? Challenged? Scared? Excited? Even if all these issues do not seem directly relevant to you, they are concerns that float through your awareness and hang on the edges of your psyche, nagging you to take them in. When you make a decision about where to send your child to school, or how to invest your money, or whether to make a career change, factors such as these are subtly making you more sensitive, tentative, confused, or concerned about your choices.

No wonder it's hard to know what you want or what is really important. No wonder we often just want to carve out a place safe from the storm. No wonder we long for simplicity and someone to just tell us what to do. We intuitively feel all this turbulence and uncertainty in our gut.

Although some are certainly in denial concerning the magnitude of challenges we face, I believe that most of us are actually in deep resonance with the spirit of our time and don't know it. That is why so many of us are depressed, frightened, or apathetic; we know what we face. We often ascribe feelings such as these to personal inadequacy, when in fact it may be a healthy and sensitive response to what is happening around us. Feelings such as despair and confusion may reveal our intuitive connection to world events. If understood in this way, they can become empowering rather than a source of isolation. In the midst of these more painful responses, we are also subject to inexplicable, unreasonable visions of hope. These feeling too can be understood as part of participation mystique. We are also becoming more finely attuned to the subtle paths that can lead us into a world that works. Whether the feelings are uncomfortable or visionary, it is vital to be patient and carefully listen to these stirrings, because these feelings hold the keys to an essential alchemy that must occur.

> *If we took someone from the middle ages and magically transported them to our time, the impact would be incalculable. It is not just that they would see so many unfamiliar things; the chemistry of modern culture would probably blow their nervous systems.*

And in fact, we are in the midst of blowing our nervous systems! And our mental models. And most of our psychological habits. In just one year, we integrate a complexity of change that our ancestors would have had a generation or two to digest. We unearth moral choices that would tax an army of Solomons. All the shaking and trembling of our economy, families, communities, and the culture-at-large has caused us to lose meaning, direction, identity, even clarity on what is real. Like Amal in our opening Sufi story, we must go inside if we want to find what we have really lost.

The Portal Must Be Personal

A culture that is simultaneously breaking apart and coming together in new ways demands organizations that can withstand this pressure. At first, new organizational shifts will lead to increases in productivity and innovation as new frontiers present themselves. But if the culture starts pulling ahead faster than an organization is able to change, eventually productivity and innovation will stagnate or decline, because the organization can't keep up.

In the same way turbulent, transforming organizations will at first unleash heightened creativity and opportunity for the individual. Chaotic, morphing organizations open doors for the individual to surf new worlds without boundaries. But if our organizations change faster than the people within them can, then once again this seeming progress will lead to decline as more individuals are left behind.

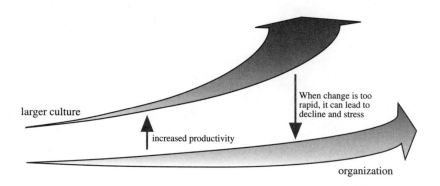

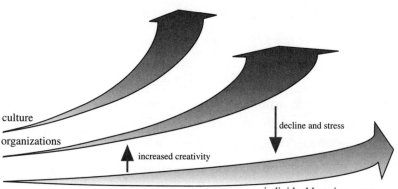

Thus, the learning curve of the individual ultimately represents the fastest pace at which a culture can move.

The buck stops there. The real challenges that our culture faces are personal. The critical thresholds are psychological/emotional/spiritual and have to do with our way of processing information, forming decisions, building relationships, managing conflict, coping with anxiety, maintaining our inner integrity, and forging new values. It is in the nature of these personal breakpoints that any cultural transformation must ultimately rest. It is at this very personal edge that the true shape of our future will be born.

Waves of social change sweep over us every night as we sleep, forcing us to awaken in the morning in a new way. This is leaving us all a bit shaky, stirring long-submerged feelings. It is quite natural to feel unexplained surges of vision and enervating influxes of despair. Our culture is waking us out of our personal slumber. There is a place within each of us, much like an internal gyroscope, that is accurately sensing this ocean of transformation and finding ways to adjust internally to a new set of forces and imbalances. This is global alchemy, the growing awareness that we must construct our personal choices out of the very unique information coded in this time.

Central Australia is one enormous, unbroken desert the size of the con-
tinental United States. Conditions are not very supportive of human life;
temperatures regularly soar over 120 degrees. Food and water are scarce
and there are no outposts. It's a very daunting frontier. For years the
early European settlers tried in vain to cross this desert, one group after
another dying in the attempt. Finally, these early settlers made it across
through sheer will and numbers, losing many along the way. Even today,
rusted out hulks of jeeps with human remains can be found in the
Australian outback, all that is left of travelers who miscalculated and
didn't pack enough gas and water.

Yet for 42,000 years the Aborigines crossed this same desert, never get-
ting lost or starving, never going without water, carrying almost noth-
ing in supplies. They raised families along the way, created magnificent
art and music, and evolved a rich spiritual tradition.

The Aborigines followed the songlines. When they came to a watering
hole, they sang the song that would direct them to the next watering hole,
telling them what to look for and guiding their imagination along the
way. Their songlines were far more powerful than the horses and bug-
gies, automobiles, and technology of the Europeans. The songlines
allowed them to sing an invisible world into existence.

We are embarking on a journey far more challenging than crossing the
Australian desert—we are crossing paradigms, shattering emotional
thresholds, and touching new realities. Often it seems we are blindly bat-
tering our way into this future, hoping for the best. Obviously, we could use
some songlines! This chapter describes eight personal skills that could
allow us to sing a new world into existence. Like songlines, they offer **a**
psychological map of the future.

CHAPTER 3

A Psychological Map of the Future

We are definitely participating in the mystique, and dare I say, "feeling the pain."

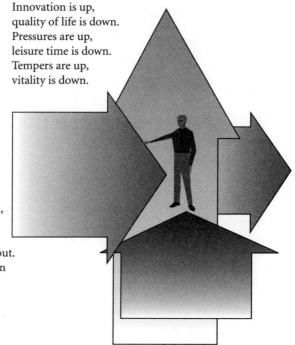

Innovation is up,
quality of life is down.
Pressures are up,
leisure time is down.
Tempers are up,
vitality is down.

Competitors are moving in,
jobs are moving out.
We are "wombing" in,
Social Security is running out.
The kids are moving back in
and often our parents, too,
and the idea of tranquility
seems very far out.

How do we keep from being torn apart?

By Discovering A Map

53

We are entering an uncharted psychological universe, unique in human history. We are bombarded by a range of stimuli and dimensions of challenge unprecedented in our entire evolutionary experience.

➢ The body/mind relationship is being torn apart.

➢ The onslaught of information makes it harder to hear our own thoughts.

➢ We are personally shutting down in the face of the massive need for change.

➢ Our sense of self is fracturing.

➢ We have lost and denied vast areas of our being, leading to profound sensations of powerlessness.

➢ It is harder to feel purposeful, because our larger cultural directions are so unclear.

➢ In many ways we are more socially isolated than at any time in history.

➢ It is harder and harder to keep up with the demands we face.

A map of the future can only be described by the edges of our own psyches. How we evolve our patterns of thinking, feeling, relating, and acting will shape the parameters of a new frontier. In the next few pages, I describe eight key domains that will allow us to walk into the future in an expanded way.

The Future Zone
We will need ways of:
increasing body/mind integration,
heightening performance,
transcending stress,
and developing a kinesthetic wisdom that can withstand a more digital world.

The biggest issue at hand is how to adapt 40,000 years of genetic programming to a culture that is approaching the speed of light. Forget more gigabytes, what we really need is a neurological bridge to the 21st century. Despite the chronological freedom technology gives us, much of modern life still requires that we constantly bow to primal biological patterns. Most people also suffer from a culturally induced chronic fatigue, because we have disconnected from the sources of our natural vitality. We sublimate very normal feelings because of our commitment to what we need to do. These kinds of discrepancies tear apart the body/mind integrity. At the same time that we are being pressed to get more done, we are more disconnected. We need to discover paths to heightened performance and heightened vitality that restore the body/mind wisdom we have lost. A high-tech world can render the body less relevant unless we use this challenge to discover ways of increasing our body wisdom.

A New Sense

We will have to sense:
faster, farther, deeper,
gaining a capacity for precognition and for seeing what lies ahead.

The diagnosis du jour is something called ADD—attention deficit disorder. With ADD, it's harder to keep your focus, your field of attention narrows, commitment to a direction is very flimsy, you change your mind a lot. Is there anyone who can't relate? Information blurs. We can't remember where we heard what. Ideas get simplified to the point we go numb. Our information-dense world depends on a more subtle perceptual style. We need to locate new levels of focus and discernment to keep pace with the flood of input entering our field. Besides more effective editing of the input, we will need the equivalent of a new sense to see through our incredibly intrusive and multilayered sensory environment.

The Emotions of Change

We will need to be:
more fluid,
more responsive and dynamic in our feelings,
and ultimately become masters of change.

Some sociologists think a new generation begins about every 5 or 6 years, with new musical tastes, aesthetic sensibilities, slang, and value shifts. With the current acceleration, these "generational" transitions could soon be down to a few years or even months. We need to be able to switch our world view, our sensibilities, and our expectations at will, or we will soon find ourselves many generations behind. All this "morphing" requires that every feeling, every opinion effortlessly flow into the next. Chaotic systems dissolve boundaries; form disappears into process. When process becomes dominant, then *how* one approaches a problem becomes more important than *what* the problem is. This requires new emotional training; it requires a kind of skill I call "shamanic change."

Mythmaking

We will need:
greater understanding of how our sense of self is built,
an ability to reinvent ourselves, creating new identities at will,
and to discover a self-awareness that transcends the fluidity of our world.

Our sense of self has never been weaker. We are inundated with so many forms of persuasion that we don't have time to develop a personal response. As McLuhan foresaw, hot medium such as TV infiltrates our attention in a way that a cool medium like books can't. We need ways of reestablishing a sense of self that can stand up to a far more seductive, "hot," and dominating environment. A more fluid cultural world requires the ability to alter our sense of self at will. Who could ever have predicted that *Reviving Ophelia*, a book about the self-image of adolescent girls in our society, would hit the best-seller list. It is indicative of a much deeper issue: we're trapped in our cultural images, we instinctively know it, and we know we need reviving.

Shadow Dancing

We will need:
skills for locating deeper truths,
since everywhere we turn, denial is being shattered.
In a world that fractures our sense of self and ability to relate,
we need new skills for confronting what we have disowned.

Every nook and cranny of the public psyche gets exposed; denial is shattered and truth is skewed. We need to detect where we are lying to ourselves if we are ever to put some truth back into the system. We will eventually have to encounter the issues and people we have "thrown out the window." And they will be a lot bigger when they return than when we casually dismissed them the first time. When a system is approaching a boil, it takes heightened skills to deal with the heat. Yet we have all allowed ourselves to shut down. Compassion fatigue, communication dullness, and relationship avoidance are all forms of the numbness that has set in. We must wake up our feelings again in order to respond to what's really happening. We need people who can wrestle with the suppressed parts of our culture, the denied parts of our businesses and families, and the submerged feelings within ourselves. "Shadow wrestling" will be a much needed talent in the years to come.

Why We Need to Sweat

We will need:
deeper roots, a deeper center,
paths for greater participation,
and sources for increased direction.

Traditional rituals are designed to prevent our egos from running rampant; they insist that our efforts flow back to serve the greater good. In western culture, we are uninitiated. In fact, unchecked self-expression is considered bold. But eventually we will feel too alone and unnourished by our actions. Only the growing hole in our soul has the potential to lead us to new vision. The most fascinating aspect of chaotic systems is that they always lead to unprecedented freedom. With an increasingly blank canvas standing before us, people are free to take incredible chances. Out of this extraordinary emptiness, vision, choice, and intention take on an importance and power that is not available in more stable times.

The Power of Intimacy

We will need:
a way to bridge our isolation,
and new levels of intimacy that can withstand increasing chaos.
Every new degree of connection will require a new degree of depth.

We are rewarded for learning to rely on no one. Self-reliance is held in such high esteem that we have been urged to weed out any signs of dreaded co-dependence. Since it is also less common to be able to count on others, we become even more focused on ourselves. We spend less time in meaningful and complex conversation, so profound parts of our being are never touched. The poetry in our souls often withers from disuse. Curiously, at the same time this self-imposed isolation is running rampant, we have the highest level of cultural interdependence that has ever existed. The new economy requires unprecedented cooperation and collaboration between diverse peoples. New social concepts will need to be created out of this seeming divergence. Understanding the true nature of intimacy holds the key; it is a concept that can be tapped for wisdom. We need to remember how to grow this fruit in the midst of a garden that rarely gets watered.

Accelerating Results

We need:
ways of collapsing time,
strategies for skipping steps,
and ways of taking action that offer a path to self knowledge.

An information-based business is said to operate ten times faster than a more traditional company, hence the expression *net time*. As information strategies filter into all business arenas, the hyperspeed characteristic of the digital world will become the status quo. The feedback loops between product and consumer, use and redesign, delivery and production have all gotten shorter. Those responsible for interpreting these feedback loops need new strategies of response. New skills and organizational strategies will not be enough. It is only by playing with our notions of reality that we can truly design a new paradigm for taking action.

The Portal/The Map

This is it. If you arrange these skills as a single image, you will see that they reveal a very consistent strategy for walking into the future. In each case our ordinary faculties are heightened as a result of teasing out new capacities.

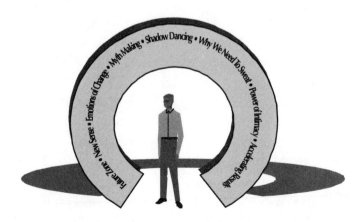

These eight domains serve not only as a map but also as a portal. They offer a description of where we must go and strategies for making it through a culture in chaos. Like songlines, they offer a way of traveling a psychological world that is often invisible to the naked eye.

Learning to Navigate

We are asked to become more fluid and resilient. At the same time, we are challenged to become more focused, better able to hold our center. We are asked to allow our boundaries to become more flexible at the same time we are discovering a deeper sense of what we want. We are asked to see further ahead, and we are asked to be more responsive to the present moment. These seemingly divergent directions mean that there is no one response to the spirit of our time. That is why the idea of navigation is far more suited to preparing us for the challenges that lie ahead.

Navigation is not a technique or a fixed solution. *Navigation is a quality of individuality.* It rests in the ability to tap into new sources of intelligence. If we gain more accurate internal compasses, we can negotiate ever vaster uncharted waters. Thus it is the most powerful way to open up new dimensions of the world around us. It is the path into true creativity.

As we further explore these eight terrains in the next section, the discussion will focus on how to use each theme as a centering device. Each theme will be explored not as a defined "how to" set of processes, but as a context for moving through a particular set of challenges.

The Inner Game of the Future

The breakthrough that our world so desperately needs can only be born within our own psyches. Coming chapters cover what happens when our habitual waves of perceiving give out and our senses must reorganize at a new level or what happens when traditional meanings collapse and we must find a capacity to create new stories. Each chapter will follow a similar pattern and will describe a new order of possibility that can arise out of very ordinary features of daily life.

Biologists have used the term *co-evolution* to describe the interdependence between the evolution of a species and their environment. They have found abundant evidence that organisms and their surrounding environments seem to evolve simultaneously. Changes in a species and changes in its environment seem to arise in mutually beneficial ways, seemingly as a shared event. Thus our morphing economic, social, and cultural environment must be inextricably bound to our own personal development.

> *This is the participation mystique. It is the part of you that can feel the birth pangs of these emerging economic, cultural, and social worlds as the seeds of your own transformation.*

Our psyches are more susceptible to what can only be called future pull. Most people are well aware that they have inherited an emotional reality from their childhood that they continue to project onto the present. It is much harder to grasp that who you are becoming is also projected onto the present moment. We have entered a moment in human history where what we must become has now become dominant.

Since work, home, and culture are all about to surpass our past experience, we will be forced to construct new solutions. We are being pulled to gain new and unprecedented knowledge. Although some adjustments are in order, such as unplugging a bit more often, slowing down, or rediscovering community, these actions alone will not be adequate.

It's too late to turn back the clock. We must *press into* our accelerating, decaying, turbulent, trembling culture and allow it to change us. We must echo the spirit of our time. Since the future is coming at us like an F-16 down the runway, the real key is whether we can allow it to change who we are.

The real power of our digital, nanosecond, third wave world rests on our capacity to transform our personal psychology. If we can integrate these larger societal shifts, then we have the potential for the first time in human history to consciously evolve as individuals and as a culture. If we can't change the quality of our personal responses, then our vast technological developments will mean little. As in the movie Stargate, we will merely find ourselves in a future with nothing more, literally and metaphorically, than a bigger gun.

A psychological map of the future rests on defining new skills that lie buried within our ordinary day-to-day activities. We are co-evolving within a more turbulent and undefined environment. We are getting smarter as a result of living in a more complex and multilayered time. The portal to a different future lies in a very simple solution, our willingness to experience ourselves in a heightened way.

PART 2

HOW DO WE GET THERE?

Eight Navigational Tools

Several years ago I attended a concert organized by musician Peter Gabriel called WOMAD, The World of Music and Dance. Twenty or so bands from all over the world played their traditional music along with more contemporary bands. On the grounds of the concert Gabriel had several stages going simultaneously and a large tent called The Future Zone. I wasn't going to miss this.

Inside, I found a wide variety of interactive games. One allowed you to create dancing images on the walls, which in turn played with the designs other people created. In another, dancers had sensors attached to their bodies that allowed their movements to create sound. They composed music by moving. As I played with these games, I could faintly hear the sounds from two different stages, as the rhythms of one country mingled with the beat of another. Gabriel was attempting to create an experience of how our culture might evolve. He was provoking a living, breathing hologram of where our world might be heading.

The experience he created has stayed with me all these years; I can call up the memory in a moment. Ever since, I have been intrigued with the idea that we could transport ourselves into a future scenario at such a high level that we could actually feel what it would be like to walk around there. It is a skill that has great relevance for our time. In order to keep up with a future that is barreling down at us like an F-16, we must each tap into our hidden abilities for entering **the future zone.**

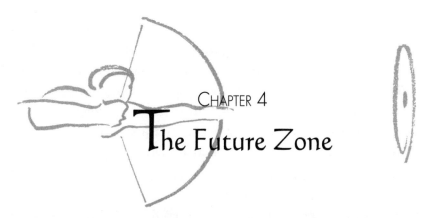

CHAPTER 4

The Future Zone

A friend of ours would sometimes begin his seminars with the provocative question, "What is your purpose in being here?" (On this planet, at this time.) People would respond with lofty statements or abstract notions. After a few minutes of responses like this, he would say, "Your purpose is to master being in a body. If this wasn't your purpose, then you wouldn't be in one."

Part of our purpose is to forge a relationship with our bodies that matches the creative pulse of our time. Ultimately, entering the future rests on having a body that can take you there. As I stated earlier, it's not more gigabytes, we need a *neurological* bridge to the twenty-first century.

There are five features of modern life that impact the way we experience the body/mind relationship.

➤ We are facing unparalleled environmental impact on our bodies causing stress to be the number one disease-related factor in industrialized countries. Allergies, sinus problems, and respiratory difficulties have officially been called an epidemic. This heightened physical distress, in addition to the feeling of bombardment from noise pollution and visual chaos, often leads us to "numb out" and try to forget the body. Increasingly, we ignore or suppress our physiological messages and run on willpower and adrenaline.

➤ We are also asked to modify primal rhythms of attention to accommodate the schedule of business. Natural rhythms of attention are about 90 minutes long, yet many meetings go way past this. For most people, the siesta is a physiological fact; blood sugar and metabolism rates naturally drop leading to a desire for sleep. Yet we ignore this pattern, take a slug of caffeine, and press on. Sleep researchers claim a vast majority of the industrialized world suffers from sleep deprivation as result of electricity and the capacity to keep working or watching TV. Sleep deprivation drastically compromises judgment, decreases attention span, and heightens frustration. In our effort to adapt to accelerating cultural rhythms, we drive ourselves even more, creating one more layer of disconnection from what our bodies naturally feel.

➤ Allopathic medicine has taught us to fix symptoms; so you learn to experience your body as isolated elements rather than a unified system. So we not only disconnect from the body as a whole; we then separate it into discrete parts.

➤ There are other implications encoded in modern technology that are further altering our body sense. The idea of "body extension" has been explored at great length by anthropologist Edward T. Hall and others.[1] Telescopes are extensions of the eye, cars are extensions of the foot and locomotion. Computers extend the mind's ability to process information. The result is that our normal physical boundaries are altered, our bodies literally feel less physical. This is what Mchuhan referred to as the "discarnate effect:" we identify more closely with mental processes and have a more abstract awareness of the body.

➤ F2F, or face-to-face contact, now requires a name. Moving the body around for work or social exchange is increasingly optional. Alternatives to F2F have become so numerous, it is highly seductive to use them. Many sociologists maintain that this is one of the big attractions of cyberspace. We feel more powerful, less bounded, able to tap into happenings beyond where our bodies are stationed. Thus the body starts to feel like a source of limitation, not as nimble as the feeling we have in this digital world.

So here's the problem. Modern life forces us to override the natural rhythms and wisdom of the body. It leads us to disconnect, separate, and consider our physical reality a source of limitation. Just going to the gym is not enough. Yoga and the martial arts come closer. What we really need are models for forging a heightened relationship between the mind and the body that not only can withstand these intrusions but also lead to a freedom that is as powerful as what the digital realm seems to promise.

Thus our body/mind relationship is being "reparadigmed" just like everything else. We all need a path that heightens vitality and decreases stress. We need a path that allows us to tap into a wisdom that is stored in the physical experience. The mind-body relationship must be more aligned than ever, for this is where we will find the seeds to that neurological bridge we so desperately need.

A Necessary Convergence

Let's briefly return to the image of the Zen archer. When the Zen archer pulls back his bow, the body/mind relationship is more unified. His action in the world is more aligned with his thoughts. It is a state of increased relaxation, heightened efficiency, and more powerful performance.

The skills of the Zen archer have more relevance today than ever before. We must make decisions with less information. We work with people we barely know on projects that require intense compatibility. We are routinely asked to solve problems that challenge our limits. The answer to the increased demands of our time may lie in the most ancient realms of knowledge. While the majority of the world's population has looked to technological advances to improve their performance, a small contingent of shamans, mystics, monks, and mavericks has always relied on entering advanced states of consciousness. Now these two powerful trends are converging.

The Zen Archer Must Learn to Shoot His Bow into Hyperspace

The states these monks and mavericks have been perfecting for millennia are a perfect solution for the stresses we now face. The tempo of modern life makes it easy to feel we have reached the edge of what we can handle. The answer does not lie in more effective time management or squeezing more hours out of the day. When we reach the end of our normal problem solving abilities, the edge of our attention levels, or feel blocked in our creative expression, the only solution is to leap into a new domain of action.

What Does the Zen Archer Know?

There are days when we just seem to be in the right place at the right time; whatever we do, the impact is powerful and positive. Maybe we intuitively call someone and something great results. Sometimes, we are able to accomplish a week's work in an afternoon or spend extraordinary hours on a project without getting tired. In these moments we naturally touch what the Zen archer experiences. It's more than being lucky or having a good day. They reveal the natural capacity we each have to connect with a more unbounded experience of reality.

In athletics, this phenomenon is called *the zone*. It's been studied for years. Hall of Famer Stan Musial said that in this state, he could see the seams of a baseball thrown at over 90 miles per hour. Olympic gymnast Carol Johnson said the balance beam would become wider when she was in the zone. The golfer Tony Jackson called it a "cocoon of concentration." Formula one race car drivers refer to it as "driving above yourself." Scott Hamilton, the world's number-one figure skater, says that when you enter the zone, you "skate stupid." Your mind lets go and the wisdom of your body takes over.

When Roger Bannister broke the record for the four-minute mile, he knew he had entered one of these moments. His words after the race were, "No longer conscious of my movement, I discovered a new unity with nature. I found a new source of beauty and power, a source I never dreamt existed."[2]

In 1968, in Mexico City, one of the most extraordinary moments in sports history took place. Robert Beamer cleared 29 feet in the pole vault, an astounding 17 inches beyond the previous record! It had taken years to move the previous record even seven inches, rising in tiny increments of sometimes less than an inch. After completing the jump, Beamer broke down in a cataleptic seizure, literally shaken by what had occurred. When asked how he felt before the jump, he said, "I was running scared. I was in a place between time and space."[3] Like Bannister, he clearly recognized that he had pierced the veil of physical reality.

Biologist Lyall Watson calls moments like these *perfect speed*. All the components of an action—the preparation, the crowd, the weather, the psychology, the release—align in a way that for the athlete seems to suspend the law of gravity. It is as if they exist in a different world that has more flexible and malleable rules governing performance.

Of course this state extends to every profession and is called by many names—*flow, the groove, peak performance*—all ways of saying *the force is with you*. Einstein said that his ideas "arrived." They appeared to him complete; the subsequent writing of theory was secondary. The great jazz musician Thelonious Monk once said, "I have been performing with such concentration that everything stopped, everything was silent, and then suddenly it was over."

In his classic book *The Act of Creation*, Arthur Koestler says that if an act is truly creative, it must allow us to touch the unknown.[4] As the creative moment peaks, normal experience collapses, and we touch a knowledge not previously available. Like the experiences of Bannister, Beamer, Einstein, or Thelonious Monk, the creative act transports us to a domain beyond ordinary space and time. Koestler uses two drawings to distinguish the creative act from the tragic act, or in this case ordinary performance. The first illustration shows the normal ebb and flow of crescendo and denouement; a peak leading to the next valley. His second illustration is much like the image from the first chapter; a discontinuous moment occurs that leads to a different order of experience.

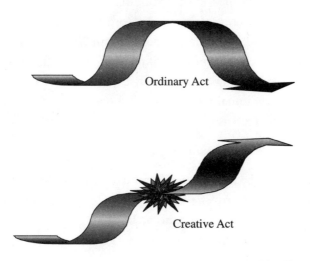

Ordinary Act

Creative Act

As you can see, the zone is a path for allowing our bodies to ride the same creative cycle that was described in the first section. It parallels the path of the morphing spirit of our time. It is what might be called a "hyperphysical" state, in which the body is more closely aligned with the rhythm of our times. It represents a quality of attention and action than can make the speed and chaos of our lives seem more manageable.

The Wall

The critical moment is the point when we choose either to leapfrog into a new domain, or to slowly dissolve until we can regroup again. When an athlete "hits the wall," if he persists, a second wind occurs and a new flow of strength more effortless than what was before. This critical juncture always appears when we feel the most frustrated òr tired; therefore, it is a key moment in any creative process.

The zone, flow, or creative act also echoes descriptions of the mystical experience. By exploring the mystical experience, we may learn more about how to negotiate the wall, this very critical moment of discontinuity.

Cosmic consciousness, samadhi, or satori involve a dissolution of the ego, a dissolution of the conditioned beliefs each absorb from our environment. What blocks entry into this new awareness is only our *memory* of what we were before and the part of us that clings to this image. Once in the satori experience, the practitioner no longer feels separation, from others, from his surroundings, even within himself.

Entering the zone may merely require "forgetting" who you think you are. The wall is a psychological state, a personal and collective memory of what is possible. There are hundreds of examples, like the four-minute mile, where once a psychological boundary is passed, then all athletes are freer to enter this new domain. One person's breakthrough paves the way for others to walk through as well.

Possibility has been permanently redefined.

The purpose of the Zen archer's practice is not to become a sharp shooter but to reorder his psyche in ways that expand his understanding of himself and allow him to forget who he thinks he is. Thus his action in the world is a path to personal evolution. This same context is available to any of us. You can seek out peak performance for the purpose of getting your sales numbers up for the week or for turning in an ace report. Or these results can be made secondary to your broader goal of learning to function in a more fluid and expansive domain of creativity. With one approach you get the stuff done. With the second approach you get the stuff done *and* you have more fun, experience less stress, become a lot wiser, and are left with a skill you can use anywhere, anytime.

So the main purpose of learning to access the zone is that it offers a practical path for restructuring your sense of self, and thus the mind/body relationship, in a more fluid and expansive way—precisely what our cultural tempo is demanding from us.

What Does This New Domain Look Like?

All indigenous cultures know about the zone and have clear rituals for dissolving their ties to ordinary perception so they can dwell in this more fluid world. Through such practices as fire walking, trance dancing, vision quests, and shamanic journeys, one is guided and provoked to enter a domain of expanded possibility. Cultures that have been evoking this state for thousands of years describe it as a location you can visit. The Mayaruna call it "the land before time began;" Australian Aborigines call it "dreamtime."

The Aborigines are so experienced at accessing dreamtime that they are able to paint it in their drawings of the songlines. They are known to be the best trackers in the world, able to follow the path of someone even a year after he has walked through the desert. When asked how they do this, they will say something like, "It's easy, I merely find the person in dreamtime and walk alongside him." In other words, their trackers seem to bypass the normal constraints of time and space. Dreamtime is not just a poetic vision, it is a lived reality.

Dreamtime Is a Place Where Desire and Fulfillment Are One

It is the same place touched by the Zen archer when the desire to hit the target and the fulfillment of a bull's-eye meld into a single experience. Every example that has been given of this state—Einstein's ideas arriving, the

Formula One racer driving above himself, Scott Hamilton's skating stupid—requires entering this domain where mind and body are more unified. It occurs when the duality of our inner experience, what we desire, and our outer experience, what actually happens, becomes a more integrated process.

Across cultures, in all professions, throughout history, strikingly similar descriptions of this moment can be found. A musician in the groove accesses a *knowing* similar to lovers who intuitively hear their partners' telepathic messages. Someone who experiences a spontaneous healing experience feels the same *certainty* about their new-found health as a physicist making a breakthrough discovery and knowing it is correct or a businessperson at the bargaining table who knows exactly the right deal to offer at the perfect moment. A shaman walking across white hot coals *perceives* in a way that is quite similar to an athlete having the game of his life. Peak performance, creative breakthroughs, personal realization, humor, and love, all allow us to touch a very comparable place of awareness.

Not only are the descriptions similar, but there seem to be very clear and universal consequences of entering this state. We access feelings, knowledge, and results beyond those typically available to us. Whether it is gardening on a spring afternoon and losing all sense of self or having a major creative or performance breakthrough, people tend to report some or all of the following 14 attributes encoded in this "hyper-physical" experience.

1. *Time is altered.* It can seem faster or slower. The sensation of linear time collapses, and instead there is an experience of timelessness. You are more centered in the present as if that is all there is. Researchers have discovered that brain waves shift in these moments, suggesting that we are processing more information than usual. If more information is passing through our awareness than normal, this could be the physiological basis for feeling that more is happening, and therefore that time is altered.

2. *Information is accessed intuitively, beyond what can be rationally explained.* Knowledge gained from zone experiences has a different quality. Ideas seem to enter the mind without intention or effort and they appear in full-blown detail. Often you are curiously unattached to your views, as if the information is not really yours but has merely come through you. Stravinsky said he did not compose The Rites of Spring but that he was merely a vessel. Rather than being pursued, creativity *arrives.*

3. *There is a certainty accompanying this knowledge; you know that you know.* Often you feel compelled by the knowing that occurs in the zone. The split between thinking and doing evaporates; so it is easier to act on the information you receive. When Fredrich von Kekulke had his now-famous dream of a snake biting its tail, he awoke with the certainty that carbon was a ring. He did not contemplate the possibility but rushed into his lab. He had no doubt, and subsequent testing confirmed his dream.

4. *Perception is both heightened and more profound.* People report seeing further, hearing more acutely, touching more intensely. Beethoven wrote some of his greatest works when completely deaf, and reported being able to fully *hear* the completed work. Sometimes your separate senses can be integrated as a single experience called *synesthesia,* suggesting that perception arises from a deeper order of experience which does not rely on ordinary sensation.

5. *The mind/body relationship is more integrated, resulting in greater strength, vitality, and coordination.* The body is elevated to the fluidity of the mind; the mind elevated to the wisdom of the body. Timing is enhanced; stress is reduced. Any sensation of fatigue evaporates. In this state, individuals are more aware of the workings of their body and are able to detect pulse rate or blood pressure level with precision and consciously modify them. You access a strength and vitality from a place that transcends the purely physical, such as when a mother is able to miraculously lift a car off of her trapped child.

6. *Actions are more focused and on target.* You operate instinctively, somewhere beyond the mind, leaping before you look, doing before you think. If you have ever reached out and spontaneously caught a glass as it was dropping off the table, even before your conscious mind realized what was happening, this is how it feels. Your mind lets go so the wisdom of the body is free to surface. This has been called *instinctual knowing,* a knowledge that occurs kinesthetically, outside of conscious awareness.

7. *Internal conflict decreases; decision-making is easier.* This is an extremely useful by-product of the zone. You experience fewer conflicting messages and are therefore more able to go to the heart of the matter. Researchers have found indications of greater synchronicity between the

right and left hemispheres of the brain in this state. This may produce a sensation of inner coherence, and therefore superior decision-making.

8. *Concentration is extraordinary.* It is like a cocoon of concentration. You are tuned only to what is relevant to the task at hand. Since you are more integrated with your body, concentration is deeper. A world-famous pianist became so crippled with arthritis that he could barely hold a glass of water, yet when he was in concert, he could play for hours without pain. The suspension of pain was possible because there was less separation between him and the act. The *doing* was more powerful than the pain. The concentration you feel in this state is like a bubble that insulates you from the distractions of ordinary awareness.

9. *Commitment is easier.* Since you know that you know, doubts and fears disappear. Action takes over in a way that makes commitment integral. People report that rather than breathing, they are "being breathed," rather than playing music, the music is playing them. In this state, you are so completely merged with a task that follow-through becomes automatic. The "doingness" carries you.

10. *There is a sensation of knowing one's larger purpose.* In this zone people report knowing why they are on the planet. For example, in the midst of having the soccer game of his life, world-famous player Pele saw a greater meaning to his life and the need to write a book explaining his experiences. Often you are moved to express yourself in ways you haven't in the past. Since it is a place of expanded possibility, it is easier to have bigger dreams.

11. *A sense of bliss and well-being often accompanies this state.* You feel as if you are in the right place at the right time. There is a sense that a particular orchestration of events was meant to be, as if a higher intelligence is guiding you on your path. There is a feeling of relaxation and grace, as if you can have more happen with less exertion.

12. *When working with others, there is increased alignment and magic.* People "catch" this state from others. When one team member enters the zone, it can trigger the whole team to become more exceptional. I am a mediocre tennis player. I once had the opportunity to play with a former Davis Cup player, and not only did I have the best game of my life, but his ability, his high, seemed to transfer to me. Heightened states of awareness seem to be transferable.

13. *Our relationship with others is deeper, more compassionate.* When zoning, you are more able to see past superficial appearances and sense the true needs of others. You feel more in tune with them, as if your mutual well-being is connected. Often people say that after entering the zone, they have so much to give.

14. *There is also a heightened connection to the planet and all of life.* Life feels more profound than the endless dramas that describe everyday activity. The late physicist Itzhak Bentov found that in states of deep meditation, our brain waves more closely approximate the frequency of the electromagnetic field surrounding the earth. He hypothesized that this physiological resonance with the earth may lead to a greater feeling of psychological resonance.[5] Jung hypothesized a similar idea in his description of the collective unconscious, an archetypal planetary wisdom into which individuals throughout history have tapped.

The Zone Is a Perfect Solution to the Heightened Stresses and Seeming Dephysicalization of Modern Life

If you could enter this state at will, life would be far easier. When Philip and I first started talking about zoning in presentations almost fifteen years ago, few people had heard of the term. It took a bit of explaining to get them to see that we were talking about something that went far beyond being in a good mood or having a good day. Now almost everyone knows the term and exactly why it is such a powerful place. Several books have been written recently equating the zone with heightened leadership and more creative management. Barry Sears diet book, *The Zone,* suggests that our eating habits can trigger a neuro-hormone associated with peak performance states, so we can diet our way to more sustained highs. The runaway success of Sears' book suggests that the general public wants to be in the zone.

I believe people are more aware of this state not just because of the media coverage but also because we are all personally having more direct experiences of it. The chemistry of modern life is ideal for inducing zoning experiences. The fourteen attributes of the zone offer a perfect solution for high-stress/high-demand times.

A Behavioral Doorway

Two of the best-known researchers of zoning are Mihaly Csikszentmihalyi and Michael Murphy. Each has documented thousands of cases of heightened performance, and they have come to remarkably similar conclusions about what this state might indicate.

In his book *The Flow*, Csikszentmihalyi says,

> *After each episode of flow a person becomes more of a unique individual, less predictable, possessed of rarer skills... Flow helps to integrate the self because in that state of deep concentration, consciousness is unusually well ordered.... And when the flow experience is over, one feels more "together" than before, not only internally, but also with respect to other people and the world in general.*[6]

And in his masterful cross-cultural survey of the phenomenon, *The Future of the Body*, Michael Murphy says,

> *Certain types of extraordinary human development, I believe, herald a third evolutionary transcendence. With them a new level of existence has begun to appear on earth, one whose patterns cannot be adequately specified by physics, biology or mainstream social science.*[7]

I share these conclusions. The fourteen naturally occurring attributes spell out an extraordinary view of the future. If the zone were easily accessed, life as we know it would be transformed. Relationships would be more telepathic. Projects would more easily attract resources and unfold more quickly because of increased synchronicities. Motivation would become more effortless, since our certainty and concentration would compel us to act. **If the future rests on finding more powerful states in the present, then the zone certainly qualifies as a taste of what lies ahead.**

Biologist Lyall Watson says that experiences of the zone are "mutational events," because they change our very definitions of what is possible. This is why I likened it to Peter Gabriel's tent, "The Future Zone." It provides tangible evidence of what might well become an ordinary state of being in the not-too-distant future. In fact, this may be the true purpose of zoning: to allow us to experiment with advancing our ability to function in the world.

Psychologists have recently expanded their notions of intelligence, identifying seven different types, such as spatial intelligence, musical intelligence, etc. The best known, emotional intelligence, is a quality some people have of being able to use and ride their emotions in a more productive way. **The zone can be considered a form of "meta-intelligience." Whenever we access and move around in this state, it brings all our faculties—emotional, cognitive, somatic, and the like—to a higher level.**

Hard-Wired Cells and the New Amphibians

Of course, many mystics and poets have explored the idea of an "emergent" state of consciousness. Emerson called it the "overmind," Bucke referred to it as "cosmic consciousness," and the Indian mystic Sri Aurobindo called it the "supramental." The Jesuit priest, Pierre Teilhard du Chardin described the mechanics of this evolution as a greater "interiorization," an internal deepening that would unfold in response to an evolving world.

Radical philosophers Timothy Leary and Terrence McKenna give a modern twist to our interpretation of this state. They recommend that more than new software (beliefs), the hard-wiring of our nervous systems needs to be reordered.

A reordering is precisely what happens in the zone. Information is processed differently, our sense of self is altered, perception shifts, conditioning dissolves, our brain waves are altered, and our physiology responds differently. After each experience we are forever changed, possessed of rarer skills.

A "muscle memory" takes place. Like riding a bike, the body retains a permanent awareness of where it has been. Once we have experienced a flow state, it is easier to retrieve, suggesting a permanent shift in hard-wiring. This is why athletes access the zone more frequently. Part of their job lies in recognizing when they get there, so they also know how to get there again. They train themselves to follow the path. It's no accident that so many professional athletes go on to success on the speaker's circuit; their proficiency at accessing the zone is something other people want to learn.

Very often, when we have a peak experience, it feels as if it has always been there and we have never left, that it is an ever-present, although unnoticed, feature of our consciousness. Every time we enter the zone, or the transcendent realm, a part of us never leaves. This is the new hard-wiring, or muscle memory. Your normal experience is subtly colored by every subsequent experience of this expansion. You are forever touched and begin to yearn for it as a permanent state.

When tadpoles are developing the ability to live on land, they slowly experience changes in their physiology. There is a time when their lungs have formed and they can breathe on land, but their gills are still functional, so they can breath under water as well. In this stage little functional legs appear, yet they can still swim around with the vestiges of their tails.

Amphibians have both sets of organs necessary for living on both land and water. In the same way, we may be developing early characteristics of what will eventually become a permanent state. **For a time, the capacity for ordinary action and the superordinary action of the zone will coexist.** Like tadpoles' gills, rational, linear thought may prove increasingly less effective. The belief that mind and body are separate may someday feel like a quaint memory. These ideas may dissolve like the remnants of the tadpoles' tail, as we spend more time in the enhanced fluidity of the zone.

The Future Only Exists in the Present

If the zone is a doorway into a future state, we need to look more closely at what we mean by the future. The future is not something that exists in chronological time. It is a construct of our minds, a metaphor for the unrealized potential of the unknown. Anything can happen tomorrow, so it allows us to entertain the notion of unlimited possibility. Whenever we tap possibilities beyond our conditioned reality, we enter the future.

The zone feels like the future because it takes you beyond the push-pull of dualistic thinking; you *know* what to do. This certainty exceeds the bonds of ordinary thought. It transports you past doubt and inertia and you effortlessly find the enthusiasm to act. Every time you touch one of the fourteen attributes of the zone and transcend your previous limitations, in effect, you are in the future.

A scientist was raising some baby fish in a small glass tank. He placed this small tank inside a larger tank with adult fish. The baby fish in the small tank could see the adult fish in the larger tank, but because of the glass barrier could not swim out.

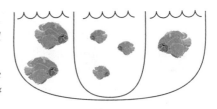

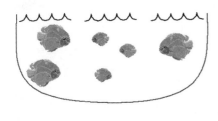

Once the small fish had grown up, the researcher removed the glass of their small tank so that they could swim out. But they didn't! They stopped at the perimeter of what used to be a glass wall. This conditioned experience was more real to them than the fact that the glass had been removed. Although the small tank was now gone, the memory persisted.

We are all a bit like these fish. We act within the range of what we have learned from the past. Our conditioning shapes the parameters of our world. The moment we "swim" beyond a past boundary, there is an exhilaration of surpassing our known existence. In that instant we have left our conditioning and habits behind; there is the freedom of no longer dwelling within a memory. All spiritual traditions refer to this as *awakening*, emerging from the hazy dream of our past.

The present is our point of power. It is the only moment in which we have choice. It is the only moment when we can go beyond the memories we project on the present. Only through expanding our sensations in the present can we ever attain something different from what we already know.

It sometimes takes time to fully grasp this idea. In the Carlos Castenada books, the Yaqui sorcerer, Don Juan, spends endless hours and about three books trying to get Carlos to understand this very concept. Entering the future means being willing to feel in ways you have never felt before. It means summoning what Castenada calls "an act of power" and redesigning the features of what you think you see.

There is an intriguing episode from the TV show, Star Trek: The Next Generation. The opening scene shows the ship's crew playing poker. A few minutes later an alarm sounds and the officers are called to the bridge for an emergency. A few minutes into the show, the ship explodes and everyone dies.

After the commercial, you see the exact same scene as in the opening, the crew playing poker and getting the same cards as before. The sequence proceeds, the alarm rings, the ship explodes, and everyone dies. Yet a third time, you see the crew playing poker. Only this time one of the crew correctly guesses what the next card will be. The poker game- emergency alarm- explosion sequence repeats a few more times. But now, each time the cycle occurs, the crew remembers a bit more about what is about to take place. They begin to realize that they have been in the situation before. They start to wake up.

With each repetition they become smarter. They realize they are caught in one of those nasty time loops that causes them to repeat the same 20 minute sequence over and over.

They plant clues for themselves that will "wake them up" to the fact that they keep making the wrong decision, however logical. Even though it is the most rational choice, the ship blows up over and over again. They must find a way to remember to make a different choice, rather than the sensible one that keeps leading to their eventual demise. Finally, they are able to forge a new pathway in their decision-making. They are able to make the less obvious choice, which saves the ship and frees them from the loop.

We are all living a version of this *Star Trek* story. Our remembered limitations function like an endless loop tape. We walk into a meeting and take on the same roles and opinions as in innumerable past meetings. Within days of starting work with a new partner, we recreate the same patterns we have followed with previous partners. We live with someone for years, yet have the same arguments over and over.

All forms of personal growth boil down to the process of placing little clues for ourselves that say, "Hey, wake up. You've done this before. Make a different choice!" Like the *Star Trek* crew, even though we are pulled almost irresistibly to make the same choice as in the past, some hazy part of our minds is vaguely awake enough to summon the alertness to do something different. We defy the attraction of the obvious path and strike out in a new direction, demonstrating an act of power. Entering the future, or truly accessing new possibilities, requires a transformation in the present, and that we break the bonds of the past.

Been There, Done That

Whenever we bring up this topic in our seminars, everyone always remembers a time when they were in the zone. A songwriter remembers a six-month period when he wrote almost all the songs that became the basis for nearly a decade of his career. A broker remembers a streak of "luck" in which every investment he made for months was right on target and this period set him up for life. These periods can be prolonged and yield fame and fortune, or they can be simple and quick, like following an urge to go to a very different place for lunch and bumping into a friend you haven't seen for years.

There really is no functional difference between what happens in these quick experiences versus a more prolonged one, or one with flashier results. In fact, in many ways the simple experiences are more relevant to understanding the zone. Major peak experiences can be more easily dismissed as once-in-a-lifetime events or a function of having been younger and more driven. The more ordinary experiences of the zone allow us to see that this expanded reality is always just a simple choice.

To Zone or Not to Zone

We go in and out of this state all the time, yet we dismiss or ignore it because it is not commonly discussed.

> ➤ Could we be ignoring all but the most extraordinary experiences of breakthrough because no one is talking about it?

> ➤ Could we be forgetting these simple moments of greater ease because all our friends always talk about how tired they feel or how much they have to do?

> ➤ Do businesses unconsciously limit people on a creative roll because of their overreliance on short-term results?

> ➤ Do we pay more attention to our hard work than our easy times because of the persistent ideology of "no pain, no gain?"

Imagine if from the time you were a child, your parents pointed out every time you were in a peak state and said, "Go for it, you're in the zone.

Don't worry about coming home for dinner. Don't mess with a roll." Suppose whenever you expressed a hunch, it was encouraged and you were not asked to explain why you felt that way, or when you were daydreaming, your reverie was considered productive. Imagine if the typical dinner conversation included everyone discussing the moments when their day became effortless and their vitality seemed endless. What if in school you studied about being in the groove, the nature of the creative process, and how brain waves tend to shift in altered states, and your teachers coached you on entering this state?

Then suppose TV talk shows regularly questioned guests about how they created lucky breaks, and the news regularly covered stories about projects that finished ahead of schedule in an effort to uncover clues that would allow others to do the same. If we were allowed to grow up this way and this was how the larger social environment was set up, zoning would be a much more accepted and frequent experience.

One of the main reasons we perceive the zone as rare is that it is still not a part of the larger culture. It is more socially acceptable to focus on how stressed we are than how inspired we are. As long as we focus on struggle, that is what will dominate our attention. As long as we have little opportunity to share the miraculous moments, they will continue to feel illusive.

The film *Don Juan de Marco* is an excellent illustration of the transitional path that we must all follow in order to live from the zone.

> *Johnny Depp as Don Juan is either truly is the world's greatest lover or more likely is delusional because of severe childhood trauma. Marlon Brando plays a psychiatrist who is on call the night Depp's character attempts suicide, and therefore becomes his therapist.*
>
> *Brando has one week left before retirement. His marriage to Faye Dunaway is comfortable, although a bit passionless after many years. He could easily slide into retirement and quickly get this patient off his hands by prescribing the appropriate drugs. Yet he fights his superiors to keep the case and resists giving drugs so he can find out what this client is really about. Deep down, Brando senses that he needs Don Juan, perhaps more than Don Juan needs him.*
>
> *As Brando halfheartedly tries to bring Depp out of his fantasy, Depp wholeheartedly tries to bring Brando in. It is a magical reality where dreams come true and days are filled with endless passion.*

Technically, Don Juan sees the same things the psychiatrist does, but he takes them in through a different filter. At one point, Brando asks him if he understands he's in a psychiatric hospital. Depp, who insists on calling Brando "Don Carlos," responds, "Don Carlos, you call this a hospital? I call it your hacienda!"

Ultimately, of course, Depp succeeds in building the stronger case. Brando is more interested in entering his world than Depp is in leaving. In the final scene, Brando enters a parallel universe where Depp is in fact Don Juan, he is Don Carlos, and he is joined by Dunaway in what promises to be nights of pleasure. The reason Brando enters Depp's world is because if he accepts that he truly is Don Juan, the world's greatest lover, then Brando can be Don Carlos and possess equal power!

The power of the Don Juan role is that he is someone who has totally transformed the world he sees. He sees the chairs and tables and all the stuff that you and I would see, but he also recognizes qualities unavailable to the normal eye. Like an athlete reaching perfect speed, Don Juan lives in a world with different rules.

I am asking you to make a similar transition to that which Brando makes. I have painted a glorious picture of a zone where dreams come true and passion reigns. You are probably intrigued; part of you, like Brando, wants to enter this universe, but the weight of ordinary life dominates your senses and reason says, "Nice concept, but irresponsible and unrealistic."

You might think: "Even if I believe in this crazy place of the zone, how could I live there? Would people call me strange? Would I lose my ability to be grounded and function in the ordinary world? And suppose I go there and can't get out?"

Johnny Depp takes his time in bringing Brando into his world. He knows that Brando must *really* want to be there or no amount of persuasion will work. It's the same here. No matter how magical I make cultivating a flow state appear to be, you won't expand your experience of this state unless you want it. Once you acknowledge a *desire* to live in and from an expanded reality, everything will begin to change.

All of a sudden it's a different world,
and infinity is just another game.

All of a Sudden by Laraji[8]

The first tool for navigating the future is our ability to enter advanced states of awareness that allow us to "bring the body along." It is the most fundamental way we have of reshaping what lies ahead.

> First, it represents a quickening of awareness, an ability to access, process, and organize information differently.

> Second, entering the zone goes to the heart of what is being transformed. Time and space, the very cornerstones of rational thought, are challenged. We access a place where the rules of manifestation are more directly influenced by our own consciousness.

> Third, it allows us to focus on the inevitability of this direction. It is an evolutionary response to a more complex and stressful environment.

> Finally, it highlights the natural hunger we each have to operate from a new level of being. Stories about "zoning" obviously fascinate us, and we naturally want to partake of the experience.

Slowly, both our random experiences in the zone and our intentional efforts to get there will begin to transform our nervous systems into a new "hard-wiring." We will cultivate the ability to consciously enter these states and sustain them for longer periods. And some day, we may even find that we have walked into this new world permanently.

Practicing the Zone

In Latin, there are two distinct terms for knowledge, *lexis* and *praxis*. This chapter and each of the next seven has these two parts.

> *Lexis* is the knowledge that rests in language. The linguistic dreaming of the first part of the chapter (which you've just completed) is designed to open your imagination and get you thinking.

> *Praxis* is the knowledge that rests in action. It can only be discovered in practice, and like learning to ride a bike, once attained, it's always there. The second part of each chapter is a practice section where I will describe ways to bring these ideas into your daily life;

e.g., how you start getting into the zone more often. Practice takes time and commitment. But if you do the second part well, you won't need to remember anything said in the first part; the ideas will have become your own.

Naming

Merely having a name for the zone and a willingness to begin noticing when this experience occurs can in and of itself increase the frequency of it's occurrence.

There was a tribe in South America that did not have a name for the color red. If a shade was closer to orange, that is what they called it. If it was closer to purple, then they called it purple. But once an anthropologist helped them make up a name for red, they were able to distinguish a color they had never seen before and they began to see it everywhere. In the same way, merely having a name and a concept for this state will probably cause you to start seeing zoning experience more often.

You might want to merely jot down an entry in your agenda whenever you feel yourself entering a zone state.

A woman we know who did this conscientiously found that with each passing week, the entries in her book increased. She came to realize that she had always entered expanded states; she just hadn't realized it. She also felt that merely by tracking it, she accelerated its frequency. This is a form of the Hawthorne effect, based on some studies that found when you decide to observe a particular behavior, people will often begin to produce the behavior just because you are looking for it. So merely naming and acknowledging the zoning state is an excellent starting exercise.

Body/Mind Synchrony

Athletes find that the zone state is always accompanied by a higher state of body/mind coherence. Here is a simple exercise you can do to promote body/mind integration at your desk.

Ask a friend to time you for 60 seconds on her watch. Or you can set a beeper for one minute. Now close your eyes. Open them as soon as you think one minute has passed. See how close or far off you are. If you are stressed or hyper, you will often think a minute has passed when it has only been 40 seconds or so. These 40-second minutes, or even 50-second minutes, create the psychological sensation of always being pressed or rushed. I once did this with a very stressed executive. She thought it was a full minute when only 30 seconds had passed!

This simple process has been used as a measure of what is called "time sickness," a recent phenomenon of being so stressed that you no longer perceive chronological time accurately. It is an exercise that you can do at points during the day, whenever you just can't seem to hold it together because everything is pulling at you. *It's a way of resetting your internal clock.* Take a few minutes to do this process and wind down again. Allowing yourself to relax until you can more accurately sense a 60-second minute goes a long way toward feeling more balanced. Balance is one of the conditions necessary for entering the zone.

Slowing and Deepening

At many points during the course of a day, you probably find your thoughts or actions becoming scattered. When faced with a project that is losing steam or a meeting that seems to be deteriorating, we tend to try harder and as a result often stray further from a flow state. If this is done repeatedly, it actually begins to trigger a muscle memory of effort and struggle, and the body begins to remember how to go there as well.

> When you notice a moment where your thoughts or actions seem to become more scattered, try stopping. Pause and do something different. Stopping goes further than just taking a rest, it involves relaxing into a different rhythm. As you begin to experiment with taking purposeful breaks, with the intent of shifting into a different rhythm, you'll discover the incredible power of this simple act.

This pause functions in much the same way as the previous exercise: It is a way of resetting your internal clock. As you become more familiar with the rhythm that accompanies a flow state, you will become more sensitive to when you leave it and automatically want to return to this sense of inner synchrony.

Cues

Aside from resetting your internal clock, there is a range of behaviors associated with being in the flow. In fact, the main difference between world-class athletes and merely good athletes is that the top winners seem to have more cues for knowing when they have entered the zone. They catch the experience early and can relax into it more fully, because they have more parameters for describing it.

The fourteen attributes introduced earlier in this chapter can serve as your body of cues. We once asked a group of people who were attending our seminar to spend one day focusing on each of the fourteen characteristics. One day they would notice every time their normal sense of time fluctuated; another day they would pay attention whenever they felt increased certainty, and so on. At the end of two weeks everyone felt they had a much better understanding of the range of cues that could suggest they were entering an expanded state. Why don't you try this.

> For the next two weeks, spend a day focusing your attention on one cue at a time. You can do this mentally or use the journaling technique, i.e., make a brief entry every time you notice a particular attribute entering your awareness.

Don't Close the Door

Philip's father, Roy, told us a great story. Roy is a long-time TM meditator. Once he went on a retreat set in Hopi territory. He asked where he could go to meditate and they suggested he go into a *kiva*, a traditional round building that is partially underground. Roy went in and began meditating as he does most every day. Almost instantly, he entered an experience of cosmic consciousness. It was a state he had heard about but had never himself experienced at this level. He was ecstatic. Then an innocuous thought crossed his mind: *He had forgotten to close the door.* Clearly aware of what a profound state he was in, he decided it made sense to get up and close the door so that no one would disturb his reverie. That done, he sat back down to continue his journey, but the experience was no longer there.

Closing the door put an end to what had been happening. In retrospect, he realized that the thought about the door was *not* innocuous. It was really a cover for an underlying terror, his fear that he would lose himself in that state and never be able to retrieve his personality. His fear masqueraded as a seemingly normal thought. Being in the flow is unfamiliar; it can feel like more than you are able to handle.

We all close the door on the zone experience because it represents more energy and freedom than we are used to having. You might be on a creative roll, innocently stop to return a phone call, and never quite get back to where you were. I have been in an extraordinary conversation with someone and suggested that we continue by getting more comfortable and going to sit down somewhere, just to find that when we get to the new location, the moment is lost. In the movie *Bull Durham,* Tim Robbins' character, the pitcher, one day puts on Susan Sarandon's black garter belt for luck, and enters a streak of no hitters. Kevin Costner's character, the catcher, subsequently insists that Robbins continue wearing the garter belt every day for months. As Costner said, "You never mess with a roll. " You don't change where you're standing, make a phone call, take off a garter belt, nothing!

> It is valuable to begin looking for the characteristic ways you pull yourself out of your zones. Next time, start a log of what happens when you leave a flow state. Do you get tired? Does your mind wander? Do you get fidgety and get up? There are infinite ways we have of doing this. Once you get a handle on how you exit the experience, experiment with it and try relaxing so you can hang in a bit longer. Every time you successfully extend the experience, you stretch your capacity to sustain it. It's a doorway that you can learn to keep open.

The other reason we leave the flow experience is because we hit what might be called an energetic threshold—the exhilaration feels like too much.

> Ask a friend to do this next process with you. Ask the person to acknowledge you, telling you all the things they like about you. As she does this, her job is also to stop whenever she feels you have in some way blocked the statement or not fully let it in. You'll give cues, like blinking faster, darting your eyes, spacing out, or laughing. Every time this happens, the person stops and asks you what's going on. Invariably, you will notice that you had an extraneous thought while they were talking or an emotion like sadness or guilt which kept you from staying present. After you describe what happened, go back to having them acknowledge you again and repeat the process.

As you learn to detect your favorite ways of leaving, you will find you can stay with the acknowledgments longer and more powerfully. Receiving acknowledgment is similar to maintaining a high-energy experience of any kind. Having done this process, you will be able to apply it in other situations, such as a project or relationship that just can't seem to break though.

Perfect Speed

We each possess very personal conditions that make it easier to touch the zone.

> Make a list of five or six key times recently when you entered the zone for a more sustained period. Spend a few moments analyzing each experience. What happened just preceding and at the moment of entering the experience? What elements were present: deadline or no deadline; working alone or working with others; quiet, meditative conditions or wild chaos. After analyzing each experience, see if you can identify any common threads. Eventually, experiment with designing your working conditions so that these threads are in place.

Challenge and Mastery

An observation that Csikszentmihalyi and others have made is that zone states are more often triggered when there is a balance of challenge and mastery. Too much challenge leads to overstimulation and stress. Too much focus on playing it safe leads to boredom and stagnation. Most people tend to fall into one camp or the other. Some people constantly keep themselves in a state of overstimulation and need to focus on building pockets of certainty and calm. Others tend to protect themselves and keep it safe, and therefore need to focus more on risk-taking and defining new challenges. It's useful to determine which camp you tend to fall into and adjust your workstyle/lifestyle by either adding or reducing risks and challenges.

Building a Social Environment

Someone we know was collaborating on a very significant creative project. Since she had done quite a few of our seminars and had a lot of familiarity with the experience of entering the zone, she began to point out to her partner when they both were on a roll and solutions seemed to be effortless. Just by pointing it out, they both found that they became more aware of their working rhythms and began to use their time more successfully.

> There are ways to point out zoning experiences without sounding too strange. If you are in a meeting, you might say something like, "I feel we just created an opening," or "That exchange felt good." Try to notice even subtle shifts where flow occurs more freely.

Recently I was involved in a frustrating series of meetings on a volunteer project. I was on the verge of dropping out because the meetings were so disorganized. By good fortune, I remembered this process and went to the next meeting with only one goal, to verbally acknowledge any time I felt some progress was made, *however slight*. After an hour of making observations like this, it seemed we had our first decent meeting ever. Eventually, this chaotic and very diverse group was able to successfully pull off a big community event. Whether these observations just kept me more creatively involved or really did turn things around as it appeared, for the first time I was able to attend the meeting without wanting to scream!

Awakening Don Juan

The real key to entering expanded states more frequently is wanting it. We all have ways of getting what we really want. Merely desiring to function from this state will cause you to find ways of triggering it.

> An interesting strategy is a technique called reframing, pioneered by psychologist Erik Erikson and made popular by a form of training called neurolinguistic programming. With this technique, you think about something you really desire, maybe a new car or a vacation to an exotic island. You think about the object for several minutes with the intention of building the feeling of really wanting it. Once you achieve the kinesthetic experience of wanting, you can maintain it while changing the object of your desire. In this case, allow yourself to feel that you want to be in the zone with the same intensity and specificity that you might feel about a new car.

Philip is constantly obsessed with some new gadget that he wants. Within a few weeks of getting it, he stumbles upon the next item he wants and finds himself thinking about it with the same intensity. He came up with the idea of transferring his obsessive thoughts about gadgets to wanting to be at the peak of his creativity. Every time he noticed himself thinking about a new toy, he reframed it. He would say to himself, "But what I really want is heightened creativity." It sounds a bit corny but it worked. Not only did it save us a lot of money; in the period he was doing this, he got a quantity and quality of work done that surpassed anything he had ever done.

The more you discern, acknowledge, provoke, and sustain the zoning experience, the more it will feel like a state of awareness that is at your disposal—a handy tool for hyperspeed, high-demand moments. Remember, the key to anchoring this state is to focus on the kinesthetic experience, the "muscle memory" of getting there and staying there. Although it is easy to get lost in the wonderful feelings of the zone; it is a neurological experience, affecting our physical rhythms, sensory capacities, and even brain waves. If the beginning research is right, it will eventually start to change your hard-wiring and serve as a neurological bridge.

Several years ago, with the advent of digital photography, a device was developed called the "Magic Eye."

> *At first glance, the Magic Eye appears as a random series of colored dots with lots of empty spaces and little aesthetic appeal. There is little about the image to catch your attention. In fact, it is somewhat unattractive and dull.*
>
> *If you relax your eyes in just the right way, a 3-D image suddenly pops out, not at all your previous perception of chaotic dots. The image that appears is fascinating, complex, and has an amazing level of detail. In fact, it is constructed from a photograph that has had so many of the dots removed that for a long time all you can see are the spaces and randomness. When the new image finally presents itself, it is as if another layer of reality is emerging.*
>
> *The Magic Eye is commonly used to illustrate paradigm shift, since the sensation goes far beyond that of a normal optical illusion. It is not just a shift in perception, but another order of experience. You keep looking, relaxing, and modifying your internal filters until finally this visual breakthrough occurs.*

Our cultural landscape often looks as unappealing as our first glance of the Magic Eye—fractured, random, nothing makes sense, the patterns are not aesthetically appealing. But as with the Magic Eye, if you relax and allow your preconceptions to dissipate you may find an image of surprising depth and detail, locked beneath your initial impressions. Chapter 5 describes a series of perceptual shifts that are more suited to catching images in our current cultural landscape. It is a shift that may at first seem like **a new sense.**

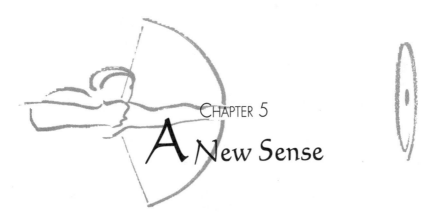

CHAPTER 5
A New Sense

Our environment is no longer one of forests and mountains, slow seasons and subtle colors. In less than 200 years we have created an entirely new sensory world.

The arenas in which we work and play are filled with ideas, information, and mind stuff. Sixty percent of the gross domestic product is now derived from activities having to do with information. The average manager reads hundreds of thousands of words a day and spends 60 percent of the time with paperwork, digital and nondigital. TV news clips flash by in increments of 11.5 seconds, down from 23 seconds just a decade ago. Every newspaper in the country has been downgraded in terms of vocabulary and grammar, partly because we have poorer linguistic skills but also so we can grab information faster. Complex sentences and less common words slow you down. In less than a year, the number of people on line will double, probably also doubling the bits that are zipping around our info highways. Product cycles decline with every passing month: an automobile can now be assembled in days; a book on a timely topic can be rushed to the stores in weeks. The decision makers functioning within these market cycles have to be able to sense trends long before they are visible to the ordinary eye.

We are entering a fundamentally new era both of business strategy and personal growth strategy. For a long time we focused on skills development and improving quality. Individuals and organizations tried to get better at what they did, to know more. The new era in which we find ourselves will be increasingly based on perception and our ability to sense where things are going. Business and personal directions will rely less on resources, products, and fixed models and more on our infinite supply of ideas and creativity and our capacity to perceive opportunities. It's no longer who you know, or even what you know, but how far you can see.

If we must learn how to see farther ahead, then we must also understand a bit more about the nature of our current sensory environment. Our information world has become not only prolific and intrusive, but fractured and disjointed. This mass of undifferentiated, unsolicited data threatens to undermine our cognitive health. Our attention spans dwindle and we have little time for subtleties. Although we are asked to see more, often we are sensing less. To make this transition, our perceptions must echo our surroundings—faster, fuzzier, and more tuned to what's ahead.

Seven Sensory Adaptations

➤ *The future is arriving faster.* A window to what lies ahead seems to be perpetually open, a permanent feature of our sensory world. The line between today and tomorrow is very transparent. Thus whatever is brewing on the edge impacts our everyday affairs much faster. We must gain faculties for dealing with this "bitemporal" experience. Our awareness of what lies ahead must be tuned and sharpened, so that it is as developed as the future itself.

➤ *The amount of available information has become so massive that it becomes background rather than foreground.* Knowledge no longer has a shape and profile that can be discerned. It is instead a field upon which our actions rest. Details drop away, information blurs. In a sea of churning data, directions, flows, and interconnections become more evident. We must adapt by learning to see with a softer focus, with entirely different kinds of filters.

➤ *The pace of modern life has made our window of attention much narrower.* Unless data reaches us quickly, we are gone. Our response time has been shortened. Feedback loops are tighter. The impact of an action shows up quicker. There is a danger that in moving so fast, issues will become so simplified and superficial they will be meaningless. To compensate, knowing must become more instinctual, arising from deeper roots, committed to more archetypal truths.

➤ *A glut of information screams at us around every bend.* In order to attract our attention, every year the volume is raised, sometimes metaphorically by making images more seductive. They have become what MTV calls "eye candy." The more candy we eat, the less appetite we have for subtle, complex, more nutritious information. We will lose all sense of ourselves and become cognitively out of shape on this sugar diet, unless we find a new set of sensory priorities.

➤ *Speed itself alters perception.* It induces a quality of heightened intuition and stretches our senses. A natural "paranormalization" of our perceptions will emerge as our normal boundaries are redefined. A project in hyperspeed may provoke strange and unusual capacities not present under normal conditions.

➤ *Our new sensory environment will require more fluid identities in order to be able to comprehend the multilayered nature of the information world.* Your history, lifestyle, and aspirations all shape your interpretations. Who you are is the ultimate sense organ.

➤ *In order to see further ahead, we must discover new sources of passion.* This will allow us to counter the increasing numbness that our growing information glut seems to provoke.

As you can see, the future will require more complex, profound, and unusual perceptions. If you have a heightened sense of what is coming, then it is easier to feel centered in an increasingly chaotic world. It's a bit like being in a vast video game. As your senses expand, it seems that the characters are not coming at you quite as fast. Heightened perception slows things down. It allows an accelerating world to at least feel as if it is moving at a more comfortable pace.

The following pages detail these seven sensory adaptations so they become more practical and usable.

1. Edging

Someone who has attended a number of our seminars owns one of the most prestigious fashion forecasting companies. One year she hired her twenty-year-old son to travel to different cities; he combed the streets from Brussels to Delhi, looking for what the kids were wearing, often in the poorest areas. These ideas from the edges of society were then bound into a glossy magazine and sold to the elites of the fashion world to let them know what lies ahead. If she merely removed the fabrics and color samples, this magazine could easily be reprinted as a hot new sociological forecast.

This same dynamic occurs in every field. The sounds on the street become next year's Grammys. The explorations of teenage hackers quickly become the basis for next year's hot stocks. Companies run by Gen-Xers are redefining the role of management. "Hot off the press" companies that function without rules are provoking others to learn their game. Many years ago I worked as a family therapist and found that the youngest child, the one on the edge because of age, often had the clearest perception of what was *really* going on with their parents.

The future always lurks at the edges, among those who are least locked into the system.

While the mainstream focuses on solidifying its power, those who are outside the loop are free to think beyond the system. A venture capitalist told us that over 50 percent of new inventions come from individuals who are not directly in the field. The greatest competition to the blue chip companies is not from their peers, but from shoestring upstarts that are free to change how the industry operates, like a Southwest Airlines or a Netscape. The information companies are quickly learning that when a programmer thinks he has a hot idea, if he doesn't get what he wants, he can quickly find the capital to form his own upstart. Thus the edges are beginning to acquire more power.

A recent survey asked a wide range of corporate staff where they thought the *real* leadership came from in their company. Ten areas were mentioned: CEO, VPs, mid-level management, sales, marketing, secretarial, etc. Each area received between 6 and 10 percent of the votes. In other words, leadership can come from anywhere.[1] There is no top; the edge is everywhere.

If the future lives at the edge, and the edge has more power, and the edge can be anywhere, then we must learn how to locate where the thresholds really are. People sometimes think the edge lies in cultural taboos, so they seek to push the limits of what is acceptable. This is the kind of strategy Calvin Klein used when he caused a stir by showing what seemed to be preadolescent models in provocative poses. Movies, books, and advertising all take this tack, trying to be more risqué, darker, more shocking, or more "something" in order to stand out. This may have been a valuable direction when rigid roles and rules were more entrenched, but in a chaotic world, increasingly, the outrageous will barely catch our eye. Screaming louder or weirder than anyone else is just more of the same.

The edge now lives in a far more subtle place. The new thresholds will be found in envisioning new dimensions. Some experts call this *vertical vision,* the capacity to see through and beyond obvious images.

Sometimes the edge resides with people who have left the system and discovering what is pushing them out. Sometimes it exists in things so obvious they are ignored. Howard Jones developed Callback, a $40 million business and a $500 million-a-year industry, from a simple observation that many before him had also seen: it was costing more to call NYC from Paris than Paris from NYC. Sometimes the edge rests in challenging sacred cows. John Stack introduced the revolutionary idea of open-book management, allowing everyone to see and participate in the finances of a company. He credits this strategy with saving his company, SRC Holdings, and leading to some of its greatest breakthroughs. Sometimes the edge rests in following new values. Real Goods, a company that carries supplies for sustainable building, is the fastest growing small business in the United States. A hit children's cartoon from Britain is sweeping the U.S. market. It stands out because the animation is low-tech, the cuts are as slow as cartoons from the fifties, and the story lines are innocent and have little action.

Edges are not so much found in a place. They can be anywhere, at any level, at any angle of approach. It's popular now to advise careerists to read magazines outside their field or attend conferences on topics unrelated to their work. In fact, the mainstream publications of most fields tend to follow the same assumption, therefore they may offer little new stuff. Real edging must go deeper. It rests less in new content than in a persistent and relentless attitude.

The fashion forecasting company I spoke of a couple of pages back did not send someone to take the same trip to foreign cities the next year. Instead, it did something unheard of. It sent out a book without any fabric samples at all; the forecasts were based completely on ideas. And the year after that their edge was somewhere else. Even though the staff has desks and they are in straight lines and the business form is traditional, it is a company with an attitude of edging. And this attitude is constantly modeled right from the top, from the world-class selection of art books in the library and insistence on breathtaking graphics to the continual insistence that staff take risks. There are no short cuts to true creativity.

The edge is not what your competition or someone else is doing, but what you could be doing that you are ignoring. It exists within your own values and beliefs. The way to begin expanding your own perceptual field is to learn how to look past your own center to the nagging thoughts at the edges of your psyche, to perceptions that lie just beyond ordinary awareness. In conversations, it may mean following an off-the-cuff remark rather than the main point. It means staying alert to subtle openings in your thought process that are so easy to miss. It means taking chances and facing conflict. It means confronting the obvious. It means surrounding yourself with excellence whatever your aesthetic may be. More than anything, it requires a sincere intention to look for thresholds.

Of all the work we do in our seminars, my favorite is coaxing out slivers of information that lead to the next direction. If the future is showing up faster, then whatever is brewing at the circumference will enter our lives before we know it. Therefore, we need a keener eye for developing this peripheral vision. The future demands a powerful commitment to this perceptual style of "edging."

2. Blurring, Fields and Flows

Much of the sensation of speed we experience in our culture has to do with the volume of information that assails us. In one day we may see hundreds of ads, read hundreds of thousands of words, and meet more people than we once saw in a lifetime. Information is cheap, accessible, and the bulk of the industrial world's activity is now devoted to moving it around. When faced with such abundance, we tune out and become numb to the details.

We seek out people or services that will predigest it for us, telling us what is important. Companies that filter the world for us and give it to us in a more personalized form represent one of the fastest growing sectors of the information economy. A technological breakthrough called Agents will allow our computers to learn our preferences and edit information for us. Critics say Agents and other push technologies will make us lazier, less discerning, and more mindless, just like with TV. Proponents say these effects are merely temporary and once the technology evolves, it will supercharge our brains. With such "cyber-attachments" we'll be able to race through mountains of information.

With or without this technical support, we are racing through a river of sensations anyway. Mattel toys determined that children can retain 80 to 90 percent of what they hear on hyperspeed ads with over 100 edits in 60 seconds. Adults find these ads irritating and retain almost nothing. At the same time, today's high school kids find the linguistic complexity and rhythms of Shakespeare or Joyce just as annoying. Their brains can't slow down enough to hear the words.[2] It's a curious sensory dilemma: Shakespeare vs. MTV—the sensory capacity for one seems to obliterate the other.

Perhaps by knowing the dilemma we can begin to develop two sensory modes, hyperspeed and hyperdepth, and learn to cultivate both. Hyperspeed requires that we focus on broad sweeps of information rather than specific ideas. Ironically, it requires a more profound ability to detach and not latch on to details. It is the kind of instinctual knowing required when you drive a car at high speed. You let your mind relax and your reflexes lead.

> *I once attended a think-tank conference which included some of the elite of biology, physics, and other academic fields as speakers. I understood about 50 percent of what they were saying and kept paying more intense attention so maybe I could catch a little more. I went with a friend whose first language is Italian and who probably has only about 75 percent of my proficiency in English. He didn't even try to get the details; he relaxed and settled for a far less literal comprehension. In our discussion afterward, it appeared that he understood the entire conference, maybe more than the speakers. Like the kids who can discern hyperspeed ads, he listened for field, flow, pulse, and direction. Maybe this guy is just smarter, but I think listening for detail actually diminished my understanding.*

Buckminister Fuller, one of the great systems thinkers of our time, had an undiagnosed visual disorder for most of his early childhood years. He is certain that spending his childhood in a visual blur was directly related to his talent for thinking in fields and systems. He was seeing the world without fixed edges. Hyperspeed viewing requires allowing the sea of data to retreat from your immediate view so that it becomes background. When viewed as a panorama, new dimensions of how information is organized can come to the fore.

It also requires a "leap before you look" kind of mindset. More and more companies have dropped long-term visioning and multiyear budgeting on the assumption that planning is inseparable from action. It is only when you are sitting with a client delivering your product or supervising a new staff member that you suddenly "get" what the next step is for you or your company. The doing *is* the analysis. We all intuitively know this; we always get smarter when we have to attend to someone's specific questions, so why this continued overreliance on predetermining our goals. It is a lot more useful to make a list of new and challenging situations we can put ourselves in. In this new sensory world it is much smarter to design your learning environment, the context in which you intend to place yourself, rather than your objectives.

Information-based companies are leading the way in this new perceptual style by echoing the nature of the digital environment in which they operate. In the new Net economy, "the business model is constantly monitored, reevaluated and rejiggered."[3] These rejiggered, loosely formed companies will even drop an existing product if they stumble upon a new one that seems better. They do not tack their identity to a product, but on a corporate intelligence that can be applied flexibly. They focus on developing responsiveness and resiliency. Their goals are loose, often not fully articulated until there is a need to define themselves, and then only temporarily.

It is now an accepted fact that the peak performers in the new information world are generally those who have a very developed instinctual, nonrational style of knowing. They consciously work at having fewer mental images of how things should unfold. Sometimes their ideas can't be fully articulated. They think with fewer thoughts. They might not be able to quantify their hunches. The new perceivers may only be able to say, "This is where we need to go; I just know it."

In our recent sensory past, if a project didn't go the way we expected, we would look for what was wrong. There is no right and wrong in the world of information flows and fields.

When a project takes an unexpected turn, instead of fixing it, *you follow it.* The archetypal story is how 3M stumbled upon post-it notes. In his search to create a super glue, a researcher came up with a minimally effective glue. Metaphorically then, if the glue doesn't stick very well, go with it. Rather than fix it, find a market for mediocre-sticking glue!

If you've had the opportunity to drive in Europe or in the U.S. West where there are no speed limits, you know that when you're going 100+ mph, you don't worry if you hear a car honking or catch a glimpse of something approaching or just sense that you need to avoid something. In fact, all avenues of input merge together. This is exactly how we are beginning to operate. It as if all our antennae are up, looking for any "ripples in the force." We know in a way that seems to transcend our ordinary senses. The new supersensory individuals trust this blurry sensory style. They cultivate hunches, pursue illogical directions, act more randomly, feel comfortable with fuzzy details, and allow their companies to move along even if they never quite figure out a mission statement.

This fuzzy, fast knowing must be balanced by a more intelligent gut response. An MVP-quarterback who makes a broad perceptual sweep of the playing field will sense very different things than an amateur. The quarterback has a greater depth that comes from more cultured instincts and a more intelligent "gut," a more refined way of experiencing the world. The broader and fuzzier your sweeps, the more commitment you must make to your craft, your depth, and your precision.

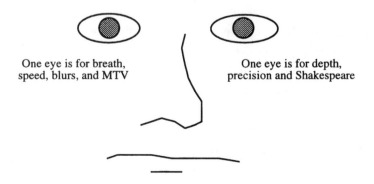

One eye is for breath,
speed, blurs, and MTV

One eye is for depth,
precision and Shakespeare

The next section deals with the second perceptual style, *hyperdepth*. You can appreciate that someone who can retain information from ads with 100 edits per minute and also grasp the nuances of Shakespeare would be a very formidable player in their chosen field.

3. Precision of Attention

To balance out these fuzzy broad sweeps, we need heightened focus. Fuzzy organizations need more finely honed individuals. The looser the rules, the more refined our skills need to be. Although we are offered more and more possibilities, most of us have had to narrow our attention in the last few years. Specialties within specialties within specialties have been spawned. Most companies have had to follow a path similar to the computer art which is created by using fractal equations, each pattern representing a more narrow spin on the original form.

Fractal equations demonstrate that the distance between any two points is always infinite. Let's say you decide to measure a coastline and find that the distance from LA to San Francisco is roughly 400 miles. But if you start measuring every point where the coastline goes in and out and forms a harbor or promontory, the distance suddenly gets much longer. And you can find infinitely longer measures by using smaller and smaller units of measure. Thus the actual distance between LA and SF is infinite, it depends on the size of ruler you use.

Most companies are becoming what we might call "fractalized," because their services rest on new dimensions of their existing product or service. Thus their range of services can become infinitely long, depending on how closely they choose to examine a market. An attorney in the legal department of a motion picture company told us that for 10 years, he provided cookie-cutter, one-size-fits-all contracts. Today, every contract is totally unique; taking into account new media, new distribution, creative quirks, the need of artists to define what they want, etc. He projects that this tailoring of proposals will become more complex with every passing year. Thus the same individual in the same job has to perceive unique spins just to get the same task done.

More and more companies are having to free up and reward individuals for following their increasingly personalized fields of expertise. Microsoft hired a computer programmer who was blind. In his efforts to create an acceptable work environment for himself, he developed a series of products that have put Microsoft on the cutting edge of programs for the blind. This was not the job he was hired to do, but he was given the space to "spin" out a new fractal curve, and the larger corporation had the corporate intelligence that allowed them to listen.

Markets continue to splinter into ever narrower fields addressed by individuals with more personalized areas of expertise and more individualized whims. Every business has become more technical and the directions more specialized. Often the person you hire knows more than you do, so old-fashioned supervision goes out the window. Knowledge is no longer concentrated in the center or at the top. The highest forms of knowledge are found in the heart of every individual. In this new fractalized world of business organization, there must be space for people to develop ever smaller and more targeted spins, thus new dimensions of the market and new dimensions of organizational intelligence.

> *In this new sensory world, quirkiness, an examined life, and personal passion are often your main assets.*

If you are seeking a solution, you don't necessarily look for the person with the most experience or organizational power; you look for someone who is placed in a way that gives them a better vantage point. Sometimes it's your customer who has the needed angle, sometimes a supplier, sometimes someone in another department. So you must discover a way to serve others that maximizes what they know rather than promotes what you know. Our new perceptual world requires harnessing each person's unique strengths and perspectives.

One of the liabilities of having things fast and loose is that the capacity to endure suffers. Enduring is the ability to persist through multiple layers, which is why Shakespeare is so difficult to hear. Developing your own quirky spins, leading an examined life, and expressing your individual take on the world are powerful ways of building endurance. It builds a depth that can begin to counter the fast and loose ways in which we must also operate.

Fostering endurance or precision requires knowing when someone "has the force" and is connected with their piece of the world at a high level, and in those moments to let them lead. It means restructuring boundaries so these micromovements can enter into the direction of the larger organization. It requires not only trusting but making room for very personalized expressions of creativity. It requires letting anyone lead, even a customer, if they happen to be the one with the unique spin that is needed at a particular moment. It also allows precision and depth to become driving values. Leadership lies in actively supporting the people around you in knowing more than you do, encouraging them to delve deeper into their own particular spins on reality, and knowing how to follow the thread in a conversation, project, or business deal that has the most "juice."

4. New Priorities

Locating priorities has to do with "following the juice," finding the directions with the most promise.

> At a certain point, the law of diminishing returns takes effect,
> the glut of information no longer contributes to our quality of life,
> but instead begins to cultivate stress, confusion and ignorance.
> Information overload threatens our ability to educate ourselves, and leaves us
> more vulnerable as consumers and less cohesive as a society.[4]
>
> *Data Smog*—David Shenk

Every increase in speed requires resetting priorities. At 40 mph street signs are important. At 100 mph signs can barely be read and staying on the road is all that counts. As your personal or corporate speed increases, the question you must continually ask is, "What information do I really need?" This question is as important as defining goals used to be. Increasingly, we will all be defined by what we pay attention to. Where we choose to look is what will eventually fill the space.

Many years ago, I was working at a management institute which used a theoretical framework called "decision theoretic." We would help organizations define the kinds of decisions they might have to make several years down the road and then help them design their data collection systems so they would feed these future decisions. The most important feature of this work was that defining information needs became a way of shaping organizational intelligence. Unconsciously, people paid more creative attention to the information they had selected as important. What you look at now becomes what you eventually will see down the road. If you change what you are looking out for, you will see something different down the road. What you choose to perceive, edit, and prioritize are unconscious forms of scenario building or visioning.

An oft-repeated quote is that the Sunday *New York Times* has more information than the average person in the 17th century encountered in a lifetime. Imagine having years to ponder the travel section. You would not need to make choices about where you spent your information resources. Since we are absorbing what was once a lifetime of information in a weekend, selection criteria is vital.

An almost unlimited availability of information can be addictive. Great graphics and catchy titles tease you into reading one more article that you won't remember. The growing information smog threatens to choke off real intelligence. Writer/consultant Tom Peters warns that soon all we may see is "garbage going at the speed of light."

Obviously, editing is a key way to filter out the garbage. If you set priorities, the mass of information that seemed undifferentiated and overwhelming can offer a path to more informed thought. Every school and business should offer a course in information management—how to select information criteria, how to know when you have a well-rounded approach to an issue and *when you don't,* how to perceive bias, how to read between the lines, how to evaluate conflicting information, and so on. If your company or school doesn't offer this course, find a way to take it anyway. Your intellectual health is at stake. Go on an information diet: turn off the TV, stop the paper, and give yourself some creative breathing space.

A lot of the so-called data has crossed the line into persuasion. Much of what we read and hear are really stories fed to journalists by PR companies employed by corporations. Is the development of a new computer or a new auto really news? Is a celebrity going on vacation really news? It sits on the page like news, but it's mostly promotion. When there is so much information being pushed at you, it's hard to distinguish between opinion, persuasion, and real news. Everything blends together unless you heighten your critical faculties.

The most serious aspect of an information-rich diet and a seductive landscape is that our senses become focused outward and we lose the

ability to perceive internal messages. Research is beginning to surface that claims children who spend hours looking at TV and computer screens may experience alterations in their brain waves that the researchers interpret as the loss of internal imaging capacity. Furthermore, this decline in internal imaging has also been associated with these children having more aggressive and violent feelings. Could this be part of the reason we have "lost our global temper," that everyone seems to be running on a shorter fuse?

Setting priorities may be the only way to ensure that you think your own thoughts. Internal imaging may be a necessity for maintaining sanity. It is a fact that if someone is deprived of REM sleep, the time when we dream, in a few days they will start to become delirious and eventually go insane. Perhaps internal imaging, having our own ideas and visions, is a waking form of REM sleep. Setting information priorities may be a key way of protecting our imaginative faculties, and therefore our emotional health.

Exercising the "eye" that can respond to Shakespeare is necessary to balance the new eye that can respond to hyperspeed ads. I believe it is important to spend a portion of every day daydreaming, with no intention of ever implementing your dreams, imagination for imagination's sake, spacing out just to slow your sensory style. Some psychologists have linked daydreaming with intelligence in children—just the data you were looking for! As you settle back for your next good daydream, tell your colleagues, "I'm just going to focus on my internal images and sharpen my intelligence for a while."

5. Paranormalization

There is a reason people become race car drivers; speed is a *rush*. When a project is in hyperspeed, it is often a pleasurable feeling. Part of workaholism is the addiction to the exhilaration of adrenaline rushes. We would probably do well to kick the adrenaline habit, but since it is an ever-present and natural part of our physiology, when you do enter an adrenaline rush, at least try using it more consciously to expand your senses and your mind.

Neuropsychologists now think psychedelics work by inhibiting the natural tendency of the brain to block out stimuli. Cultural speed or project acceleration may operate in a very similar way; we are sensing more than what is familiar. When dramatic breakthroughs happen, or a project or idea speeds up, people suddenly get smarter, their perceptions heighten, they hear things beneath the words, and they sense patterns that were previously undetectable.

Beyond the adrenaline rushes that expand our senses, we are also dwelling in a more complex environment that is stretching our receptivity. The way our sensory system operates is that receptors create the nature of the sensation. Rods in the eye are receptors that allow us to see line and shape. Cones are another form of receptor that allows us to see color. Other kinds of receptors cause frequencies in the world to appear as sound or touch. In reality, we are swimming in a sea of undifferentiated frequencies that our brain then forms into shapes, colors, sounds, and smells. Thus, the medium is the message. Receptors shape the nature of input. Theoretically, if we developed new receptors, we would begin to distinguish experiences not currently available. If we are being subjected to a new range and speed of cognitive stimuli, then we may indeed be developing entirely new receptors.

One form this may take is through linguistic evolution. We are in the midst of a language explosion. Entire dictionaries are now devoted to the new jargon. A surprising number of the words in the New Webster's dictionary did not exist 20 years ago. It amazes me when the spell check on my brand new program cannot recognize words that I already consider to be common usage. The futurists are big contributors to this growth industry. Toffler may have started the trend over 20 years ago when he introduced the concept of *Future Shock*. Now everyone is hot on the language trail; we define our unique niche by creating new words. Your bio can even contain a reference to a wonderful word you coined. Faith Popcorn entered the public eye as the creator of the terms "cocooning" and "wombing in." Watts Wacker is hyping the term "downward nobility," a reference to messages that don't play to materialism. Terms like these can launch entire new marketing strategies for companies. New words are a powerful way of creating receptors and identifying previously unrecognized phenomena in ways that can make them usable. Eskimos have hundreds of words for snow, seeing distinctions we wouldn't care about. We have become the "Eskimos" of marketing, having hundreds of words for social forces that people in the past didn't know or care about.

In 1954, Alan Freid, the most famous DJ ever, went on the air and said in effect, "Rhythm and Blues is out; from this day forward, we will call this music Rock and Roll." On the strength of a new phrase a new era of music was ushered in, and an entire generation had a new identity.

Every month, the magazine *Fast Company* profiles a person with a trendy job title, such as Troublemaker, presumably to spark ideas for the reader. It is interesting to analyze your personal dreams or new business directions in terms of creating a phrase that will open new doors. Philip and I know a guy who created a job title that didn't previously exist, a "fractal spin." He then approached a company with it and was hired to fill the position that he himself had conceived.

6. Remasking

One of the most interesting features of the increasing speed of information flow is that it alters our sense of self. The way we refer to ourselves becomes less tied to stories and past events and more focused on what lies ahead. People on job interviews used to stress past accomplishments. Now job hunters are coached to talk about their *intended* directions, what they *propose* to offer down the road. The shift is from a historic focus to an intentional focus.

An atmosphere of continuously changing rules and priorities requires being able to change mindsets at will. Since the Net allows us to assume constructed identities, we are all gaining some practice. This fluidity of persona is an extraordinary cultural development. Shifting identities is one of the most powerful ways to allow new perceptions to emerge and it represents a substantially new mindset. (There's more about this in Chapter 7, Mythmaking.) Creativity consultants often try to get us to act like children, shooting each other with squirt guns and playing with brightly colored toys. By becoming kidlike, they suggest we are more likely to experience spontaneous and unbounded ideas.

When Philip and I lead seminars for couples, one of the key processes we employ is a role play in which the partners are asked to change places. When husbands "become" their wives and vice versa, mimicking body language and using their partner's favorite expressions, they are always blown away to see themselves through their partners' eyes. Not only is it usually incredibly funny, often it is the first step to healing. Colleagues can also benefit by stepping into each others shoes, or looking through a client's or supplier's eyes. A workplace and culture in flux requires the ability to look through ever shifting sets of eyes. Thus, *who* you are is *what* you see. As I said earlier, *our identity is the ultimate sense organ.*

7. Passion and Perception

When you are in love, your lover sometimes seems to move in slow motion, because you are willing to see him or her so deeply. There is an intensity about what you notice. You know what your lover is thinking and feeling without having to ask. In the same way, when we are involved in an absorbing project, everything around us seems to remind us of our work. Passion lies at the heart of perceptual style; it affects how profoundly we allow ourselves to see.

The reverse may also be true; expanding perception may in turn increase passion. There are many examples of this, but I'll let the tale of a project manager named Ed make the point.

> *Ed had a way of speaking which seemed numb. No matter what he said, you felt bored when he talked. His girlfriend complained that when he came home, all he wanted was to watch TV or surf the Net. Even having friends over was a radical idea for him. We knew this numbness had to be coloring everything he did. We began to offer Ed the suggestions we will present in this chapter's practice section: how to see beneath people's words, sense feelings he was ignoring, exaggerate perceptions he thought were inconsequential, look past his customary descriptions and make up words for experiences he could not explain. He was part of a seven-month leadership program we were offering, so we got to see him change over time. Not only did he increase his income, he started traveling, to the delight of his girlfriend, and has formed the kind of upstart company you'd like to buy stock in.*

Merely opening his perceptual style resulted in a more natural motivation. By letting go of his habitual numbness, he became irresistibly attracted to the future.

Passion is probably the most powerful tool for breaking out of the three dimensional boundaries of ordinary perceptual experience. When we feel passion, we are compelled to break down walls and see past the ordinary. When we are passionate about what we do, we want to see more. And conversely, when we allow ourselves to see more, we feel more passion.

Foresight

Although each has its own twist, these seven sensory developments rest essentially on the same dynamic. They involve locating information you have previously ignored.

In Greek, the word for prophecy is *profitia*. The literal translation is "before you take a position." All that is necessary for allowing foresight, or prophecy, is to practice operating from a perceptual stance that does not involve already having a position. Every time you experience information without any prior bias, you are beginning to sense the future.

- When you practice "edging," or peripheral viewing, you are less biased because the habitual or the status quo is less dominant, and ignored information comes to the fore.

- When you look at the world as streams, flows, fields, and vortices, the loss of detail allows predispositions to drop away.

- When you become more precise, individualized, and unique in your views, programmed responses and other people's opinions begin to disappear.

- When you establish new sensory priorities and take information breaks, complete with far out daydreams, then new data can inch its way in.

- When you allow yourself to be "paranormal" and stretch your senses, you see beyond the expected and shatter preexisting boundaries.

- When you modify your identity, you begin to see through different eyes, and therefore tap into previously unavailable perspectives.

- When you add passion to your vision, you awaken the drive to seek out a longer view and naturally attend to more subtleties.

Every time we engage any of these strategies, we experience "prophecy." By seeing dimensions of information that were previously unavailable, we begin to see through the barrier of time.

The image of the Magic Eye is at first unavailable because all you see is space. When your mind fills in the spaces, a previously unrecognized image suddenly appears. The spaces we are starting to fill in with this new sense are not so much new content, but the ability to see the unfolding and evolution of experiences. Thus entirely new images are beginning to form in our cultural landscape.

Part of our mind still persists in seeing objects and events as if they are flat, static, and separate. But a part of our mind is naturally beginning to sense in terms of relationships and connections. Developments like hypertext force us to see ideas as levels of organization. The fracturing and blending of markets forces us to loosen boundaries and release the notion of fixed territories. The heightened need for collaboration and work teams leads us into a more flexible interpretation of intelligence and power. Factors such as these challenge us to see the invisible fabric of organization that links events and people to each other.

Many are calling for the need to think in terms of systems or more holistically, in order to gain a deeper grasp of the world around us. In order to think in terms of systems, we need to perceive that way. *Perception precedes thought.* Until we can sense the underlying connections of our world, we will not be able to think in these new patterns.

Practically, it means that we need to pay less attention to the mere expansion of our business and careers. Instead we begin to ask questions like: What is the next dimension of my relationship with suppliers, clients, staff, and the community? What is the next dimension of my product, service, and creativity? Most new frontiers will not be found in lateral expansion, but rest in discovering a new depth and complexity of relationships.

Our new cultural and economic environment requires that we operate in a sensory, not a conceptually, dominated mode. Individuals and businesses with long-term visions and carefully articulated plans of action may not be suited to this new world of opportunity. Strong conceptual biases freeze information and do not allow us to experience the movement of ideas. More and more, we will need to rely on our sensory acuity, our ability to detect changes in the wind. Sensory acuity requires dropping conceptual dominance. Dropping our need to always understand allows us to take in information without such strong filters.

Our current cultural climate demands that we all look further ahead and rewards those who can catch trends before they are evident to others, seeing patterns which are not yet obvious to the ordinary eye. The more developed our perceptual style, the more our culture will appear to slow down and stress will be reduced.

Our second tool involves truly sensing what lies ahead, beyond the mirages our culture flashes at us. Heightened perception frees us to feel a deeper attraction to what is already pulling us forward. Allowing yourself to perceive wider, farther, and deeper into your surroundings will awaken a natural motivation.

When your habitual styles of sensing drop away, you can literally see the pull of the future, how it is shaping, attracting, and rejecting flows of information. When you view ideas through the lens of time, you can instantly evaluate their depth. When you view your relationships through a temporal filter, you naturally sense their purpose. The rhythm of a project becomes more apparent because you can see the natural pulses and flows of an evolving idea. Each of the seven sensory adaptations I have described is a way of sensing the pull of the future.

When time is added to your sensory style, it is much like my original story about the Magic Eye. A sea of random pulses and dots suddenly transforms into clear and detailed images. Since every arena of human endeavor is being pulled into the future; the seeming chaos of our cultural patterns will start to make sense. You can see where the "drag" is, and where the areas of release are. You can sense contractions and expansions. It is a different way of processing information. Seeing what were once static experiences moving through time is key to making sense of the deluge of data that may at first appear smoglike and overwhelming. Those who can catch information *before* it has been influenced by a concept will be at a distinct advantage.

Practicing a New Sense

You can look at any project or relationship and ask these questions:

> ➤ Where's the edge? Where are the thresholds that hold new information?
> ➤ What's the broad sweep (no details)? What's the fast take on what's happening?
> ➤ What's my unique position, my unique spin? What's the unique spin of the other key players?
> ➤ What are my info priorities? What are the key questions we need to be asking?

> When I am on a roll, what do I see that is not ordinarily there?

> What other eyes or identities do I need to look through.

> Overall, if I look at this idea over the course of time, what do I see? What's moving? What's not? Where are the sticking points? Where is it most dynamic?

Merely answering these questions should bring up previously unrecognized information, i.e., foresight and prophecy.

Zooming

Here's a quick eye opener, or what you might call sensory gymnastics.

> Look at the room around you; observe it as you normally would. Now imagine you are looking through a microscope, adjusting the lens so it focuses on smaller and smaller levels of detail. The room might slowly disintegrate into spaces, energy particles, and finally waves of information. Try the same process of magnification for looking at a social situation, a meeting, a project, or relationship.

> Now reverse it. Turn the microscope into a telescope and look at the room, situation, whatever, from farther and farther out.

> You can also zoom with time. Bring a result toward you, closer and closer in proximity. Take yourself farther into the future, looking back at some moment in time, and note the changes as you get more removed.

> Try using different filters. Look at a social setting through a filter that only senses attraction and repulsion. Then look at the same setting through a filter that only senses whether social boundaries are rigid or loose. There are infinite filters you can make up. Notice how each filter creates a different "reality."

The main point is to practice allowing your eyes, literally, to relax and shift focus.

Exaggerating, Reversing, Softening, and Glimmers

Here are a few more quick exercises. If you want, you can use the same idea or project all the way through and see if it stimulates additional ideas.

> Take your idea and exaggerate it. Imagine it taking over your life, reorganizing your company, the planet. Imagine it becoming a

guiding thought for our time. What's making this idea so huge? What is the key factor that would cause it's expansion?

➤ Reverse it. See yourself going in a direction that is exactly opposite. What is it that would allow something to "be" opposite. The features that allow something to become opposite may be the critical variables to your project.

➤ Project yourself into the future, 6 months, 1 year, 2 years. Speak about the idea in the past tense, describing how it unfolded.

➤ Find an edge. What would be dangerous, unacceptable, bold, wild, or unique to look at? What would represent an edge of more commitment, more kindness, more trust, or more imagination?

➤ Look beneath the words; what are the true motives or powers underlying this project? Ask questions of people who are not directly involved with your idea and try to see through their eyes.

➤ Try a body/mind reversal. Experience this idea/project as if it was your body. Where does it feel good, where is it stuck, where is it tense? What do these experiences mean?

➤ Look at the idea with a soft focus: disregard any details and just try to see what the key pulses or flows are. You can practice this by slightly blurring your vision. If this idea or project had shape, color, or music, what would it be like? If it could dance, how would it express itself?

➤ Play with the meanings you have placed on this project. Write down all the things it means to you, such as excitement, opportunity, more work, stress, etc. One by one, take each of these meanings and change it. Continue shifting the meaning as if you were placing new frames around a picture. Notice how each frame shifts your motivation.

Masks

Step into the shoes of different people. Imagine yourself an historical figure, celebrity or expert in some field. Imagine their perspective. Become the people representing different facets of the project, like the customer, supplier, marketer, designer. Imagine what they would each see when they look at your idea.

Word Games

Design at least three words that this idea/project will need in order to make it happen and three words it will offer to the public. See if you can find a word or words that will create the kind of sea change transition that moving from "rhythm and blues" to "rock and roll" triggered.

For example, today you might be a "shoe store;" tomorrow you are a "foot-wear technologies company," handling everything that makes walking and standing easier, every product related to the foot, including books and products to help your posture. With the ideas triggered by this redefinition, your foot-wear technology store could network with podiatrists, dance schools, yoga studios, massage therapists, etc. You might publish a newsletter and become a national resource. You might even develop your own line of shoes that are stylish *and* therapeutic, complete with research studies backing up the value of your product. This example shows how a change of word can trigger other realms of possibility.

> Try finding several different words that would redefine your business or project in a new way. This is a great game to play in a group. See how each redefinition opens new possibilities.

Perception and Passion

For this process choose a project that is stuck or moving slower than you would like. Here, you will be experimenting with the premise that a wider, deeper, longer perceptual field will automatically increase speed. First go wider; look for people, ideas, and a range of impact you haven't considered. Next, go deeper into levels of meaning or subtleties you haven't considered. Finally, go longer—6 months past where you have been looking, 1 year, 5 years, even 10 years. See if your motivation feels different with various time frames.

If you are feeling disillusioned, tired, and numb, make your perception more vivid. Interview other people about what they think. Talk about the project in a different way. Take it through any of the above exercises. See if perceiving at a higher level makes you more excited, more in love with what you are doing.

Overall, make a commitment to foresight. *Before* you go forward into a new endeavor, set some time aside to look around with fresh eyes. Perception is one of the most powerful tools for redesigning what lies ahead. When we *see* new dimensions, then new worlds come into being.

A wonderful book called Amazon Beaming *tells the story of a South American tribe called the Mayaruna who are undertaking the shamanic journey of a lifetime; they are traveling to the beginning of time![1]*

To prepare for their adventure, they ritually shake up every belief they have. They get up in the middle of the night, eat at odd hours, take the young children through the adolescent initiation rituals, and finally leave their homes, burning all possessions as they depart. They are purposely shaking up their world, because only with this level of change can they let go enough to touch the beginning of time!

The explorer who discovers this tribe is inadvertently taken along for the ride, since he gets lost and cannot find his way back to his camp. After a few weeks, he awakes one morning to find his watch missing, his camera being dismantled by a monkey, and the awful smell of his sneakers being burnt in the fire! These are his only three links to western civilization, his life as he knew it and his identity. Once they go up in smoke, he loses his grip on reality. At that point, he has no choice but to really surrender to the trip. At this point in the story, when he finally surrenders, he develops a capacity to telepathically communicate with the tribe's shaman. The shaman had been beaming him messages all along, but his links to the outside world and his habits associated with that world had kept him from hearing the messages.

We are on a path much like the explorer who stumbled upon the Mayaruna, perhaps involuntarily. The collapse of tradition, the chaos of values, the looming specter of the unknown, and the premature arrival of adolescence in our culture are all provoking the equivalent of a shamanic journey. Metaphorically, we have lost our watches, seen our image-making abilities ripped apart, and now we are beginning to smell the distinct aroma of our sneakers burning, our last link! Since we are all losing our grip on an old reality, we have little choice but to surrender to the trip. We have no choice but to master **the emotions of change.**

CHAPTER 6

The Emotions of Change

Philip and I travel about half the year, usually about six to eight weeks at a time. We always procrastinate about packing until the last moment, resisting our imminent departure in any way we can, although once we are on the road, often we don't want to stop and will even spontaneously extend the trip. It is neither staying home nor traveling that we resist; it is the change.

Ask almost anyone to do something different, and their spontaneous, first response will be, "Can't make me." A graphic artist we know put off buying a computer for years until she almost lost her business. A retailer with a rapidly growing company delayed hiring more staff until he almost had a nervous breakdown. Recent studies show that the majority of all attempts to re-engineer a corporation will fail, principally because of the resistance of the people involved. There is also the now-familiar quip, that many of us are still on the "information dirt road." We are all actively resisting a necessary change that is right at our doorsteps. Why?

Resistance to Change Is Not Only Our Genetic and Cultural Inheritance, It Is Locked Deep Inside the Core of our Personal Identities

Biologists say that man has the equivalent of three brains—the reptilian brain, the mammalian brain, and the higher cortex—each linked to a different period of our genealogical history. The oldest of these is the reptilian brain, which controls arousal, attention, and the involuntary nervous system.

Locked in the reptilian part of our brain is the desire to want the world to move slowly. Like a lazy lizard, we have been programmed through eons of evolution to seek out a kind of stability equivalent to lying in the sun with no greater mission than our next meal. Ask someone to conjure up a vision of ease, and invariably it will look something like lying down in the hot sun on a beach.

This primitive part of our brain is linked to the most basic aspects of survival—breathing, arousal, fight, or flight. So when we feel threatened, we instinctively resort to a reptilian like programming and dig our heels in, emotionally looking for some safe rock to sun ourselves on.

And the plot thickens. Our resistance to change is also coded in the more complex parts of our brain. Our ancestors lived in a harsh environment. Those who survived were the ones who could create stability, insulate themselves from the ravages of nature, and keep their social interactions under control. We had to stay fairly close to the cave, just so we would have enough time to make babies. The really adventurous types were killed before they had time to hand down their genes. So the wise elders slowly wove it into our cultural traditions not to rock the boat.

And there's more. Then our culturally ingrained resistance to change gets intertwined with our personal history. Starting school may have been stressful, our parents may have divorced, a friend may have moved when we were young, or a favorite uncle or grandparent may have died. So the process of change gets associated with pain, loss, or other unpleasant feelings. We begin to equate stability with emotional survival. We organize our personalities and life scripts so that we steer clear of events that could trigger these past programs. In other words, we stay on the safe side.

Our current predicament is that this long-standing equation, survival equals stability, has shifted. The largest proportion of our environment is created not by fight or flight, not by storms and seasons, but by our cultural milieu. Our culture has turned the evolutionary tables and now demands the opposite of what once ensured survival. Survival now depends more on the ability to encompass new possibilities.

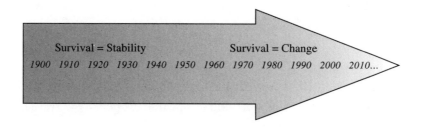

Survival = Stability   Survival = Change

1900 1910 1920 1930 1940 1950 1960 1970 1980 1990 2000 2010...

This is an era awash in change. One in four people will change homes this year. One in five will switch jobs. Two or three times in our lives, we will undertake whole new careers. Feedback loops in the workplace are tightening, so we have to make decisions more quickly. Relationship parameters are more thoroughly defined, and our partners have less patience. If we don't shift our behavior quick, often they are out of there. We have been programmed and designed for stability, and now suddenly we're expected to have the flexibility of a chameleon.

This is why almost all psychologists equate change with stress. A clever table has been devised that lists various kinds of changes—moving to a different city, changing jobs, learning a new skill, etc. Each type of change is assigned a point rating. You then add up your points. Total scores over a certain number are linked with higher stress levels, increased likelihood of high blood pressure, nervous breakdowns, depression, and a host of maladies. According to these charts, the average person now experiences higher point ratings than at any time in history. Since our cultural turmoil is not likely to abate, we need to find ways to move with change rather than resist it.

Although that British explorer who stumbled upon the Mayaruna was likely off the charts in his potential stress level, he probably did not experience it as stress. He was on an adventure and was focused on discovery, not stability. The Mayaruna were even a step past the explorer; they were consciously, willingly throwing themselves into the heart of the profoundest change possible. If we follow the model of the Mayaruna and the British explorer, we can reframe the multitude of shifts we are asked to make as a journey into the self rather than a series of stresses to be dodged.

In our current environment, rigidity is creative suicide, flexibility is opportunity.

When I hear people complain about the pace of things, I think, "Get used to it, it's only going to increase. You can learn to enjoy it or you can go crazy."

Few will argue that the coming years will be shaped by unrelenting and unprecedented transformation, so our next tool for dealing with the future must focus on transforming our primal propensity to resist change. We need a more fluid emotional style that allows us to easily move from one tempest to the next.

You Won't Move until You Really Want To

Try the following simple experiment. Continue reading this page and simultaneously think to yourself, "I'm going to get up and walk into the next room."

Now think this thought once again even harder. One more time, as hard as you can, think the thought that you are going to get up and go into the next room. Now let's talk about what probably happened.

You most likely stayed in the same position as you continued to read. Although you were thinking a thought about getting up, you probably did not act on it. You will not get up and walk into the next room until *you want to*.

We do not act merely because of a thought. Most people try to turn making a change into a rational process, weighing alternatives, selecting the most sensible ones. This is not really how we make choices. We end up doing things mostly because we want to. Feelings are what spark action.

Thought gives the direction. We make lists of things we want to do and rarely get through the list. But if you're in love, you don't have to put on your list "call my honey." In fact, we probably call much more often than necessary! If we could relate to the other things on our lists the way we relate to someone we love, it would be easier to get through the list. Our resistance to change is locked in at the emotional level. That is why an emotional exploration is where we need to go to address the resistance.

Psychic Surfing

Change stirs up:

➤ Primal, "reptilian" survival feelings

➤ The higher cortex, self-esteem, and acceptability issues

➤ All our very personal neurotic quirks

The bigger the change we embark on—shifting values, changing our workstyle, getting used to the experience of being in the zone, or seeing things in a new way—the more feelings it stimulates. Since we resist some of the emotions change can trigger, like terror, grief, fear of the unknown, confusion, frustration over not knowing what to do, loss of identity, heightened insecurity, we shrink from trying new things. As a result, we stay in uncomfortable situations far longer than we should.

How to Save the Empire

To set up and illustrate the three stages of emotional change, let's examine a scene from *Star Wars*.

> In the third movie of the trilogy, Luke Skywalker, the foremost Jedi warrior, is once again protecting the Empire from the forces of evil and is locked in battle with his arch enemy Darth Vader. Luke's world view is simple, the lines between good and evil clear-cut. His mission is clearly mapped out.
>
> Luke knows Darth Vader was once a Jedi warrior like himself and somehow shifted his allegiance. He flirts with the idea that maybe this weakness is also within him, or that perhaps the dark side holds irresistible powers of persuasion beyond what even he can withstand. He is always able to push

away these doubts; asserting to himself that this could never happen to him. Every time he suppresses his doubts, the world is familiar again and he is safe in his image of being good, while Darth Vader is evil. More important, he reestablishes a familiar boundary: Darth Vader is fundamentally different from him, weak, susceptible, corruptible. Sometimes he reinforces this more powerful sense of self with fantasies that maybe his goodness could even bring Darth Vader back to the Jedi fold.

Finally, Luke can no longer push away the nagging doubts that have haunted him for years. In the midst of hand-to-hand combat, he asks Darth Vader what happened so many years ago to cause him to relinquish his role as a Jedi warrior? Darth Vader proceeds to tell him that he is in fact Luke's own father, whom Luke has not seen since he was a baby!

The shock stops Luke cold. His entire world view crumbles: his idealistic fantasies about his father, his notions of good and evil, his own self-concept of purity and innocence are smashed. In that moment, he cannot even pick up his sword. He is empty, without volition.

This is all Darth Vader needs. He quickly seizes the advantage, and Luke, defeated, is marched to central command to watch the final destruction of the Empire. As things become more hopeless, any possibility of getting out by his own power dissolves. Luke has been conquered. The Empire is lost.

Since there is no hope, Luke begins talking to his long-lost father as a son. He reaches out without any agenda. He merely wants to get to know his father in what he assumes are the last hours of his life. Without revealing any outer changes in his behavior, something mysterious and powerful begins stirring deep inside Darth Vader, and in a dramatic turn of events, he surrenders his own life to save his son. It is he who saves the Empire.

Simply put, this is a story of what happens when our world view crumbles. We are forced to enter a space of emptiness which will eventually organize into a new world view. Like Luke, when we surrender to our vulnerability, it frees others to become different. Had Luke remained in his role of warrior, Darth Vader would have as well, and the Empire would indeed have been lost. Only a change as fundamental as becoming a son could release Darth Vader to become a father. Although not intended, it was the most brilliant strategy available.

Any change we might make, whether it is starting or ending a relationship, beginning a new job, or developing a new marketing strategy, entails the same emotional sequence revealed in this story. Can you see it?

Luke's journey was primarily emotional, not analytical. It parallels the morphing spirit of the times detailed in the first chapter. As Chapter 4 showed with our bodies and Chapter 5 with our perceptions, our emotional style too needs to adapt to riding endless waves of change. Whether you are initiating a new direction or responding to a shift in your environment, change rests on a profound emotional journey. True change always confronts our need for security, thus it must be encountered through a reorganization of this very primal place within our psyche. To further understand this, let me describe in more detail what happened for Luke.

The First Stage—The Call

Rumblings. We are capable of doing something the same way for decades without ever questioning why. In the first movie of the *Star Wars* trilogy, Luke hardly thought about Darth Vader's origins; he was absorbed in developing his own skills as a Jedi warrior. It is not until much later that the serious rumblings begin.

Rumblings are those moments when we start to ask ourselves:

> Why am I in this same predicament *again?*

> Why don't I do something *different?*

> Why am I so bored, tired, apathetic, frustrated?

> Why am I beating my head against the wall of a situation that just won't change?

Questions, doubts, wanderings, parallel scenarios, fatigue, giving up, all are forms of rumbling. When an organization begins rumbling, managers call more meetings, reevaluate procedures, randomly fire people, rehash things from the past that can't be changed, make sure everyone understands the rules. Whenever these things start happening, stay alert, big change is on the horizon!

Resistance. What is the first thing we do when we start to question our familiar circumstances? We resist, of course. Lizard-brain kicks in with its 500,000 years of genetic programming, the higher cortex with its 40,000 years of cultural programming, and the corpus colloseum with the aggregate of all our personal stories, and they all scream out in unison, "Don't rock the boat!" Our primal programming tells us not only that we should-n't rock the boat, but if we do, we will probably die. So we answer our doubts by assuring ourselves that everything will be just fine. We justify the present position, defend our traditions, and tell ourselves to shape up and think positively.

Refusing the Call.   Bad move. As we all know, resistance is futile. We were consulting with the founder of a start-up, call it the Smith Company. Everything that could go wrong was going wrong: mistakes on orders, can-celed contracts, flaky staff, costly delays, loss of promised funding, you name it. Smith eventually came to us for support more out of emotional fatigue than for business reasons.

For a year he had responded to every difficulty by fighting back. When staff flaked, he worked more. When promised funding evaporated, he kicked in his own money. When mistakes occurred, he rationalized why it happened and carried on. When the product was not received well, he rein-forced his beliefs about how special it was. It's not that all these solutions were wrong, but when so many things go off track, sometimes it is better to stop, or at least pause. Instead of consistently ignoring the rumblings, try thinking, "Something is seriously out of balance here. Let's look at it."

Rather than pressing into the pain, the founder of the Smith Company continued to focus on easing the rumblings. Only when he was in a state of exhaustion would he look at deeper issues. When he reached a place that I would call "soft and stayed there a bit," openly feeling the pain of what was happening and looking deeper at his motivations, curiously, events in the company would start to move again. Repeatedly, however, he would snare these inklings of renewed success and revert to the previous patterns. His tone would become opinionated again and he would reel off a stream of ideas about what he would do next. This attempt to overpow-er difficulties would inevitably trigger another crisis.

Refusing the call means pushing away doubts and fears which may hold critical information. If you sweep away the emotion, underneath every fear, lies at least a kernel of truth, and sometimes a mountain. Underneath most physical blocks in projects are psychological blocks that need to be addressed.

At a similar point in his development, Luke declared to his teacher, Obi-wan Kenobi, that he was unshakable; he would never turn like Darth

Vader did. The mentor listens with a wan smile on his face, knowing the difficulty of the path that lay ahead. It's like a business firing anyone who doesn't tow the line or a person who in the face of difficulty becomes even more rigidly committed to a path. Resistance to these rumblings always demands that our lessons repeat with greater force.

Dissolution.   Given enough pressure, at some point any dam will break. If our rigidities are hammered on long enough, we will fold. Finally, Luke's assurances to himself and others could no longer hold back the wave of curiosity he had about Darth Vader. He had to ask. The more we say we are not interested in something or that it doesn't matter, the more it eats away at our unconscious, building pressure until it breaks through with a force capable of dissolving everything we know.

The Second Stage—The Bardo

Loss of Volition/Emptiness.   When our old views collapse, we enter the second stage of change. When this happens to Luke, he is stunned, unable to take action. Nothing from the past is available to him. He loses volition.

This is often what people feel. With great excitement they start a new job or discover a new solution and then find themselves incapable of doing anything. Someone we know called us in dismay. He had hired a new sales director who at first appeared to be a real go-getter. This man spent the first three weeks in his new job decorating his office and organizing his personal life, since he and his wife had just moved to a new city. The owner of the company was horrified, thinking maybe he had made a very expensive mistake and this guy would never do anything.

When we first leave a familiar belief system, a comfortable situation, or relationship we have known, often there are intense feelings of confusion, being lost, being without grounding, even grief, and despair. We pine for the past. Secretly, this new sales director was as horrified as the owner. He thought of himself as a go-getter and now he just couldn't get going! I find it helpful to think of this as a stage. It gives me more courage to endure these uncomfortable, ego-challenging spaces. It's the "burning the sneakers" stage of the Mayaruna story, when our favorite beliefs about ourselves begin to emit a terrible stench.

The founder of the Smith Company could never really let go into this stage. He would reach this point over and over, but could never accept the "stench" long enough to make any progress. Burning sneakers smell awful. When his favorite pieces of self-image came into question, he would unconsciously pull back and begin focusing on external problems in the company. This is probably the most challenging stage. It's an awful feeling to discover that what you used to like most about yourself has suddenly become malodorous.

Bardo—The Moment between Forms. Tibetan tradition has a term for the space between lifetimes; they call it the *bardo*. It is the interval where you have left your physical body and have not yet chosen a new one. Tibetans feel the real key to spiritual advance lies not only in what we do in this lifetime but also how we negotiate the bardo. It is a very different framework from how western thought is structured.

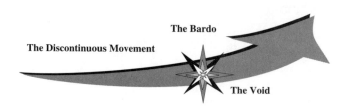

I use the Tibetan bardo because, of any tradition I've seen, they have one of the most keenly developed understandings of emptiness and how to travel from one world view to another. The bardo is not without danger, however. Supposedly, the womb and an unconscious rebirth appear to the traveler between lives as a palace filled with temptations. Illusions of treasure, gold, and beautiful lights tempt the traveler to take another birth. Similarly, when we have the opportunity to enter a space between one decision and the next, we must watch out for the temptation to figure it out, to be smart, to look good. The more we let prior understandings fall away, the more new possibilities can come to the fore.

This phase does not have to be long, *but it must be profound.* In the "new sales director" situation, we offered the owner and the unproductive sales director a description of the bardo. We suggested that they both actively let go of their expectations and give each other more space. Many months later, both reported that those initial weeks were probably more important than they realized. In retrospect they were able to link future successes to this "empty" time, although they could never quite explain how.

More and more organizations are finally realizing the power of empty space, the value of allowing people to be undirected, even the power of failure. New findings show that traditional activities such as brainstorming become far more effective if the talkative moments are balanced by silent, reflective breaks. Other studies show that when we work continuously without a break, it can lead to as much as a 50 percent decline in productivity. Even Bill Gates admitted in a recent interview that the ferociousness of the current economic climate now requires that he take two weeks off every year just to reflect, rather than the one week he used to take.

When our old world collapses and we allow ourselves to feel the emptiness, the helplessness, and the loss of identity, we eventually begin to tap into a realm where anything is possible. This freedom should not to be dismissed lightly. Often in retrospect people will acknowledge the power of bardo-like times; yet when they are in the thick of it, it is almost impossible to make people understand the value of this space. High achievers are the worst. They not only have a hard time letting their sneakers burn, they have an even worse time with not knowing.

There is very little support in our culture for such periods. Secretly, people are horrified when they hear you say, "I don't know" or "I'm not sure." It threatens our notions of power. They immediately offer you advice and referrals to their favorite "fixer uppers" so you can quickly get out of your confusion. Imagine if people began to respond to our vagueness by saying, "How lucky, you're in the bardo, take your time, don't even try to figure it out." Imagine telling a colleague "I'm not sure what we need to do here." and having him respond, "I'm with you, sounds like you're on the right track." Suppose we could fill those empty gaps in our resumes with the statement, "Spent time in the bardo," and the prospective employer would read this notation with *respect* and we would be more likely to get the job than someone who was "bardo-less". Much of the intensity we experience, many of the quick and unsatisfactory fixes, arise out of our inability to understand and stay with the power of the bardo.

The Third Stage—Recognizing the Unknowable

The biggest danger we face in the third stage is trying to choose too quickly. Skywalker handled the situation well. Had he pulled himself together and tried a last-ditch slugfest, Darth Vader would also have resumed his past role and nothing would have changed. But the shock was so deep, Luke had to let go and allow the creativity of not knowing to work its magic.

He entered the creative moment. He reached out with total innocence and without ulterior motive, and it was absolutely the most powerful move he could have made! Darth Vader was rendered helpless. He had little choice but to assume a father role in response to Luke's new role as son, which changed the course of destiny.

Destiny is merely an old story living itself out. Creativity is the destroyer of destiny; it is the only way to allow new directions to emerge. The moment of choice has a freshness and unpredictability about it. Even though Smith never totally entered the bardo and continued to refuse the call and avoid the worst part of the stench, the company was finally brought to its knees. At the end of his financial rope, the owner finally gave up his picture of how the business needed to look. An individual appeared offering a radically different way of distributing Smith's product. This knight in shining armor lay invisible until they were willing to see things differently.

Remember in the opening story the shaman who had been beaming the explorer messages all along? Miraculous solutions are being beamed at us all the time, but they cannot be heard until we drop our attachments to the past world.

Riding a Paradigm Shift

This is what the three stages of change feel like:

> ➤ The first stage, The Call, often feels like attack. It feels like we are being asked to let go of what we have. It often breeds defensiveness, rigidity, and conservatism. We go either into clingy-manipulative or warrior-combat mode, trying to maintain what we know.

➤ In Stage 2 we feel powerless; our old reference points have been annihilated. Our self-image suffers and can seem seriously flawed. It feels like we don't know ourselves any more. Since we don't have a new path yet, it is impossible to gain traction. Everything we try seems to evaporate. Internal dynamics dominate our external actions.

➤ Out of powerlessness, the past is swept away. Only in this way can really fresh solutions emerge. In the third stage we have to watch an insidious desire to want to fix things, to get things back to normal, to return to what we had, to find the good old days or a pace that feels familiar. This stage requires that we feel different about ourselves, stay receptive and move slowly with increased softness and sensitivity. It requires going forth without an agenda and feeling oddly off balance. We also have to be aware of the subtle temptations to shut down on the increased energy that always accompanies breakthrough.

Each stage requires different handling. If you are in the letting go stage, the fastest way through is to give yourself space to rant and rave and vent your resistance. Increased conservatism is often the key to making the balloon pop. If you are fighting off the forces of change, eventually you'll get tired and give up.

When in the bardo, embrace not knowing, not acting. Enjoy the opportunity for having fewer opinions, for listening rather than talking. As hard as it seems, it requires sinking into what feels like your greatest weaknesses and letting go of your favorite strengths. It is a time for becoming aware of the emptiness between events, the spaces between you and the people in your life. It is a time of emptying out.

The choice stage emerges naturally; you only need to focus on being willing to feel different and allowing a mild case of uncertainty to persist. It only requires staying with and enjoying a "shaky on your legs" kind of feeling.

We consulted with a surgeon who had said for years that he wanted to change professions and become a management consultant. Years went by and he did nothing. Every time he came to the moment of actually taking action, a feeling of uncertainty and confusion paralyzed him. He was so frightened of the feelings, he stayed put. Our work with him focused on developing his capacity to feel these emotions and talk from these feelings rather than about them. Within the seminar, he became used to staying in these feelings and even enjoying the intensity of experience they offered. Then we didn't hear from him for over a year. One day he called from a hotel in Seattle where he had his first job leading a training seminar for a local corporation. He was deep into the shaky legs feeling, but he said his increased ease with the emotional side of the trip is what made the external change possible.

We saw the same cycle of feelings occur when the founding partner of a small advertising firm wanted to leave. Soon after he announced his intentions, the business experienced a downturn. It was everyone's way of holding on, saying in dollars and cents, "You can't go." He brought us in at this point to see if there was something that could be done to make the process easier.

We followed the same sequence as with the surgeon, showing them the stages of change, allowing space for them to verbalize and even exaggerate their feelings. The exaggeration and acting out of their imaginary disaster scenarios eventually became humorous. People started to feel "permitted" to go through some very natural emotions and could even joke about things like their terror of having to call new clients or make speeches, since they had already role-played the worst possible disasters. We spent a lot of time having his staff practice not knowing, feeling shaky, and staying vulnerable. The transition ended up going far easier than expected and the founding partner was able to leave sooner than he had originally planned. By resisting or denying the feeling side of change and trying to stay "professional," they were actually slowing down the process. Feelings usually move very quickly when you don't resist them.

Shamanic Change

Some people call this the Age of Anxiety, because we all have so many fears about what might lie ahead. But there is a transformative value to be gained from living in a time where you are constantly shaken. By breaking from tradition and conditioned beliefs at the level our culture is offering, we can each access a level of freedom never before available.

A shaman can be defined simply as a *shape shifter*. Changing our fundamental attitudes about ideas, projects, the economy, and even relationships on a near daily basis could qualify as shape shifting. If we proceed with the right context, we all have the opportunity to walk in the shoes of the shaman.

Anyone who has been downsized and is able to break through by creating their own business, a new direction, or reselling their services to the company most often reports a tremendous sense of freedom. Relationships that have almost ended but survived both people's worst fears inevitably become more playful and light. Companies that have successfully weathered seemingly imminent defeat emerge on the other side much more powerful and resilient. As you gain more familiarity with this cycle, change is never quite as frightening as it was the first time.

What distinguishes shamanic change from ordinary change is allowing ourselves to be transformed by the process.

We routinely take on new directions or learn new skills without it changing us in any substantial way. Change in and of itself is meaningless unless it touches your core experiences of security and freedom. When you allow change to reshape your understanding of yourself, then and only then does it begin to become transformative. When you travel the emotions of change in the way I have described, you learn to use these external shifts as a path to greater emotional freedom. If felt in this way, our dominating cultural change will begin to make us more fluid, sensitive, and responsive. I have known people buffeted by a series of changes who are left tired and disillusioned. I know people who have weathered very similar external dramas and have been left more empowered. Once again, its not *what* you change but *how* you change, that makes the shifts more shamanic.

Like it or not, you are in the midst of the equivalent of a shamanic journey. We all are. Our third navigational tool focuses on allowing the relentless external change we face to also change us internally.

Almost every day some part of the rug is pulled out from under us. Every day we are thrust into a no-man's land, some unfamiliar territory with no rules or signposts. Every day we must discover the subtle omens that will lead us to safety. Used wisely, our unrelenting social change has the potential to bring about an awakening of our spirit. Like the explorer, if we surrender to the trip, we may be more open to the telepathic messages our time is beaming at us.

This emotional path allows us to join the Mayaruna in a journey to the beginning of time, the source of creativity. If we just cycle through repetitive patterns, we become trapped in time, tied to history. Many individuals and businesses continuously implement new ideas and trendy techniques, yet they remain essentially the same. It is only by feeling the emotions of change that we can forge a real path through our habits and into the bardo—and into the possibility of doing something truly different. The Mayaruna relentlessly shook up every feature of their known reality. Entering into the void or the unknown, feeling it so deeply it sometimes hurts, is the only way to touch true creativity. Riding the emotions of change can feel like psychological death. Something unimagined can only enter when we have emotionally allowed the past to die.

Practicing the Emotions of Change

Starting to Feel

Obviously, the big key to this tool is *learning to feel*. This may at first strike you as easy, but true feeling, emotion that really moves energy in a permanent way, is rarer than you might think. We live in a society deep in denial. We have devised many ingenious ways of avoiding what we feel in a given situation, either because we think it's not cool, or it's unprofessional, or we are just so frozen, we don't even know when we are feeling something. In all our experience of leading seminars and consulting to businesses, if we had to choose one factor that keeps things stuck, it would be the habitual denial of real feelings. Scott Peck explores this issue brilliantly in his book *A World Waiting to be Born*. Peck calls this lack of real feeling a "loss of civility."

It's possible to mistake talking about our feelings for actual feeling. I can say I'm sad or frightened until I'm blue in the face without ever really sinking into the experience. Often in the deepest states of feeling, there are no words or thoughts or even any external drama. Our deepest feelings are held close to the heart; there is little to see.

The true expression of feelings is usually intelligent, focused, and efficient. Expressing them in a relaxed and natural way is brilliant at clearing away unnecessary fluff. External displays can sometimes be right on target. Some people are just more expressive, and it is the fastest path for them. But big displays can also be a trap. Continuous displays of anger, fear, or sadness are usually more about control than real emotions.

Recently, I had an experience with a woman we had known for a long time. She was describing her difficulty in committing to her career as an architect. She broke into tears, as I had seen her do many times before, yet as I watched her, I felt nothing. I'm usually fairly empathic, so it was unusual to have this response. Then I realized that although tears were streaming down her face, it was a convenient habit, and she was experiencing very little real emotion. I took a chance and told her I didn't think she was really sad. At first she was hurt and put off. Then in an abrupt turnaround, she agreed and tuned into a much more interesting facet of her fear of commitment.

There are a lot of things we do that masquerade as feeling but are often just habits. There's no easy way to discern this, but if you find yourself habitually entering the same feeling states over and over, it may not be as cathartic as you think. Familiarity is the key word. Transformative feelings are fresh. They always offer the sensation of entering new territory and are almost always accompanied by a feeling of relief.

It is also valuable to shake up your understanding of feelings in general. Ask yourself the question over and over, "What am I really feeling? What underlies this sensation?" And the next sensation, and the next... Try to be aware of any tendency to go into your mind, to think rather than feel.

It is a common pattern from childhood, when parents would ask, "What are you feeling?" when they knew very well what we were feeling. Asking the question served to bring us up into our minds. The implied message was that feeling is not okay, that no one will connect with us when we feel, so it's better to describe what we feel than to actually be there.

It is valuable to shake up your characteristic ways of labelling an emotion. If you become aware of a sensation that you typically label fatigue, you might try thinking of it as tenderness. If you feel frightened, try relabelling it awe. Let sadness become kindness, anger become love, and so on. Also allow the reverse, kindness to become sadness, love to become anger, etc. By playing with how you label various feelings, it shakes up and resets your emotional reality much like changing perceptual filters.

Feeling the Rumbles

Now that you've become wiser about *how* to feel, let's surface some rumbles that you've been suppressing. On separate pages:

➤ Make a list of the main judgments you have about people in your life.

➤ Make a list of the times when you are most likely to want to withdraw and give up.

➤ Make a list of what makes you the most tired.

➤ Make a list of everything that bugs you about your present job. Make a list of your five most frequent complaints.

➤ Make a list of the worst judgment you have about yourself.

Arrange these lists in a semicircle around you so you can view them all. Forget specifics and look for themes. What is the shape of what is brewing inside you, underneath all these complaints, irritations, fatigue, and annoyances? Imagine that this theme is a ball of energy. What does it look like? What does it want to do? Experiment with moving into this energy. How does it feel? What scares you most about these rumblings? What would happen if you paid attention? Try exaggerating and intensifying these rumblings. What does it make you want to do? There is no end point to this exercise; the point is merely to learn how to pay attention to the rumblings we all experience and connect with the deeper truths that underlie our normal labels of things.

Understanding the Void

I'm going to describe a one-month sequence of exercises geared toward exploring empty spaces. I am suggesting a month, not only because this phase is important and undervalued but also because it requires the kind of patience that a month can provide.

> Try breathing in a rhythm of four counts in, four counts pause, four counts out, four counts pause again. Pay special attention to the pauses, what you feel when there is neither an inhale or exhale. At first, it may seem like nothing but slight discomfort. Try doing this exercise several times a day for an entire week, focusing on the pause. During this week, also pay attention to the spaces between thoughts, a difficult task but enlightening and interesting to try. Pay attention to pauses in conversation and to when you are likely to pause when speaking.

> In the second week try another experiment. You can buy one of the miniature rock gardens that have white sand and small rocks in a bowl. Or you can make one by using a wide, slightly curved plate; even a wide soup bowl will do. Fill it with sand and two or three beautiful rocks. Now, get a fork, knife, or something that will allow you to make paths in the sand. Several times a day, once again for a full week, merely comb the sand into different shapes. (If you're really committed to this process, you can make a life-size version, with a real rake, boulders, and pebbles.) During this same week, whenever you walk in a room, focus on the nature of the space between people, the distance between their chairs, the relationship between their nonverbal gestures, etc. If you look at a picture or painting, focus on the space between elements. If you listen to music, try to focus on the quiet spaces between notes.

> In the third week, try to arrange at least one day, or several hours every day, when you are in complete silence. Even when you are not in complete silence, spend the week trying to focus on listening and asking questions. If it is at all possible, try to go a week without offering your opinion about anything. Of course, don't lose your job over this! (Although that can be a very effective way of experiencing the bardo at a very high level.)

> Are you ready for one more week of experimentation? See if you can stop doing everything for five minutes of every hour, for an entire week. When your five-minute break comes, just sit, without thought, without a mantra, without an internal agenda. For this whole week, every time you think you need to do something, like turn on the TV or radio, call

someone, or run an errand, pause for a moment or two before you take the action. Pay particular attention if the pause leads to a different action.

At the end of this month, I guarantee you will have a very different understanding of the bardo. You will begin not only to enjoy it but to see how full emptiness can be.

Shaky Legs and All

There are probably many times during the course of a day that you feel shaky, that you feel on the edge of what feels familiar and what feels unknown. We tend to dislike this sensation and try to do something so we can feel comfortable again.

> Experiment with feeling that shaky feeling a bit longer without trying to fix it, e.g., feeling shy and continuing to talk from that shy place; feeling an uncomfortable amount of attention and continuing to hold the limelight; feeling like an idea you have is weird and detailing it a bit more. I find that when I ride that edge, I begin to notice the freshness and creativity that goes along with it.

> For a moment cross your arms the way you ordinarily do. Then recross your arms in the opposite direction, with the other hand on top. Unless you are ambidextrous, this shift will feel very uncomfortable. Do it a few more times in order to get a real taste of the shaky legs feeling so it is easier to recognize.

> If you want to go further, try shaking up your normal routine. When you wake up, do things in a different order. Conduct a meeting in a different way than you typically do. Do something completely unexpected in the middle of your workday. Notice both how uncomfortable it makes you feel and also how it wakes you up a bit.

Our most amazing story concerning this process was told to us by the founder of a company that was about to go public. In the months preceding this offer, all his prospective investors changed their minds and the company was about to go bankrupt. Remembering this idea, he decided to shave in a different direction than he had every day of his adult life. He was flooded with new ideas and enthusiasm and within a few weeks came a wave of new investment. It's a pretty iffy connection, but according to this guy, shaving his beard differently was instrumental in saving his company!

Shamanic Change vs. Ordinary Change

So this was all fun, but how does it relate to something practical like trying to move into a new job or changing how your sales force is approaching customers?

> Take whatever specific thing you need to transform and try running yourself through the three emotional phases. Find your areas of resistance and exaggerate them. Spend some time looking at the spaces surrounding this particular issue. Spend some time systematically surfacing every possible solution and then letting each one go. Experiment with only talking about the issue when you feel shaky and uncertain, and sometimes disregarding those times when you think you know what to do. See if you notice any difference in your results when you do this.

We are all subjected to intentional and unintentional changes every day. What makes these transitions more shamanic is when we use them to become more self aware, when we use these shifts to provoke and release our deeper resistance and habitual paths of action. When change is shamanic, each successive shift in our lives leads to a feeling of increased personal freedom.

The spider woman is at the heart of many Native American creation myths.

Spider woman! It is a strange image for one considered to be a creator.

She is a mysterious character. She lurks in the shadows and is rarely seen. Only at very special moments in the human saga does she emerge. She comes forth in times of powerful transition.

When she does arrive, she slowly pulls apart the threads that formed an old world and begins spinning the stories that will bring new forms into existence. We have much to gain by learning her ways, unraveling and weaving new stories in order to make new realms appear.

According to Native American legend, spider woman only appears when it is time for us to enter a new world. It's a fascinating bit of synchronicity that spiderlike images seem to permeate everyone's description of the information wave.

We use the tricks of the spider woman's art to describe the webs and nets of the cyberworld. Information is dependent on the width of the bands and is linked where fibers cluster together. We describe the corporate structures that arise in response to this new landscape as spider-weblike, with threads reaching in and out of new markets. The role of the individual is to create content, to spin stories.

We must be alert, for it is not often that the spider woman makes her presence known. Her appearance has traditionally been a sign that it is time to master the art of **mythmaking.**

CHAPTER 7

Mythmaking

Everyone is feeling a bit lost. No matter how collected they appear on the surface, everyone is either a little or a lot uncertain about the next step, for themselves, their businesses, the market, their lifestyles, and the planet.

Large-Scale Assumptions Are Unraveling in the Twinkling of an Eye

- For example, the record industry is being battered by bootleg recordings. As quality improves, the potential for people to download music from the web and the ability to make professional quality CDs on home equipment will begin to have a profound impact. Yamaha and Stanford University are licensing technology that will allow users to synthesize sounds which are indistinguishable from the real instruments. Sampling already offers the ability to create music without producing a single original note. It won't be long before the music industry as we know it will be completely reformulated.
- Here's the same story, yet another field. People in the medical field now feel that profit is dictating health care more than they are. The Association of Physicians and Surgeons is even contemplating forming a doctor's union because the attacks on their expertise

have been so relentless. Nearly 60 percent of the public has used alternative practitioners, and the practice of energy medicine is at the forefront of many bestselling books, forcing everyone to pay attention to what was a fringe element just a few years ago. In less than a decade, the practices and assumptions of medicine have been disassembled, and they're being reassembled before our eyes.

➤ Same story, one final angle. Middlemen, such as car dealers, travel agents, insurance salespeople, and brokers for industrial products, find their role being eroded with every passing day. Virtually every business magazine now warns that if you are a middleman, start looking for new job skills. Any job that involves brokering information or products is collapsing because increasingly, people can do business directly with the suppliers. Increasingly, it's a do-it-yourself world.

A closer look will tell you that there is virtually no industry or position that will be untouched by the unraveling and reweaving of new stories. And as I touched on earlier, these reworked stories are enmeshed in a larger cultural fabric that is undergoing the same process.

Culture is merely a set of agreed upon meanings that tell us what is important and what is not. It typically evolves over tens of thousands of years and slowly enters the fabric of day-to-day relations so that everyone knows the expected way to greet someone, how best to reply to most questions, etc. Yet the advent of a universal, media-induced culture is so seductive that it quickly causes people to forget everything they once knew.

There is a nomadic tribe in sub-Saharan Africa that delayed their annual migration, a tradition that had been untouched for tens of thousands of years, so they could watch the final episodes of Dynasty!

That's the power of a hot medium. The sub-Saharan nomadic culture is so finely tuned that even in the way their grains are cooked is coded an acknowledgment of the powerful desert they have chosen to call home. Merely darting your eyes at a slightly different speed indicates to all that the wind is picking up and it is time to take cover. Yet all this wisdom paled when confronted with the flickers of a TV screen.

We now exist in a cultural milieu that has not been thought through, that is extremely turbulent and mercurial. It did not develop slowly out of the roots of the earth. What's hot flickers across the collective screen, and within days it's no longer hot. Even so, this loosely rooted body of meanings we now call culture is weaving itself into our chemistry just as powerfully as the deep-rooted belief systems that once formed our world. When an entire industry and all the individuals involved have to rethink their core assumptions, it shakes us cognitively, emotionally; we feel it in our bones.

It's a Myth. Not.

We are in trouble personally and culturally because we lack transitional stories. We don't have myths that can take us from one set of beliefs to another. A culture that is unraveling needs an army of storytellers that can build new images.

The movie *Jerry Maguire* offers an excellent illustration of this problem.

> *Tom Cruise is Jerry Maguire, an up-and-coming agent for sports personalities, getting them new playing contracts and lucrative endorsements. One day, he has what might loosely be called a spiritual awakening and decides to dramatically and overtly question the greed that permeates his firm. He stays up all night writing a manifesto about how they can return the firm to integrity and truth. With great passion and hope, he delivers the speech.*
>
> *He is promptly fired, his client base gutted, and only one client remains with him, an out-of-control football player (Cuba Gooding), who is not quite making it. Cruise gets him as a client because his firm no longer wants him.*

But despite all the upheaval that Cruise creates and all his impassioned speeches, little changes in his relationship to money, clients, or even his own ambitions. There is really no way out. Even though he leaves his corrupt firm, he is still neck-deep in a system that operates on competition, win-lose, and making deals. Instead of rewriting the story, Maguire reenacts it.

There is a lot of Jerry Maguire in all of us. We complain and become cynical. We know a lot of our motives are not as healthy as we would like. We make impassioned speeches and then go back to what we have always done. We don't know how to get off of the moral, emotional, and creative treadmill we are on, or how to get from a situation that is increasingly unpalatable to one that is more interesting. We don't know how to tell a new story. And there are no longer minstrels or troubadours, or even much of an oral tradition like the stories our grandmothers learned from their grand-mothers. Therefore, we know very little about the art of telling stories.

For an idea to qualify as a myth it must touch the core of our emotional programming, how we see things, how we make decisions, how we evolve our actions. Unless it connects with this core "wiring" of our psyche, it is not a myth, it is not capable of shifting reality. To enter this realm of making myths, you must first understand how stories function. I will backtrack a bit and first look at a simpler notion, the stories we tell about ourselves and others, and how to tell stories that are deep enough to touch our cellular wiring.

A Story Is Always Subjective

We think we can tell a story and it has nothing to do with us. We describe a business problem or analyze why a particular project is stuck and assume that there is some level of objectivity in our description. We might say something like: "The problem with this project is that no one is willing to take a risk." or "The reason I don't feel supported by my boss is that he is always changing his priorities." We all make hundreds of statements that are constructed much like this and think we are actually describing an external situation.

Our journey into mythmaking must begin with an understanding that every story and description is also subjective. On some level, every analysis we make is ultimately a statement about ourselves. If Jerry Maguire could have kept talking about the vacancy in his soul, he might have had a fighting chance at discovering a new myth. Unless we become the story-teller, there is no chance to ever change the outcome of the story. Every statement about your objective world has a subjective source that is the driving power of the story.

> We know someone fairly high up in the movie industry. Don has confessed to us he is plotting not only to leave his job but the industry. He is tired of the ruthless competitiveness, the emptiness, and the lack of quality. The final blow was that Don's favorite screenwriter, who turns out one beautiful script after another, soon won't be able to get his films made because his lack of commercial success has put him out of the loop. Our friend sounds a lot like Jerry Maguire.
>
> I like Don. He's well read, funny, kind, a good father, a good husband, and truly is not overly materialistic. He and his family live simply and appre-

ciate life. It's understandable that he would feel increasingly frustrated by corporate life. Yet when I look at this man a little more deeply, there is a certain hard-to-explain lack of connection. We have wonderful, politically correct conversations, yet I always feel strangely untouched at the end.

I would say that the emptiness and lack of true connection that permeates his industry lives right there in his own psyche. He looks so right that it took a great deal of courage for us to suggest that for a while he should banish all thought of leaving his job and focus on the part of him that was content to be part of the system for so many years, easily playing the game and rapidly moving up the ranks, the part of him that is just like the movies he makes. Since he was confused about his next step and a courageous guy, he agreed to start with a much more honest assessment of the story he had built about his world.

All storytelling begins with examining your most frequent statements about someone else to discover the subjective meaning, *what it says about you*. Hatiyam Tyabi, CEO of Verifone, has developed this simple idea into a companywide strategy. When someone comes to him with a complaint, he holds up a mirror.[1]

The Narcissus Factor

In the famous Greek myth, Narcissus catches a glimpse of a beautiful reflection in the pond. He is so entranced that he can't tear himself away. He stops eating or caring for himself because he only wants to spend time with this image in the water. Finally one day, he leaps into the pond, seeking the owner of this reflection. It is only when he leaps to his death that he discovers that the image in the pond is in fact himself.

Most people analyze this story by thinking that leaping into the pool was a bad move for Narcissus. It is important to keep in mind that it was only when he leaped that he finally discovered the source of his illusions.

Part of Don's personal myth was to somehow feel he was more refined, more spirited, more interesting than those around him. He was in love with his story about the movie industry and his notion of himself as the Lone Ranger. In order to be free of the myth, he first had to see how entangled he was in the web. He had to leap in the pond. He had to find the part of himself that was quite comfortable with the feeling of superiority that was also insidiously invested in continuing the lack of quality in his industry.

We all project our thoughts on the world and think they are real. Then, like Narcissus, we fall in love with our own stories. We use them to bolster our self image, to reinforce our brilliance, so we get to play the same role over and over in the myriad plays that will make up our life. We tell and retell them, seeking out new listeners who won't be bored by what we have heard ourselves say a million times. Eventually, we no longer distinguish ourselves from the stories we tell.

The first step is to stop telling the same stories about yourself—that you are a nice guy, or that you are a risk-taker, or that you are afraid of commitment, or have difficulty making decisions. There are thousands of tales we tell and then find others who have similar stories so we can commiserate about the challenges of the particular part we play. Only when you stop the story can you begin to locate yourself as the source of the tale. Unless you can locate yourself as the storyteller, there is no possibility of changing the script.

"We Don't Like Their Sound, and Guitar Music Is on It's Way Out."

This statement was issued by Decca records in 1962 upon rejecting the Beatles. Our friend Kevin wisely places this phrase at the end of *every* e-mail he sends out. I notice whenever I read one of Kevin's messages I pay just a little bit more attention that I ordinarily might. It's a brilliant strategy. It's been almost a year now of reading this same quote at the end of every message and I still take incredible delight when I see it. It is a statement about the threshold.

There is a point in every idea, every project, and over and over in the course of long-term relationships when you have the choice of rejecting some piece of information as irrelevant. For example, your partners may tell you that you get defensive whenever they give you feedback. You respond by saying, "I don't like the sound of that and guitar music is on the way out." In other words, they'll get over it. We continually toss out information that doesn't fit our pictures.

Yet, It Is Precisely at This Edge That the Spider Woman Lives

New ideas are easy to sell. Whole new stories, like the Beatles were in 1962, are a much more difficult proposition.

A friend approached a record company with a simple, brilliant, relatively low-risk idea for creating new markets and developing talent simultaneously. The president of the label was so impressed by his initial take on the idea that he flew him out immediately to discuss it further. Yet as the meeting unfolded, the president spent the entire time explaining why it would never work! It's an old story; good ideas often go unrecognized. The reason this executive could not hear the idea was because he was hanging out at Narcissus's pond, in love with his own story. He did not like the sound (of our friend's idea) and thought guitar music (changes in the music industry) was probably on the way out.

But, remember, the idea was cheap and held relatively little financial risk. Logically, what did the president have to lose? Metaphorically, it was a $2 lottery ticket, not much skin off his back and potentially a big jackpot. The issue was not the money; the real problem was that the president was afraid to hang out with the spider woman. Besides, the old web was still catching plenty of flies.

In the native traditions, they know that the spider woman is scary. They know how hard it is to be around her. Opportunities to join her are deeply respected and revered. It is important, therefore, to know when she's inviting you to hang out, to approach a truly creative edge. The president of the record label did not have a cultural model for helping him recognize and deal with threshold energy.

Wherever history is being dismantled, you'll find spider woman pulling apart the threads of meaning. **The moment where ordinary perception becomes foresight, where ordinary action transforms into a zone state, or deep in the heart of the bardo where destiny is being rewritten: this is spider woman's domain.**

Rewriting the Story

When we play with this idea in our seminars, we ask people to rewrite core personal stories to get a feeling for the power these tales hold. If you can get a feel for the spider woman within your own heart and mind, you can more easily translate this experience to a broader area such as your business.

For example, if your father was distant and critical, you might describe an imaginary scene where he was instrumental in encouraging you. Frequently, the new story sounds so far fetched, it creates laughter. Other times, there is resistance and anger. Someone with an abusive mother might ask, "How can I possibly pretend my mother was gentle and sensitive?" In other words, "How can I let her off the hook for all the pain she caused me? Holding onto this story of abuse is part of who I am. Like Narcissus, I love this image, it makes me feel interesting."

> *Bill, a lawyer we know, did this retelling process. He had developed a well-articulated and very interesting story about his past, refined through 20 years of psychotherapy and a rich background in Jungian analysis. As a child he attended boarding schools and was ruthlessly teased by the other kids. He felt abandoned in different ways by both parents and had spent years developing a very complex character, complete with idiosyncrasies and quirks, based on this early loss and abuse. We asked him to tell a new story about being captain of the football team and a big man on campus, noticed and acknowledged by all, including his parents. It took him many tries to be able to tell it without laughing and to tell it with a conviction comparable to his previous tale. When he did, twenty years of therapy-structured stories crashed in peals of laughter.*

The most extraordinary development was that after doing this, Bill looked physically different. He had been trapped in his story; he thought it was a result of painstaking self-analysis. His posture revealed instantly to all that he was an adult with a painful past. And being able to walk into situations with a different story contributed to career breakthroughs he was able to make in following months.

The purpose of telling a new story is not to go into denial about real and often painful events. It's to allow yourself the experience, if only for a moment, to feel differently about yourself.

Here's where this discussion breaks from cognitive therapy or even positive thinking. The point is not merely to exchange an old story for a more productive one, although that can be useful. Nor is it to find an affirmation that will counter a previously negative thought about yourself. In fact sometimes it is interesting to try on stories that are *worse* than the ones you already know. A successful business executive decided to create the experience for himself of being an ex-con. It provided him with a lot of very valuable insight. The point is to discover how to discern and play with the layer of knowledge that is encoded in stories. You come to find that what you experience as the *I* is a very ephemeral experience.

In truth, the experience of *I* is really a moving center. We continually move this sensation of self around so it can best organize a chaotic range of experiences in our lives. Our identity is also one of the most powerful ways we limit the world; it predetermines the experiences we consider relevant and how we assign meanings. It is also an efficient tool, allowing us to negotiate a role for ourselves in a discussion, project, or relationship. There is a consistent body of opinions and characters we tend to play. Only by loosening the grip that your story has on you can you become more open in how you perceive the world.

Reinventing Ourselves

So, one of the ways we keep ourselves tied to the past is by the stories we tell, and one of the most powerful ways we will shape the future is also by the stories we tell. Our personal, organizational, and cultural myths all operate in similar ways, invisibly compelling us to act within the framework of an image we ourselves have invented.

> *A well-known TV personality whose very successful show had been over for several years felt ready to create a new one. He embarked on a one-year, conscious, well-orchestrated plan to "reinvent himself". He even designed stories for the tabloids that would reshape the public's perception of him. Only after he created a new public persona did he go knocking on doors.*

How Hollywood; how clever. We all focus on gaining job skills or items to add to our resumes, yet we rarely focus on building the identity, the personal story, that will support the next step. Sometimes in seminars we ask people to impersonate public figures they find interesting. Once they get into character, we ask them to reanalyze a personal issue or business problem as they imagine this person would handle it. Often, they experience insights that they could not have had just being themselves.

This is the kind of fluidity of identity that the cyber-world provides for frequenters of the chat rooms. After taking on a few different identities, it starts to click that shifting your personal story is a way to access new information. Personality becomes merely a cloak. Like our Hollywood star, it is interesting to describe your future intentions in terms of the character needed to carry off these visions and then to build a story that allows you to step into this new future.

Cognitive Modifiability

Once you get a handle on playing with your own self-image, you can begin locating and redesigning the more complex assumptions that limit behavior. Psychologist Robert Ornstein calls this cognitive modifiability, the ability to alter your cognitive structures to accommodate new information.[2] Memorizing, repetition, the notion of right and wrong answers, needing to look smart, needing to please others, an obsession with profits, efficiency at all costs: all squash our capacity for cognitive fluidity.

Without cognitive modifiability, surviving in our new psychological world will be much more difficult. A continually morphing world demands the ability to shift identities. As we suggested earlier, identity is the biggest sense organ. It underlies every other sensory experience we have. By reshaping our sense of self, we walk into an entirely new world of meanings.

We all walk around inside a self-created bubble, seeing the world reflected in our own repetitive stories. Is it no wonder we keep meeting people that seem like people we already know and having encounters that seem strangely familiar? If you want to catch new ideas, see new directions, develop heightened leadership, or enter into arenas of heightened performance, you must begin telling radically different stories about yourself and the world.

We also need more flexible identities because no one does just one thing any more. Doctors write film scripts. Carpenters become currency traders. Accountants start construction companies. The old joke is no longer just about LA or New York; it's not just waiters and cab drivers waiting for their next script, everyone is.

Our politicians warn us not to expect lifetime careers; to prepare for entire fields to close up shop, regularly. As organizations become more undefined, career paths fracture, so individuals have to be more dynamic in shaping their upward climb. We need to be able to change course when an old path closes down or a new one beckons. Nowadays, the fastest way up is around, through, and in between.

So Is There Really a "Self"?

If we are changing our personal history at will, purposely telling lies about our past, then who are we anyway?

In Hindu tradition, there is a path to self-awareness called self-inquiry, and made understandable by Ramana Maharshi. In this teaching, you name various ways you have of referring to your self, such as "I am a man; I am a teacher; I am a husband;" etc. With each reference your mind offers, you say, "I am not that." The idea is to slowly pull back from any objective references.

As you slowly reel in the most subtle and tricky of these layers, your mind begins to collapse and you finally begin to experience a sense of self untouched by personal history or cultural references. In this tradition, there is a self that is permanent and ever-present. It is the part of ourselves that is self-reflective. In the Fourth Way School, developed by Gurdjieff and Ouspensky, this more permanent self is accessed by cultivating the capacity for self-observation.

At the moment you touch this experience, you touch a place of maximum freedom and ultimate individuality, because you are at the source of all your stories. Although some articulate this path more explicitly, it is the ultimate goal of all mystical traditions to find the true self. So isn't it interesting that our current environment is pushing us to follow this path? With a work environment in total flux and a history about to collapse, we are being compelled to separate our sense of self from the stories we tell, if we are to survive.

I've already shown how a hot, seductive, and intrusive culture thrusts ideas on us that are not our own. Sometimes the barrage is so relentless, we give up and allow mass opinions to become our own. The stronger, yet more fluid self that I am advocating is the only way to withstand this cultural onslaught. Learning to consciously shift identities is a powerful way to recapture a sense of self that not only is stable but also is the source of all our imaging capacities.

Group Minds/Group Myths

You can play with organizational myths the same way you change personal stories. When Bill changed his past story from a kid who was teased to someone who had always been a big man on campus, it was not unlike the resistance a business faces when it has to relinquish a cherished piece of organizational history.

Or the president of the label who heard our friend's proposal saying, "We have always been powerful decision-makers. That's what made our company what it is. How can we let go of this control?" Or Jerry Maguire saying, "I've always been a ruthless dealmaker, what other option is there?"

Personal and organizational myths are embedded within what we hold dear. Styles of control and leadership that once worked are being smashed in this new economy. We are encouraged to have ideas that were once unthinkable. Consider the following list of suggestions found in just one month's issue of a popular business magazine:

> ➤ Give away your products for free so that you can create customers who will need you to then service these products down the road.

> ➤ Join with future competitors to expand a market so that someday in the future there will be enough room for you to also provide the product you envision.

> ➤ Ask your customers to chip in and buy you a new computer so you can give them better service.

> ➤ Go public with a company that has never earned a penny and whose 7-year plan does not project any profits whatsoever. Assure investors that it will be a very long time before any money is ever made. Your forthrightness will make them think you are hiding a good thing and shares will be snapped up like hot cakes.

These suggestions are not standard logic. It is spiderlike thinking and the spinning of crazy tales!

Levi Strauss & Company embarked on a journey of reinvention much like the Hollywood star looking for a new TV show. They literally created a parallel company with new organizational relationships, new interfaces with the market, and new job definitions. At the same time, the real-life company continued to operate. Gradually, people from the existing company applied for jobs in the new company.[3]

Recognizing what a challenging task it would be to go from one organizational myth to another, the company provided individuals with a manual called "Individual Readiness for a Changing Environment," a program for discovering a deeper level of who you are and what you want. Levi Strauss was well aware that the survival of this new organizational myth hinged on the ability of each individual to change his or her own personal story. The stress would be intense; therefore they gave psychological support. With no one "manning" the myth, the old business form slowly withered away and the new company was fleshed out with real-life people playing new parts in a new story.

Levi Strauss began this spectacular process of organizational mythmaking while it had great profits and a highly motivated employee base. The result was an even more creative and responsive company. As with personal mythmaking, on the other side they gained a much more powerful sense of what made the company unique. Mythmaking requires that you claim your role as an author of stories and to continually be inventive, visionary, and clear about the new stories you want.

In *The Fifth Discipline,* Peter Senge calls a similar idea *mental modeling.*[4] He shows how organizations mistake their mental models for facts about the world, i.e., they mistake subjective statements for objective truth. He uses the example of American car makers in the seventies. They had a successful working model: *Americans want style, not quality; they want big, not efficient.* Their failure to recognize that this was a myth subject to change caused them to be blindsided by Japanese automakers.

The more we can describe our operating assumptions as myths or mental models, the more we are free to observe their usefulness and change them as needed. The more we learn to change these models at will, the more we solidify a real freedom to express our personal and organizational uniqueness. The ability to change our organizational myths is the only way to respond to a culture that is beginning to ask for heightened corporate responsibility and more social vision. Problems like global warming or social decline can only be addressed by new myths and companies willing to truly change their fundamental stories.

Working the Story

In 12-step programs they say you have to "work the program," staying diligent, one day at a time. In the same way you have to work a story in order for it to become a lived reality. The verbal description is only the first step; the new story has to be integrated into real life. It must be developed at a level that offers new ways of speaking and new parts for others to emerge. When individuals or businesses are able to flesh out their visions, change is far more likely to occur.

Realizing the very sensitive nature of what he was presenting, our friend with the new recording idea got much better in his presentations,. He finally got the head of another label to *play* with the new story he was offering, to try it on, to detail how it might look and imagine how it would feel. As a result of getting a feel for what it would look like to walk around in this new story, and by having some fun with it, this new record label began a more serious discussion of what contracts might look like.

You can't understand a new story unless you can walk into it, move the furniture around, and get a feel for what it's like to live there.

As long as you keep your distance and observe a new story as if it were an object, you can never understand what it really offers. Entering a new story requires shifting how you organize information, structure your perceptions, even design your language, which is why Levi Strauss specifically addressed these kinds of personal issues in its companywide makeover.

As the coming decades shatter the boundaries of tradition, we will have almost unlimited freedom to enter new stories. We need skills for walking into these myths, or like Jerry McGuire, we will continue to frame the future using the parameters of the past. The ability to discern ideas as stories, to retell them, and walk into new ones will afford us a new cognitive fluidity to enter into new realities.

Back at the Web—Will the Real Spider Woman Please Stand Up?

So why has the spider woman *really* appeared at this time? Mostly because we are due for a big change. She has appeared because it is time to start telling some really new stories, not just new personal and organizational tales, but some big new cultural myths.

Companies are advised to prepare for this new world by becoming spiderlike themselves. They are advised to break down walls and link people through information needs. Forget chains of authority, cluster people in teams at nexuses where several kinds of input meet. Markets are created merely by placing yourself where you can catch what you want. Expect increased tensions, because a tug at one point in the system will be felt at all points, much like a fly getting caught in mid-flight. Webs are more integrated and holistic, so it is natural that tensions as well as strengths rapidly get communicated throughout the system. Treat breakdowns like torn fibers, i.e., forge a new link to a different part of the system, much like a spider repairs her web. Think relationships, access, and connections, not content and rules.

Cyberspace is the most powerful new myth to come along in a very long time. It is a myth in every sense of the word. Although there is a lot of hype and unnecessary jargon, it does carry with it a new language, a new way of putting concepts together, a new set of values which are essential features of any myth. More importantly, ordinary people and power brokers alike are all talking about entering a new world.

We do all the same things with this myth that we do with any story. We deny it because we are in love with the old story, and besides, a part of us wants to think that the Net is on the same train out as guitar music. We transfer images but persist in trying to structure our activities the same as always. We don't want to "get it," because change means all those nasty feelings we hate.

Also keep in mind that although it was many years ago that *Time* designated the computer its Man of the Year, not only is the vast majority of the world's population still not on-line, they don't have computers or phone lines. Many people live a mere subsistence lifestyle. Even in a country as industrialized as Japan, only 7 percent of the population has personal computers. In the U.S., with the numbers on-line doubling almost every year, most are only using it to read the headlines, check out an airline ticket, or purchase a book. And despite all the advice to get your company on line, hardly anyone has figured out how to make any big money.

With all that said, the Web style is still the driving force behind a new myth. The people who call the shots are beginning to think in these patterns. It allows individuals with few assets to approximate the information clout of large corporations. We will also see digital, spiderlike thinking become the dominant language of the coming decades. It is a language that started at the edge, and like all good futures, is slowly driving its stake into the heart of our culture.

All the books about the digital economy are attempts to help us understand how bits and bytes require new attitudes, new modes of leadership, new ways of thinking. If you are serious about absorbing this myth, then immerse yourself in at least some of these explorations. (See suggested readings listed in the References section.) Focus on the new language and sociological relationships that are emerging, because this is where the new landscapes will lie.

Some will say that cyberspace is not really all that different from what has gone before. Sure, there is more access, but with a little savvy and commitment, those who wanted could always gain access to the public. And in fact the unedited access that the web provides in some ways makes it harder to distinguish your message and get heard. Sure, moving lines of authority help the digital company achieve the necessary fluidity to deal with bits and bytes, but Ben and Jerry's did it many years before just to sell *atoms* of ice cream. Sure, everything moves a bit faster, but with our nervous systems about to give out anyway, who wants to move faster? We've always had tribes and communities that developed shared cognitive spaces, so what's the hype about virtual communities?

The main reason the Web is so powerful is that we are collectively using it to try and tell a new story. In less than a decade, it has simultaneously ushered in the greatest breakdown of existing structures we have ever encountered and has offered the greatest playground for new games. There are ideas emerging that parallel concepts from new physics and that are utopian in their flavor. There are sociologies emerging that are very eastern and echo beliefs about the nature of consciousness. The talk about the Net is passionate and soul searching, much like that which surrounded the writing of the Constitution. We are asking questions about fundamental human rights and freedoms. People are using this opportunity to discuss core assumptions about control, greed, democracy, capitalism, and a host of other things. People are publicly wondering if we want it to be a massive supermarket or more closely aligned with the building of a collective intelligence.

It is one big mirror for our collective dreams. Sorting out what we want this shared space to look like could be a way to build new stories from the ground up. Needless to say, the old stories are captivating and have quite a hold on us. We must learn the art of unraveling and reweaving stories and locate a sense of self that transcends these changing tales. Learning to tell new stories about our self, our culture, and reality itself is the way of a mythmaker.

At this point in time, by far the most fascinating aspect of the Web is the language it inspires, the dialogues and sociologies that have been triggered. We will need that army of mythmakers to carve out new conceptual paths through the collapse of meanings that it has left in its wake. From almost every front, once familiar images are being dismantled and new stories put in their place. Mythmaking is the real job skill of the future.

For now, suffice it to say that the spider woman has definitely appeared. The old stories are boring; the new ones are taking over. The new language is based on notions of fibers, webs, matrices, spins, bands, widths, clusters, bursts, fields, currents, string theories, and emergent complexities. If we don't learn this new language, we will find ourselves the equivalent of newly arrived immigrants who do not yet know the customs of a new world. We must get used to unraveling and reweaving stories like putting on a new coat. We must also locate a sense of self that transcends the variables of changing meanings. Learning the ways of the spider woman and claiming our role as a mythmaker is the fourth navigational tool.

Practicing Mythmaking

Locating Core Stories

If you want the kind of experience the accountant who went to boarding school was able to achieve, you need to make sure you locate a good story. There are several places to look:

> ➤ What are the most frequent stories you tell about your personal past?

➤ What is the most challenging event or dynamic from your past?

➤ Was there a time from your childhood when you gave up your power? When was it? What happened?

Once you've chosen a story to work with, experiment with rewriting it either in your own mind, in a journal, or by telling a friend.

> For example, you might tell how your whole family showed up at your graduation with special gifts and a party and how wonderful it felt to receive this attention. (When in fact, no one showed up or even acknowledged your graduation in real life and it has always been a source of hurt and a reason you hide your accomplishments.) Or you could go in another direction and tell a fantasy about leaving home at 16 to climb the Himalayan mountains, forgetting your own graduation, because you have always been such a free spirit.

Speaking a Story

You can enhance the value of this exercise by telling the story out loud. There are three ways to do it and I recommend them all.

> First, if you find yourself in a situation where you accidentally meet someone whom you are highly unlikely to meet again, such as on an airplane or sitting in a waiting room, experiment with telling this person a bald-faced lie. Tell them a lie about your past and who you are. Tell them your new story.

I guarantee it will bring up extraordinary resistance and the strangest feelings that you are doing something incredibly wrong. The resistance goes far beyond our training about not telling lies. Our rehearsed and polished story has an incredible grip on our being like a boa constrictor that won't let go. It feels like our skin, and we would be very raw and tender without it. Remember, this is an imaginary story and you will probably never meet this person again. It does not in any way hurt them and in all honesty, in a couple of hours they will not even remember they met you, let alone what you said. Try it. It will give you an extraordinary feeling, as if somehow you are a different person than you really are. And that is the point, to experience that odd sensation of feeling differently about who you are.

> The second way is to tell a friend your new story about the past. Their job is to have you retell it as many times as you have to, until it sounds

completely natural to them. When you get the new story to this place of sounding natural, once again you will experience an odd sensation, as if you are somehow betraying something very profound.

The third way is to use a constructed personality to enter a chat room. Personally, I found this even scarier than the previous two. Particularly, I found assuming different sex or age amazingly challenging.

If you are bold enough to try all three parts of the experiment, you will notice a curious exhilaration. It's almost like being set free.

Moving the Furniture Around/Working It

There is not any specific exercise to do here; it's more a matter of observing yourself. Once you have rewritten your story with a friend, and preferably also with a stranger, then commit to living from this new story for a week or a month. Every time you see your mind returning to the old story, actively steer yourself away. For example, if you were "working" the graduation story, you would steer clear of thoughts like, "People don't pay attention to me." and instead look for evidence that people are going out of their way to acknowledge your accomplishments. If you were working the "Himalayan Mountain" story, you would "work," or notice, every time you were bold, and steer clear of wondering what others think about you. You can even keep a journal recording daily evidence of this new story becoming reality.

Reinvention and Future Loops

You can do this one in your imagination, but it works best to drag your friend into this one again.

You begin by making positive statements about things you want to attain in the future, and then you loop back into your past to recall an imaginary story (lie) about why this future event will be easy. So, for example, you might say: "I really want to get a raise in the next three months and expect it will be easy because whenever I needed backing to take a big step in life, my parents were always right there with financial support (lie). I also want more freedom to become more creative in my work, and I know that will be a breeze because I always had a lot of space and support to be creative when I was a child and all the art and dance classes I could ever want (lie).

Once again, your friend's role is to give you feedback when you're finished about which "loops" worked and which felt like lies. You continue to replay them until they all work and all your future intentions are supported by a fabricated lie about your past or at least an enhancement of the actual events. When you've finished this process, you will notice that your future intentions feel so much lighter and playful. Once again, you've loosened your belt on what was a very tight self-concept.

Mick Jagger and Tina Turner

I just want to remind you about trying on personalities of larger-than-life figures who might have solutions to your problems or whose energy style could be useful. Some people love it and get a lot of ideas; some people find it irritating and silly. It's just another strategy for loosening up. Remember how the press made a lot of fun of Hillary Clinton for having imaginary talks with Eleanor Roosevelt, so it's probably best not to advertise your adventures with this process. Our myths haven't changed that much yet!

Self-Observation and the Transcendent Self

> Meditation or Ramana Maharshi's system of self-inquiry are powerful tools.

> You may also want to try the path of self-observation. For example, for a week, as much as you can, go through your normal activities but also cultivate the ability to watch yourself at the same time you are doing them.

> Subpersonalities, psychosynthesis, and voice dialogue are all systems for beginning to isolate personalities that have formed in response to our past for the purpose of emotional survival. When you begin to communicate between these subpersonalities, you begin to gradually develop an emotional space within yourself that is also the mediator or integrative capacity.

I believe the transcendent place that meditation fosters is very comparable to the observer state and is also very comparable to the emotional capacity to integrate subpersonalities. Skill in these areas is very important to any up-and-coming mythmaker.

Reality Myths

The kind of stories I have described so far are those that are based in your personal history. There is another whole set of stories that are based in your beliefs about "reality," for example, how fast, with what kinds of support, or under what conditions events can happen. We have seen many people astound their lawyers, managers, doctors, friends, and families by rewriting the script of how fast or at what level results can happen.

Bernie Siegal describes a hospital which now has the doctors, nurses, orderlies, and anyone else in contact with a patient align around a vision of the patients' recovery, being careful to only say things that correspond with this shared vision. Since they started doing this, recovery rates are higher and faster. Why can't software companies and clothing manufacturers use the same principles to rewrite their scripts about how fast or how well things can happen? We've personally witnessed many people who have altered normal expectations, achieving results faster and greater than any one could have believed. (More about this in Chapter 11)

Rewriting organizational myths is a much more involved process than what can be covered in a few paragraphs. However, your experience with rewriting your own personal stories will give you more insight into the kinds of organizational myths that are told, and which are just stories, not factual, and could easily be rewritten. The Levi Strauss model of creating an imaginary parallel company is an extraordinary strategy to use. Make up a new organizational structure and design a creative strategy for moving into it.

Ultimately, maybe we can collectively design a parallel global culture that works for everyone. Once we get a really good story in place, then as at Levi Strauss, we can all begin to apply for roles in this new myth.

Robert Bly tells a story about the aspects of ourselves we disown. A queen is giving birth, attended by a midwife. First, a small, ugly garden snake slithers out. The midwife, not wanting to alarm anyone, throws it out the window. Just moments later, a beautiful boy, the future king, arrives and the midwife proudly hands him to his mother. The prince grows up to be handsome and strong.

One day, the prince leaves the kingdom in search of a wife. As he enters the forest, he is met by a ferocious dragon who says, "First mine." In others words, first you must find me a wife before you can have yours. The prince agrees and brings the dragon back to the palace to find him an eligible woman. The problem is that the next morning, this "would be" wife is found eaten and the process must begin again. This continues, the dragon eating all prospective wives. The prince realizes this predicament is beyond normal problem-solving.

With the help of a sorcerer, a new prospective wife is taught how to deal with this dragon. She arrives wearing seven layers of clothing. Whenever the dragon asks her to remove her clothes for bed, she says, First you remove your skin; then I will remove mine." The dragon has to peel away seven layers of dreadful, scaly skin.

At the bottom of all this is a handsome man. In fact, it is the prince's own brother. The small snake that slithered out first, which seemed meaningless, grew into a powerful dragon with the power to prevent his brother from having what he wanted. The dragon had to be encountered. The first brother needed to be freed for the second one to be free as well. An important lesson these tales teach is that dealing with the shadow always goes beyond normal problem-solving; it always requires some special potion, twist of logic, secret charm, or amulet.[1]

If shadows are not attended to, they grow larger, uglier, and more frightening as the years go by. There comes a day when you can go no further unless you confront the shadow side. Since we have all thrown a lot of snakes out the window, our future will demand knowing a lost art called **shadow dancing.**

CHAPTER 8

Shadow Dancing

The potential of the future may sometimes feel like a bright light on the horizon, but at it's feet is always a shadow that can't be avoided. To entertain any dream of a tomorrow that is better than today requires looking at issues we would prefer to pretend do not exist.

The research for this book revealed two notable trends:

➢ There are books, utopian in feeling, that lay out incredible visions of a future seemingly without limits. Most often these books end with a cautionary word about how many fundamental challenges we still have to face, such as environmental issues, social decay, rapidly growing income discrepancies, heightened political instability, etc.

➢ Another slant is offered by books that go straight to the heart of these issues, pointing out how persistent and intractable these problems will be and how far we have traveled away from fairness and real caring. These kinds of books tend to end with a chapter or two describing some ray of hope.

The key missing in both these approaches is building a relationship between the shadow and the dream, between despair and optimism, between our escalating problems and our unprecedented opportunities. We often miss that our problems and opportunities may be two aspects of the same thing. Perhaps our current technological renaissance arises from the same source as our growing social chaos, a hunger for something more. We tend to call things good or bad, be optimistic or pessimistic, and avoid the fine art of creative tension, personal and organizational alchemy, using both the dark and the light to design new paths. Any truly skilled painter is a master of both shadow and light.

In every ancient teaching, in all psychology, encountering our worst fears *and* heeding the call to greatness are hopelessly intertwined. The prince does not even know the dragon exists until he decides to go forward in his life, symbolized by choosing a wife. Moving forward always involves facing whatever we have denied.

When the Genie Gets Out of the Bottle

In a recent seminar, we completed a strong section on rewriting myths. One of the participants was a former art director who now ran his own ad agency. Steve's personal and professional life had always been about creating a great image. When he let some of his favorite stories go, decades of feelings were released, years of fear and rage over what he had missed. He calmly told what seemed to be a very simple new story (lie) about what his life could have been and he nearly fell apart. The story he'd been living for so many years was so rigid and tight that he didn't know until he let it go just how awesome the dragon had become.

We sometimes don't realize that when we let go of a past story, we also have to encounter the feelings that may have been suppressed by this tale. The story we have told always sits on top of a story that couldn't be told.

> After years of not saying what you really want, it may at first feel like you've unleashed a seemingly bottomless pit of rage.

> Decades of denying your spontaneity may surface as an irresistible urge to make irresponsible choices.

> Years of unconsciously letting people go from your business eventually results in a very demoralized and passive work force.

> A lifetime of blocking your creativity may result in a depression and fatigue that becomes chronic.

Small snakes have a way of growing up. Yet our big problems nearly always begin as very small communication patterns or thoughts.

When Levi Strauss changed an organizational myth at the level Steve, the art director, did, they experienced a very similar reaction. People who had been with the company for many years felt betrayed and frightened. There were many who did not see the reason for purposely invoking chaos, especially when the company was doing well. The leaders of this change were smart enough to know they needed to provide constant outlets for dissent and resistance. Levi's Vice President Tom Kasten, who was in charge of remaking the company for the 21st century, said, "Your change agents, the people who really see the future, pull the organization along. But if they get too far out, if they don't circle back, they lose people."[2]

Shadow Work Is the Circling Back

Shadow work is collecting the feelings that have been stirred up by a new story and using them to forge the next step. You can temporarily avoid circling back and override these problems, or get rid of the so-called "resistant" people, but the issues they represent have a way of gathering steam until they are more in charge than you are.

What happened for Steve is happening for all of us. Whether we like it or not, everywhere we turn stories are crumbling. The myth that most families look like Ozzie and Harriet is long gone. In a few short years, the myth that a college education leads to a good job and a healthy retirement pension has almost evaporated, and a lot of people are mad. Hardly anyone believes politicians are focused on protecting the common good, so we are dropping out and harboring deep suspicions. Even such sacred cows as the brilliance of capitalism are starting to show an ugly side. Beliefs such as these organize our social world. When they crumble, the control they provided also dissolves.

And the Shadow Is Definitely Rising

The dark side of many stories is beginning to surface. You know we are in the midst of a staggering level of mistrust when 20 percent of the public believes the U.S. government may have had a role in the Oklahoma City bombing (*USA Today* poll) and 40 percent think the government is covering up what happened in the TWA crash (*George* magazine poll). Only 12 percent of the public thinks that media stories tell the real truth. Forty years ago, most people would not have entertained such suspicions. The Net fuels these fears; it's a haven for conspiracy theories. Thus our worst fears are mascarading as fact. Or is it our biggest cover-ups that are mascarading as truth? We're lost in a house of mirrors.

The Bigger the Front, the Bigger the Back

This is a well-known Zen teaching. If it's right, modern culture, with it's great big front, is bound to have a mighty big back. The more our myths crash, the freer the shadow will be to operate. If this is so, then the coming decades will require much more advanced skills for dealing with this domain of our psyches. Here's another growth industry for you. Every community and organization will soon need not only a team of myth-makers, but their own resident shadow expert.

Our mainstay stories are becoming brittle. The 6 o'clock news announces a deal to benefit the public has been struck with tobacco companies. By the 11 o'clock news the concessions reveal how insignificant the settlement is. The next day tobacco stocks rise. Furthermore, our news stories tend to have increasingly short life spans; they are easily shattered. We are told a bill was passed to end welfare as we know it. Several months later statisticians reveal that between loopholes, union concessions, and natural shifts in the population, all the stated goals can be met without most states changing a thing.

One outcome of living in a linguistic environment where there is little truth telling and what few stories we believe quickly unravel is that shadows become a huge part of our daily life. We have separated ourselves from our problems. We are terrified to look at what might be chasing us. Cynicism, doubt, and denial have become permanent features of the collective personality. As we are forced to enter this realm, we will find that the shadow is a wild place where fear and trickery abound.

Finding the Shadow

The shadow is the sum total of all the feelings and aspects of ourselves, our organizations, or our culture that we have judged to be unacceptable—

the lost, disowned, and denied parts. It is formed piece by piece, every time we cut off from an experience because we think we can't or shouldn't feel what we do.

Reasonable people can't talk about their rage. Nice people don't talk about their needs for power. Once you're in a committed relationship, you're supposed to say "we." If you want to move up the corporate ladder, you don't talk about organizational patterns that disturb you. If you are committed to your profession, you don't take a summer off; serious people don't take side trips. People who really want to make money don't slow down for the environment or social issues. Recently, we saw an article advising people about how to handle corporate retreats. It said whatever you do, don't let your guard down, and don't change your normal reserve.

We become increasingly fragmented because there are so many areas we must now avoid. Soon we are left with a very narrow path of feelings and thoughts which are acceptable. Any remaining ideas become more entrenched, our emotions more superficial, and we stay away from people who express opinions that could take us over the edge.

Slowly, aspects of ourselves are supressed, along with our power. We become numb, empty, tired, and apathetic. Unless we locate those lost parts of our personal and organizational psyches, we'll never get our vision and vitality back.

Locked in the Shadow Is Always a Missing Piece of Our Power

Whenever someone talks about a project, one of the first things Philip and I look for is where the energy is numb, rigid, or repetitive. Shakespeare gave us a clue for finding the shadow when he said, "Thou dost protest too much." Whenever someone supports an image of themselves, their relationship, or their business a little too vigorously, then there is always something they are afraid to look at.

My brain sometimes works in a funny way. I sometimes hear a spouse saying over and over how great their partner is. If they say it one too many times, their words change shape and I hear instead that they are losing respect for their partner. I'll hear a businessperson say over and over that the strength of the company lies in the quality of its relationships. But if I hear this same phrase one too many times, my auditory reversal kicks in and I start hearing the opposite. When we are brought in as consultants, one of the first areas we look at for weakness is often the area that everyone says is their strength.

The shadow is also locked in our numbness, the times when we say we are excited or committed and there is no real energy there. You have probably noticed this in others and can feel it in yourself. We all have "dead spaces" in our personas. Someone acknowledges us and we can't really feel it. Someone says they are upset with us, and something inside freezes. Someone offers us a great opportunity, and we pretend we didn't hear it. We are asked to take on a challenging task, and suddenly everything seems to wind down as if we are in slow motion.

Your personal shadow is always locked in the feelings you don't want to admit. A family's shadow is always locked in its secrets. Sometimes the secrets are big. Sometimes they are seemingly insignificant, like everyone catering to a father's temper tantrums or a mother's forgetfulness.

"You Are Only as Sick as Your Secrets"

This is a saying from 12-step programs. It means that what you deny is also what runs you, because you must spend more and more psychological energy pretending it doesn't exist.

Mort Myerson, CEO of EDS at Perot Systems, tells an amazing story about his journey into his company's shadow.[3] He unveiled such things as abusiveness to staff, inflexibility that made life unnecessarily difficult, power-tripping customers, avoidance of problems, quick and costly judgments, and on and on. His journey to begin healing these corporate shadows began with taking them out of the closet. Ugly little issues like verbal abuse were acknowledged. People were called on it and coached on how to speak differently. Bringing the shadow to light is always scary at first, but truth always brings relief. Even the simple admission of a secret or denial will often bring a feeling of renewed energy. The main thing that keeps us from looking at our shadows is our embarrassment about them. The embarrassment holds us back more than the problem itself. For example, being called on your verbal abuse is the hard, embarrassing part. Dealing with it is far easier.

Many years ago Philip and I were on the Greek island of Santorini with a few friends. We walked over to a volcanic cone where the explosion originated that destroyed Minoan civilization. To get there, we had to leap over a small chasm in the rocks. When I looked down, the drop was almost 200 feet, complete with waves crashing against jagged rocks.

Everyone made the leap and I stood there on the other side frozen. Everyone encouraged and called out to me. I finally leaped, figuring it was more painful to die of embarrassment than to crash against the rocks. Of course, I was fine. I went back and calculated the leap was about 18 inches. Typically, I would negotiate such a trifle without thought. It was my mind that embellished the 200-foot drop and made it so huge and symbolic that it dwarfed the very short and safe leap I faced. Every leap through the shadow is like this. It plays on our minds creating unreasonable perceptions.

Entering the Chasm

Once you identify where some of your shadows lie, you have to go in there.

Fred ran an advertising agency, making lots of fast money during the 1980s. He described himself as a shark, willing to do whatever it took to make a deal. One day, he was in a terrible car accident, which left him in chronic back pain. At 50, he was retired. Whenever he talked about his life, he made a clear separation between life before and after the accident. Before he was a shark; now he was a nice person who took self-improvement seminars and could afford not to deal with the ways of the world. Our only clue something was wrong with this picture was how often he would say how perfect his life was. It just didn't ring true.

A highly motivated, somewhat ruthless workaholic was now spending a lot of his time in endless introspection on his personal growth. We supported him in reconnecting with the "shark" he was in the eighties. Initially he became furious with us and said all we cared about was getting people to accomplish more. Part of what made the shark period feel so dangerous for him is that it was also a time when he made some very self-destructive choices. Going there felt to him like a 200-foot drop into crashing waves.

A few months later, he settled down a bit and deep inside knew there was some truth to our observation. Although challenging, slowly he felt the feelings he had disowned. Curiously, every time he made this connection, he reported that he felt a little less back pain in the following week. It was as if

the "shark" he had disowned was still inside, eating away at him. After gain-
ing confidence that this direction was supporting his physical health, he also
noticed that he spontaneously began to feel some small inklings of motiva-
tion. He eventually formed a small investment club to support people in his
life who needed financial help. It's not so much that he discovered a more
truthful understanding of himself, but rather that what he most feared about
himself and his past was also tied to his power and his healing. This is the
personal alchemy I spoke of, where our darkness is also our strength.

The same dynamics happen on an organizational level too. We consulted with a small business which had significantly expanded its physical
space. Soon after making this financial commitment, sales dropped and the
owner was very scared. They had to follow a similar path as Fred. They
had to admit and connect with a degree of arrogance and greed that had
accompanied their expansion, the ways people were left out and diminished in the process. As long as this material was suppressed, the business
was stuck. When it was brought out into the open, the insights which resulted were a vital key to moving ahead.

When John Stack introduced open-book management, allowing
employees to see company finances and participate in decisions, it was
regarded by some as irresponsible. The finances of a company are sacred, they
hold power, they should only be viewed by the elite who can handle this vital
data, the lifeblood of a company. Stack found, and so have many others, that
it is a way of releasing secrets and dispelling a major piece of any company's
shadow. Everyone can see exactly what's going on and many report that staff
respond with profound interest in the good of the company. With many of
their worst suspicions dispelled, a greater creativity is released.

Paradigm Drift

Paul Hawken opens his book, *The Ecology of Commerce*, with a striking personal story.[4] His company, Smith and Hawken, had just received an award
for excellent ecological practices. As he was walking up to the podium, the
moment stretched out in time and it dawned on him that even if every
company in the world operated at the level of sustainability that Smith
and Hawken did, it would not be enough. Issues far more profound than
mere recycling and careful buying had to be addressed.

This was his 200-foot freefall. He could have easily brushed the thought away, patted himself on the back, and continued enjoying his public acknowledgment as a leader in this area. He could even have verbalized his concern in his acceptance speech and left it at that. Instead, he took the leap and wrote an extraordinary analysis of the true cost of doing business and excellent suggestions for reframing our economic myths that would lead not only to a more stable and earth-friendly financial system, but also to an avalanche of economic opportunity. A thought that was originally annoying became the source of a new creative inspiration.

This is the value of shadow work. We avoid the uncomfortable stuff and wish it would just go away. Yet at the core of where a business or an individual is most stuck, why they are resisting a change, what they are questioning, or where they keep their biggest secrets is often where you will find the source of breakthrough.

When people don't look at their shadow material, they merely reenact the same dramas and no real change ever occurs. We refer to this as "paradigm drift"—new ideas, same stuff. We need to mobilize the feelings and events that we call negative in order to access a deeper level of our potential.

Don't Forget That Encountering the Shadow Always Requires a Special Potion, a Magic Sword, a Twist of Logic, or the Help of Some Sorcerer

It is not a domain of normal problem-solving. For example, in normal problem-solving, if you are feeling angry, you try to discover why, explore whether it is justified, and analyze how to best deal with it. When you are in the domain of the shadow, this kind of logic is irrelevant. Anger is a cover, a ruse. It is a ploy to keep you from your true power. You need to go into the anger, wrestle with it in it's purest state and just be. You are looking for alchemy, not solution. You are looking for power, not a quick fix or a momentary release.

Paul Hawken knew he did not need to vent his self-doubts and pull his self-confidence back together, or even make lofty admonishments in his speech to the crowd about his efforts not being enough and the need to be even more vigilant. These were not the issues. His moment of doubt and hesitation was a ruse, a cover for a deeper level of creativity that wanted his attention.

In the book *Moby Dick*, Ahab becomes obsessed by the great white whale, merely because the whale dared to elude him in their initial encounter. The whale's escape causes Ahab to chase it across the ocean. Symbolically, Ahab is the conscious mind, obsessed with the idea that negative feeling must be conquered, the shadow subdued. Yet Ahab's obsession is also his downfall: eventually the whale does him in. The shadow can never be dismantled by the conscious mind. If you try, it will always win. It is not a place for logic and reason. If we observe and respect it's significance, then and only then will the shadow share it's power. Shadows, like whales, require reverence. If they get it, they can become something beautiful and magnificent.

Curiously, the Shadow Often Has a Way of Rearing Its Head Just Before Moments of Breakthrough; Therefore, It Is Critical to Expansion of Any Kind

We have seen many people experience their deepest blocks just before they create the very opportunity for which they have been working.

> *A woman we know had been working very hard to create a personal and career breakthrough for herself. Finally, she was offered her ideal job in the city where she always wanted to live, and she found a great house at an incredible price. Two months before everything was about to take place, a fairly minor legal problem appeared to threaten her ability to make this move. Her response was a throwback to her past. She became depressed, almost catatonic, unable to take the least action to unravel these logistical barriers. She was rendered helpless. For a few weeks it seemed as if she would cancel her plans.*
>
> *Her shadow was rearing it's head. In effect it was saying, "Are you sure you're strong enough to transform what I represent." And for quite a while, she wasn't; the shadow was winning. At the eleventh hour, she found an even deeper source of commitment, strength, and persistence to continue into the vision she had set in place. She handled everything and showed up for her new job on time. She later saw that this deeper strength she accessed was right on target for the challenges she faced in that next year.*

We have seen this happen many times. We all seem to need a last battle with our fears before really being able to break through. Those in the health professions call it a "healing crisis," when an illness takes it's last shot at the individual. After a healing crisis, recovery often proceeds rapidly. We have also seen businesses go through the same pattern. A software company we know almost lost everything. Everyone in the business had to tap into their last kernel of faith and willpower to keep showing up. It was weeks of working without salary and nearly admitting that maybe their product wasn't as advanced as they thought. It was only after this last and most decisive battle with failure and loss that their success finally appeared.

There is a story often told at motivational seminars. It's based on a true story of a man who was caught in winter wilderness conditions and walked for many days without food or water to try and find shelter. Finally, he gave up. Later, rescuers discovered that had he walked over just one more small hill, he would have seen the city lights! *He was two minutes before the miracle.*

Studies of highly successful salespeople compared to moderately successful salespeople have found that top salespeople do not get significantly fewer initial rejections. The difference is that the top salespeople know how to go the extra few minutes past a rejection, when often a sale will turn around. The woman experiencing a breakdown before her breakthrough, the two minutes before the miracle, or the little extra push that leads to greater results all reveal a similar pattern of our psyches. If the shadow represents the denied and lost parts of our self, the areas we don't want to look at, it will always appear with ever-increasing power just when we are about to break past them. In order to make a breakthrough, we must look at these issues at a higher level than we ever have before.

The shadow has a curious way of lying down directly in front of the spider woman, obscuring her whereabouts and preventing you from seeing her craft. Just before entering the zone is often when you have the clearest thoughts of wanting to quit. Just before perceptions reorganize into a new sense; what you see in front of you seems to be utterly incomprehensible. Just before surrendering to the Bardo is often when we hold on tightest.

In the same way, our personal disillusionment, the deepening of an organizational shadow, or even our cultural despair may in fact be the darkness before the dawn. When things get worse, the critical elements we have ignored rise to the surface. If we are willing to take the frightening step of really looking at them, they can become the alchemical keys which allow us to develop transformative solutions.

Shadow Wrestling

Before too long, we will be called upon to go into psychic territories far more intimidating than any we've met so far. The dissolution of the social and organizational fabric that is already in progress will entail each of us becoming masters at facing our denied energy. The faster traditions crumble, the more we will be called upon to deal with the emotions locked in the stories we were never told.

If we continue to ignore the grave social injustices of many of our current practices, the garden snakes will come back as boa constrictors and then as real fire-breathing dragons. At the heart of where people feel most apathetic, angry, or frightened—ecological problems, social decay, scandal, and increasing income disparity— is where you'll find the keys to organizational breakthrough. We can no longer afford to look at issues simplistically, as good or bad, right or wrong. We are in an era that demands every person to look at his or her part in every issue.

Virtual Shadows

When people talk about "cybershadows," they mean things like information terrorism, loss of privacy, people stealing your identity and using it to buy stuff, government control, the extreme gap between information haves and have nots, and disembodied techies who have lost their grip on reality. As real and important as these issues are, they do not represent the greatest shadow the Net culture holds for us.

The new information world holds real promise, like the kind we missed with radio and TV. In the early days of radio and TV, the thinkers of the time said they would offer a forum for artistic expression and the cultural uplift of the population. Since everyone would know about world affairs, political involvement would reach new heights. Sound familiar?

Unfortunately for TV and radio, the content and its distribution were too easy to control by the forces of unchecked personal gain. What will happen if we leave cyberspace to the same fate? It will be the same game with possibly a few, but not many, new faces. The economic domination that characterized the industrial revolution has become more extreme even faster with the information wave. Already this field is top heavy: Intel controls 80 percent of the market in chips; Microsoft controls 90 percent of the software market. A few multinational media giants control increasing amounts of the content. Unless this shadow is addressed, there will be no new myth.

The rising threat to freedom in cyberspace is routed in the failure to address the shadows of the industrial age and the media age. The shadow can only be found in the obscure voices relegated to the fringes or underground—National Public Radio, PBS, public access TV, even the far right. Computer use might not be an educational panacea. It could even harm a child's intellectual and social development. Digital town meetings might not be the answer to greater participation in the political process. The problem is not lack of information.

Militia movements, crazy cults, angry ghettoes, an armed public, and youth dropping out earlier represent the ever-broadening shadows of issues we have been throwing out the window. We need the same courage that Mort Myerson used to surface shadows at Perot Systems. Although a bit more complex, we each need the courage to insist that cultural secrets be brought to light before they become unmanageable. A sincere commitment to look at our real shadows is the only way for our personal and public dialogues to become more complex and useful.

The shadow demands alchemy. Our fifth navigational tool requires the ability to bring submerged aspects of our consciousness into full view and transform this encounter into new directions.

We need to remember that:

> ➤ Often our shadows don't appear until we go forward or try something new.

> ➤ Locked in the shadow is always a missing piece of our power.

> ➤ You or your organization are only as sick as your secrets, because denied energy always shapes our behavior.

> ➤ Confronting the shadow may feel like a 200-foot freefall but usually it's only an 18-inch baby step.

> ➤ Just before a breakthrough is often when the shadow looms largest.

> ➤ The shadow cannot be understood through logic. It cannot be conquered, but must be respected and encountered artfully.

What we have called entering the chasm or shadow dancing will be one of the most significant leadership skills in coming years. As stories continue to fall apart, life events mock our denial, and chaos reigns, our shadows will creep closer to the surface. Individuals and organizations alike have the chance to go face-to-face with their shadows, and discover an alchemy that will recast them as tools for growth. Unless we commit to these skills, we abandon the field to the dragons.

Practicing Shadow Dancing

It's illusive, subtle, and disappears when you look.

The hardest part about locating the shadow side is that it's not just the opposite of what you like. It's a bit more complex and subtle than that.

Let's start with a few short processes and then explore how they work together.

> ➤ First, imagine what you would be like if you were the opposite sex. How would you look and act? What would you be able to do as

the opposite sex that you can't now? Spend a few moments developing this visualization.

➤ Now, go into the dark, ugly stuff. What would you least like people to know about you? What do you hate to admit about yourself? What trait is most responsible for things not working out in your life?

➤ Let's look at the shame and embarrassment stuff. When are you most likely to feel embarrassed? What from your past or present embarrasses you the most?

➤ Now, take a look at your projections. What is it that irritates you about others? What kind of people do you dislike the most? What traits in others are most likely to make you lose your patience? Take a moment to locate these characteristics in yourself.

➤ Finally, what parts of yourself have you lost? What did you once love to do that you've stopped doing? What secret dreams do you have that you've given up on? What values have you lost sight of that were once dear to you? What talents or loves do you have that no one knows about?

➤ Who or what have you thrown out the window? What have you dismissed?

If you put all these feelings together, you start developing a sense of the shadow. Try putting each of the previous visualizations or responses into your awareness one by one. Try building a single experience, a composite of them. What is it like? Does this composite image feel familiar? Can you remember ever before having this sensation hovering at the edges of your awareness?

Remember, the shadow is the lost, denied, unacceptable, and projected pieces of your experience. Merely paying attention to these feelings either separately or as a composite is extremely powerful. The shadow is most likely to fade and lose it's negative power when it is put under the light of attention.

Diving In and the Special Potion

In every myth the hero is given a special potion. In this case the special potion is the way of feeling I suggest in this chapter.

For example, suppose you surfaced your lost dream of making hand-carved furniture. You had always thought you'd have your own wood shop one day. In the "busy-ness" of life, you gradually forgot your dream. Normal analysis might yield something like this: "Why did I forget this dream, it's important, I'm going to resolve to do it." Shadow feeling is different; you go beneath specifics and feel the sensation of wanting to use your hands and express your creativity in that way, feeling the physicality of your dream. Then you notice how and how often you have made these feelings unimportant. You feel the sadness, not for losing the act of woodworking, but for the part of yourself that became lost when you slowly forgot this dream. What is the part of you that really got lost? How has this need for creativity left other areas of your life? Feel the separation that you have allowed with this and so many other things. Just be with it; don't try to make it better. Just stay open and relaxed, sensitive and persistent in your discovery. Don't make any resolutions to yourself about being different in the future. Focus on connecting with deeper and deeper levels of what you have lost.

Slowly learn how to do this with the other areas that are denied, projected, shameful, or unacceptable. Just be with each memory or experience. Don't ask why it happened or analyze its solution. With practice, you'll begin to see how much power is awakened by doing this. You slowly start to feel that there is nothing about your being that is frightening. You don't sit there being afraid that your right hand will unexpectedly fly up and hit you! The reason is because you are connected to your right hand. In the same way, once you connect with these shadow sensations, they will no longer feel separate and capable of sabotaging you.

Returning to the example of the wood shop dream, you will find that whether or not you ever take action on this particular dream, connecting with the feelings brings a sense of greater completeness. Just the act of paying attention allows you to notice when other secret dreams or hidden talents come up during the course of an ordinary conversation and you will be less likely to push them away.

Shadow as Process/Staying Jung Forever

Shadow work is not a one-time shot; it is a way of looking at experience. It means not dismissing, overriding, or reasoning your way out of discrepancies. If someone says in a hesitating voice, "I don't feel good about this decision," it might be easy to convince them to your way of thinking. When shadows become more acceptable to you, you might say instead, "Tell me everything that concerns you. Let's give it a thorough look." Then you would try to step into the person's shoes and let it concern you as well. Some piece of this person's opinion—sometimes very small, sometimes unexpectedly large—would be included in the final decision.

I see over and over that when I don't apply this attitude, conversations quickly become polarized and people take their marbles and run. I did this the very week I was writing this section. My excuse was that this other person was trying to dominate a meeting, so *I was going to show her.* I cleverly dismantled her point and won the discussion. The only problem was that when I got home, I had to admit that the concern was valid and if we didn't look at it, down the line we might have a huge problem on our hands. I humbly had to apologize the next week and suggest that we look at this other person's concern. Powering over someone or even yourself *always* creates a shadow that will someday demand its due.

A few years ago we met a senior vice president of one of the largest multi-nationals. We didn't meet him in the large city where he lived, but in the tiny town where we live, when a mutual friend told him to look us up. He was not here to ski, but to spend time at a local Zen monastery. His company was a major player in the Chinese market and he was concerned about the rapid environmental degradation he was witnessing. He knew there were no simple solutions. What set him apart from other executives was the integration between his corporate and spiritual life. He was not a Zen Buddhist, but he was participating in the retreat because he knew that the time spent searching his soul was essential to his integrity as a leader. More and more people are making choices like this.

Call it an Aquarian conspiracy. Call it "Celestine Prophecy," quantum healing, or the new spirit of business, but it's not going away. Spiritual and self-help books lead the best-seller lists. Eastern thought and personal development work are among the fastest growing movements in the country. The *Wall Street Journal* recently reported that yoga is now the rage with Washington politicians and lobbyists. Architects are taking classes in feng shui. Most corporate training now openly incorporates ideas that were once considered "new age."

Some people still say, "Don't mess with my soul." But to ignore this dimension, which is now such a huge part of the public psyche, is like sticking your head in the sand.

We seem to crave something to fill a void in our current reality. We have always been willing to work hard for answers and solutions, but we are realizing that that may not be enough. We are begining to understand **why we need to sweat.**

CHAPTER 9

Why We Need to Sweat

A strange emptiness is sweeping through us. It leaves apathy and a lot of lost souls in it's wake. As big and bold and graphically stimulating as everything has become, we are often left strangely untouched by the increasing glamour of our world. Like junkies looking for an excitement fix, it takes more and more thrill just to catch our attention, and the high becomes more and more fleeting.

A popular group called Smashing Pumpkins had a big hit on MTV. The repeat line says in effect, "Even if I feel my rage, I'm still just a rat in a cage." It's a takeoff of Charlie Chaplin's movie *Modern Times,* but the images the video paints are a few decades darker.

As our shadows become more undeniable, we won't be able to turn away from hard questions. Since everything is continually shaken, we need ways to stabilize. With big myths awakening, we need doorways inside.

Intuitively, we know we better start making a difference, before everything in sight starts looking the same.

The skills covered in the previous chapters—exercising the freedom of choice that change affords us, entertaining the possibilities of expanded stories, encountering the power of our shadows—push us to connect with a deeper level of our selves. This chapter will take you a bit further down that road.

Hope

Several years ago, Frances Lappe and Paul Du Bois began research for their upcoming book, *The Quickening of America.*[1] They were looking for examples of individuals and groups who were providing innovative community service. Their investigation turned up so many more examples than they could have imagined, they formed a news bureau to create ongoing visibility for such efforts and a magazine called *Hope,* based on the promise they saw in what was happening for ordinary people. Although corporate giving declines with every year, the slack has been more than taken up by individuals, mostly by those making *less than $50,000 a year!* Statistics like this and findings like those of Lappe and Du Bois suggest that the general populace seems to be moved and is doing something about it.

Books on voluntary simplicity are making it to the best-seller list. Entire subcultures focusing on such ideas as sustainable living, conscious consuming, new community, right livelihood, and ethical business, are growing by leaps and bounds, supported by Web sites, conferences, and successful magazines such as *Mother Jones, Utne Reader, New Sojourner, Ethical Business,* and *Yes!* (See additional books listed in References section.) Among celebrities, Oprah is tuned most closely to this pulse. First, she moved the focus of her show from sensationalism toward substance. Now she is showcasing, networking, and forming her own televised efforts to support good works. Marianne Williamson, a best-selling personal growth author, told her constituency they now need to use their personal healing powers for social change and titled her recent book *The Healing of America.*[2] Colin Powell leveraged his visibility as a potential Presidential candidate to advocate voluntarism. Recently, *Newsweek* ran a cover story focusing on a growing movement of individuals who are voluntarily leaving high-paying jobs for lower-paying ones because the new jobs involve helping others.[3]

When cultural movements such as these hit the mainstream press; you know they must already be huge! *In the same way that personal growth influenced the last few decades, we may see purpose—finding meaning through right livelihood—becoming the next conceptual wave.*

It's easy to see why. Our problems are more critical and undeniable. Our leaders have few answers and little freedom to really lead. We are disillusioned with chasing a receding economic carrot. With 25 percent of the working public acting as "free agents," essentially self-employed, and small businesses driving the job base, our entrepreneurial spirit is gaining momentum. And with increased access to communication; our creative juices are flowing. It's simple:

Increased problems + growing disillusionment + heightened creativity + access = the desire to participate more deeply in shaping our world.

Yet our desire to participate more deeply in the world is often blocked by our difficulty in finding an appropriate channel. More people are hearing the call, but many are not sure what direction it's coming from.

The Role of Initiation

Researchers in psycho-immunology have made the startling finding that the immune system is boosted by helping others. Moreover, even hearing about other people doing good appears to boost our immunity. A group of college students merely watching videos of Mother Theresa exhibited elevated T-cell counts. There is evidence that not only are we physiologically wired to need others; we are also wired to want to be needed. Our bodies are wise. The desire to ensure our collective survival is woven into our drive for personal survival. In other words, our immune systems know that helping others ultimately helps us.

Let's look again to our most ancient knowledge for clues to a uniquely modern dilemma. The search for meaning is a natural and ordinary part of all indigenous cultures. These cultures have always known what the psycho-immunologists are now proving. There is no indigenous tribe or spiritual tradition that does not have a ritual for entering adulthood that involves finding a deeper meaning to your life. The adolescent initiations and vision quests were set up so that you could not become an adult without a vision and a rite of passage.

Unless You Take on the Cloak of Purpose, You are Forever a Child

In modern cultures, for the first time many of us remain uninitiated; we are offered no path to a vision. The men's movement popularized the notion: we are uninitiated children of parents who are themselves uninitiated children. Much of modern culture is now based on a tradition of avoiding the tough stuff and acting without ever discovering a deeper source of your motivation. Everyone is running around, keeping busy, even participating in very exciting developments, but often feeling untouched, as if their actions are not tied to anything real.

We are all expected to make money and strive for power, yet there is little support in discovering *why*. Someone in one of our seminars said it like this, "I'm doing well. I have no real problems. But deep down I know there's no cheese at the end of this tunnel."

Recent polls show this same kind of shift happening for a lot of people. In a *Working Woman*/Roper Poll, 87 percent of those polled said they would trade a high-paying job for a job with adequate income if it involved doing something to help the planet. When asked to rank a list of ten items that were most important, quality of life, time with family, etc.; money was ranked last. Many of our emerging social myths revolve around a growing sense that there may not be cheese for any of us at the end of a purely capitalist, market-driven tunnel. Many of us are tiring of feeling like rats in a cage, and our immune systems are hungering for a hit of social health.

Even though we often feel disillusioned, we often resist looking any deeper. The desire to stay carefree is seductive, especially when we work so hard, feel so pressured, and have so little time for ourselves. Therefore, we must look hard to discover doorways into this realm. Although many paths are available, I will use images from the Native American sweat lodge ceremony as a metaphor for the journey we are now ready to take.

I chose a model that is not from a western tradition because it is sometimes easier to look with fresher eyes at something from outside your own culture. Even though sweat lodges have made it onto *Newsweek's* list of what's trendy, I am not in any way advocating that anyone begin doing sweats. I think you will see that the process of a sweat is a *model* for the stages that happen in a deep spiritual encounter of any kind and the ideas are applicable to any tradition or form you choose.

Feeling the Heat

A sweat lodge has traditionally been used for many purposes, for prayer, when a very significant decision needs to be made, for initiations, and sometimes as a social experience.

In a sweat you get down to basics fast. First you are purified with prayers and brushed down with eagle feathers and sage. After each step you repeat the phrase "All my relations" as a way of honoring the past and inviting the support of your ancestors. *The attitude with which you enter such a process shapes everything.*

Then you enter a small round space, created out of bent saplings embedded in the earth and covered with tarps so that, once the "door" (a flap) is closed, it's pitch black. In the center of the circle is a fire pit. White hot rocks that have been baking in a large fire outside the lodge are brought in one by one. They are so hot that sometimes they split as they are lowered into the pit. You may wonder what on earth you're doing here. Then the prayers begin, sung in a Native American language. Sage is sprinkled on the rocks, then water, steam, aromas, and even more intense heat. You lower your head toward the earth, where the air is slightly cooler, and the heat builds and builds.

Just when you think you can't take it anymore, something indescribable happens. It's no longer hot. You are no longer uncomfortable or worried. The Blackfoot/Cree grandmother who leads the sweat I'm describing asked us the same four questions over and over:

> Who are you?
>
> Where did you come from?
>
> Where are you going?
>
> Why are you here?

Imperceptibly, your mind moves away from the heat and thoughts about physical comfort, and you are transported into the realm of these questions. Things that just hours ago seemed urgent, drop away. Priorities dissolve and reshuffle themselves. Layers peel away and you hear a voice in your head that is somehow clearer and louder than normal.

The ingredients are simple; there's you, your sweat pouring on the earth, the fire, and the darkness, and out of this intensely basic and simple sensory experience a deep feeling of connectedness arises. And out of this connectedness comes a dawning sense of purpose, of why you are here, that transcends the smaller issues that have been filling your awareness.

Sometimes you experience messages and directions as to your next step. I find it is most profound when I can't even remember the answers that have appeared, but am filled with an indescribable feeling of commitment. Purpose is unattached to any particular thing we do, yet it's capable of instilling a passion and drive into *everything* we do. People with purpose tend to be spirited in all their endeavors. It is a relationship to life and is not located in any specific solution.

Feeling the heat is an excellent metaphor. It is the first step in finding a deeper connection to the issues that will personally touch you. You must find a way to allow the kind of questions that the grandmother asked us to burn more deeply into your psyche. Unless you give yourself space to feel the heat, it is too easy to be distracted or numbed by the smaller concerns that shape our lives.

Rounding, Waiting, Steeping

A lot of the sweat ceremony involves waiting for the pipe to circle through fifteen or so people. Then you wait for the water to circle around. Then you wait to be fanned with cooling air. Then you wait for everyone to say their prayers out loud, one by one. Like tea leaves steeping in water, each phase seems to tease out new shades and flavors.

I like speed. I take pride in being a speed reader, in having finished college at a young age. I like it best when I can finish projects ahead of schedule. I certainly don't like waiting, and have often left a store without my purchase if a line seemed too long. We named our company *Accelerating Results* and talk a lot about the idea of collapsing time. It's hard to feel that waiting around is very efficient. Yet much of the power of the sweat resides in the waiting.

For me, the wait is the most intense part of the experience. It's like the the hours when we sleep. We only remember our waking hours, and sleep is when we get to forget. *The wait is when the forces of nature sweep in and reorganize your personal plan.* The wait is strangely unexamined in modern culture. Like the bardo, it is most often left untouched, unfelt, and unattended.

In all traditional cultures, more attention is paid to the space. The caretaker of a Zen garden will endlessly rake the small stones that fill the space between boulders. It is the nature of the space, the path of the small stones, that is more significant.

The sweat teaches you the same thing. *How* you wait determines the depth of purpose that can emerge. *How* you ask a question is also the core of your answer.

It's not the heat, the aromas, or even the prayers that hold the greatest power. It is the spirit of how you enter and hold the entire experience that determines the depth. We tend to define purpose as what we want to do. Rarely do we understand that the level of purpose we can access depends entirely on how profoundly we are willing to wait, on how deep a space we create to offer our question.

The Sacred

The sweat shows you that true purpose can only be found in the realm of what might called the sacred. That is why purpose is so absent nowadays. Purpose can't be found in learning about how cultural heroes handled their difficulties or searching around for some role model. It is rarely found through blind ambition. It is seldom found by following the rules.

The sacred is a moment which transcends the mundane. The sacred is the space where all poetry and music flow. It is where creativity lives, because it is a realm that cannot be controlled by our minds. It is a dimension from which new myths and extraordinary solutions can be birthed.

The sacred is mostly easily accessed when an experience is also deeply physical. This is because purpose is not an intellectual pursuit. In fact, philosophies and intricacies obscure the obvious; a sense of purpose is simple, basic, and immediate. All indigenous ceremonies draw their power from what might be called a cellular level of knowing.

Whether it is a sweat, walking across hot coals, the fasting and isolation of a vision quest, chanting, or drumming all night, thoughts begin to evaporate and the form of knowing that emerges is outside normal experience. This instinctual knowing is a form of motivation far deeper than the more superficial ebb and flow of everyday enthusiasm. *You are moved, rather than motivated.*

The Smashing Pumpkins' song and thousands of others like it are actually a positive sign. They are a call to break through the vacancy that permeates our culture. Only a deeper level of purpose can restore the enduring passion and vision that so many have lost.

They Called Their Decision "Taking Back the Dream"

We watched a high-level advertising executive leave her six figure job to help market a company formed by a group of kids from South Central L.A. Although she was having trouble paying her bills, she said she's never been happier. An extremely wealthy individual we know asked for our help in designing a new business. We suggested to her that this business not be about making money, that she already had enough. We suggested to her that the focus of this business should be about giving back. Curiously, she experienced our comments as a great relief and could not wait until our next meeting. A couple we know, after much soul searching, consciously decided *not* to expand their small publishing house and *not* to hire more staff.

Taking back the dream does not have to look any particular way. For some it means simplifying, for others it means expanding. For others it may mean going about your same activities with more vision and compassion because you have gotten in touch with the deeper level of purpose we talked about in our description of the sweat. It always means entering into a bigger story than our own personal dramas.

Many are saying that the age of philanthropy is over, the new rich are far too self-centered. Maybe so, but perhaps something else is at work. Perhaps the myth of philanthropy and charity needs to break down just like everything else. Since the boundaries between all forms are disappearing, so will the boundary between giving and receiving, business and public service, between the one who supposedly has and the one who needs. Some are pioneering new philanthropic forms that are part business, part education, part consulting, part all sorts of things; like Paul Newman's Salad Dressing and his line of food products which function as a business and steer profits to community service. Perhaps the new philanthropy needs to be entrepreneurial. The only signs of hope in rain forest management seem to be those that are centered on creating economic opportunity that requires maintaining the forest and cultural continuity. This, too, is taking back the dream; envisioning social innovations that fit with the crazy, creative wave we are in. Service must become as fluid, undefined, and able to morph as everything else.

At no time in history have the edges between our individual and social worlds been more closely linked. Our clothes are made halfway across the globe, and this simple choice of what to wear affects labor unions in our country and working conditions throughout the developing world. The simplest everyday choices touch the lives of others in a way that is building a more fluid cultural reality and allowing us to create meaning from new sources. In many ways opportunities to make a difference have never been more accessible.

Much of what we are up against is a social environment that does not support these kinds of questions. At best, community service is considered good public relations, not its own reward. The quest for profit is currently our dominant myth, and it is tough to think outside that box.

> There was an extraordinary ethnography that came out in the sixties which described the training process of medical doctors. A large percentage entered the profession with big plans and lofty motives. By the time they graduated 10 to 12 years later, most spouted the company line about keeping a professional distance, making sure they made a lot of money, and they had mostly forgotten their original motives. The entire book was a study of how deeply we all need to fit in and how much we are willing to let go of in order to feel like we belong.

The greatest punishment in any traditional culture was to be made invisible. You physically lived with the tribe, but no one talked to you or even acknowledged your existence. This is why it is so hard to break from your surroundings; we all have a primal fear of not belonging.

Maintaining a sense of purpose, or bringing a heightened social consciousness into your work, often requires becoming very artful in how you talk about what you want. A confrontational stance is often the fastest way to feel alone and discouraged. Unlike the way Jerry Maguire went about it, you must build a social context for new directions or people will feel threatened, and a new myth will never be born.

What we most need is an understanding of what purpose feels like. In this way, we can begin to discern when we are acting from a place of greater purpose and when we are not. Out of this simple discernment, a greater vision will naturally emerge. When we experience the knowledge of who we are and what we are really about, a sense of relief will follow. The emptiness that characterizes so many people's lives comes from having lost this connection; they have nowhere to stand.

Purpose allows us to feel the part of the larger world that is connected to us. The reason for locating a deeper meaning to what you do is not necessarily for helping someone else. It is for your own sanity; the connection that occurs is nourishing, defining, and vital.

Emergence

There are usually several "doors" to the sweat. A door refers to a cycle of closing the flap, building the heat to white-hot intensity, and then reopening the tarp. With each cycle you go deeper. I find that it always shows me how superficial I am; I am usually satisfied with the equivalent of the first door. A sweat forces you to experience a place of breakthrough, and then go deeper. And breakthrough again, and then go deeper.

It drives home the idea of finding greater depth, of not being satisfied with a first, second, or twentieth draft. Much like the spirit of our time, the sweat graphically demonstrates the importance of committing to continual reorganization.

Finally, the last door is complete. If the sweat has been really strong, sometimes you are so weak you can only crawl. The curious thing is that the weaker you feel physically, sometimes without even the strength to lift a jug of water, the stronger you feel internally. Sometimes I just want to laugh. I see how much faith I put in my physical strength and how fleeting and temporary it is. Yet the spirit inside me is unshakable; it merely grows stronger in the face of challenge. After many, many experiences in a sweat, I am slowly discerning how to shift my allegiance and locate new paths for accessing power.

With this new feeling of strength, you look around you for the first time in hours. We do our sweats in a beautiful mountain setting, and the first thing we see is one of the most magnificent landscapes you can imagine. This moment of emergence from the lodge echoes the experience of birth. You are able to see with more innocence. You are with less thought. Like a child, your perception is more immediate, more directly connected to forces that seems to vibrate all around you.

Naturally as the days go by, the ordinary world begins to return. Once again I begin to obsess about tasks I don't feel like doing, or a project that's not going the way I think it should, or my favorite preoccupation with someone who is not behaving the way I would like and my private conversations about what I need to say to them, that I usually never do. Did the sweat make a difference or is it a drug, a great high that for a time takes away what Thoreau called a life of quiet desperation?

It is both. A lot of the high I leave behind in the darkness of the womb of the lodge. A lot dissipates like the smoke from the fire. There are also threads of awareness that I am learning to integrate and maintain and slowly weave into the actions of my life. I believe that spending time with our purpose must become an essential feature of daily life. Truly entering the domain of purpose can rarely be found in a weekend seminar, vocational testing, or a single experience, no matter how profound. It is built out of long, hard, and wonderful hours. This is why a sense of purpose rarely shows up in huge, dramatic declarations; it is a slow, subtle process that is most likely to be sustained when it is slowly woven into the everyday fabric of your life.

The most important feature of the sweat is that the lodge is always there. It sits on the same piece of land day in and day out, through storms and often without any people. I leave, travel, and get involved in all sorts of things, yet the lodge is always there. Purpose is not an event, a decision, or even a particular solution; it is a context, a way of life.

The sixth navigational tool entails putting on the cloak of purpose and constructing rites of passage that will continually add meaning to your life. It is a natural direction. We are living in an era when one is more likely to want to give something to others.

Here's a thumbnail summary of this chapter's six simple guidelines for achieving a higher level of participation.

> ➤ *How* you ask questions about your life direction, not so much *what* you ask, will have the greatest impact on the quality of answer you find.
>
> ➤ Clearer direction always lies in the realm of the sacred, breaking through our mundane level of thought and experience.
>
> ➤ Finding purpose requires taking back the dream that we have absorbed from our culture and dreaming a direction that is truly of your own making.
>
> ➤ Service does not have to be separate from your career vision; in fact, it is often most satisfying when they are merged.
>
> ➤ Purpose thrives when we can build a social context for our new directions.
>
> ➤ We need purpose for our health and sanity; by serving others, ultimately we serve ourselves.

Sweating, or feeling the heat, is a metaphor for a depth of questioning that can lead to new directions. There needs to be an element of sacrifice or discomfort in order to shake up the ordinary. There needs to be heat to make us stretch.

Practicing the Sweat

This practice section will read more like ideas than actual exercises. The point I have tried to make in this chapter is that finding purpose is a slow and steady uncovering that requires experiences which will take you beyond the ordinary mind. Because there are no quick and easy answers, I have not introduced any specific strategies for exploring this theme.

Finding a Sacred Space/Circling/Waiting

For some people, their religion provides this. Others need to follow less familiar paths. And some people need to create a design that is strictly personal. The main point is to choose a form that really touches you and stay with it. Don't expect a single experience, decision, or "high" to produce everlasting commitment or meaning.

There is a great story about Maharishi Mahesh Yogi, the founder of TM. An experienced meditator comes to him and says that he is seeing visions of Jesus and Buddha in his meditations. The Maharishi says, "Very good. These are signposts along the way. Keep going." A second meditator says he is experiencing lights, tasting nectar, and feeling very pleasurable sensations. The Maharishi says, "Very good. These too are signposts along the way. Keep going." A third meditator comes to him and says he is having a difficult time, "Nothing is happening, I feel and see nothing!" To which the Maharishi says, "Oh, this is very, very good. You are traveling so fast you have no time to look to the right or left."

Purpose is a bit like this. Sometimes we get all excited about a new plan or decision we have made that gives us a temporary sense of purpose. But often a sense of purpose strikes us most profoundly when it seems like nothing is happening. It is a way of approaching all problems, as much as any particular answer.

Reentry/Emergence

Suppose you start getting "hits," little kicks in the behind about where you need to be heading or mysteriously compelling clues about what lies ahead. What do you do? Nothing.

True purpose tends to build until you have no choice.

The first glimmers are sometimes accurate, and sometimes they are distractions. True purpose always feels deep, relaxed, and integrated. It is not proven by manic enthusiasm or a temporary rush. It is a sensation more like knowing your own name. You can't forget it; it's always there. You are looking for a sensation that feels as close and ordinary and easy-to-use as your name.

A Place to Go/A Home/A Context/The Lodge as Path

Any true path is always a context. The sweat, a Tibetan Stupa, or Chartres Cathedral, each offers a physical metaphor for the cosmos. In their shape and proportions lie hidden truths about the nature of reality. All the elements of how to take action in the world are coded in these forms. By immersing yourself in the *form* of any tradition, the codes are slowly revealed. It becomes not so much a body of information but a way of living that allows deeper knowledge to be revealed.

You, Inc.

"You, Inc." is a trendy expression now being bandied about. It stems from the belief that we are rapidly entering an era where jobs as we once knew them will no longer exist, nor will company loyalty or many of the rules that now govern employment. You cut deals based on your value to the company, and if you stumble upon a new resource or client, you use it as leverage to cut an even better deal. What you know becomes your value. How you leverage that value determines your deal.

It sometimes comes off as a rather mercenary strategy, but it is healthy in the sense that you have to begin focusing on yourself and your vision, since your job title or particular company no longer provide that definition. In almost every chapter, I've made the point that challenging cultural trends—such as information density or rapid-fire change—also have a positive side. They force us to become "smarter." You, Inc. is a consumer society's way of saying, "Get a purpose!"

Obviously, individuals who know how to sweat will have an easier time of it. Visions integrated at this level make managing easier. A culture that is flying apart at the seams, that has fewer and fewer meanings of it's own will likely be driven by those with the deepest centers and the deepest values. In other words, start sweating and you'll always have work.

In 1967, toward the end of one of the most dynamic creative relationships in contemporary history, Paul McCartney and John Lennon wrote "A Day in the Life."[1]

> John had written a wonderful dreamlike sequence, the one about reading the news and the lucky man who made the grade. It goes on through a series of surreal connections. John plays the piece for Paul, since he can't figure out how to end it.
>
> Paul says that he too has a little piece that he can't take any further. He plays a piece with an entirely different energy, tempo, and key: "woke up, fell out of bed, dragged a comb across my head." The two pieces were totally different in style and content, so they decided to merge them into one song. For this to work, they needed to create a substantial bridge between two such different elements.
>
> In the Beatles Anthology, you hear as John completes his part and the engineer counts "1, 2, 3…13, 14," with lots of reverb, crescendoing into 19 and 20. Then Paul's part begins. After creating the space, Paul suggests that it be filled by an entire symphony orchestra, which producer George Martin arranges—not without difficulty.
>
> The genius of this collaboration is twofold. First, each side of the piece was powerful and unique in its own right, yet equal in effect to the other. Second, the power of a space, gave enhanced meaning and effect to the two parts to yield a spectacular synthesis.
>
> When you hear the finished song, the orchestral part obscured the incredible power of the space in the earlier take. The space was so large, it needed something extraordinary, like a symphonic piece, to fill it up.

Many contemporary sociologists say that a technology-based connectivity is the main dynamic that defines our interpersonal world.

But the real future of relationship may lie less in connection and more in understanding the spaces between us, the magical 20-count windows that invite true genius and foster the **power of intimacy.**

CHAPTER 10

The Power of Intimacy

One area that has borne the brunt of our cultural chaos is relationships. Parents, on average, now spend less than 8 minutes a day talking to their children, and some studies show that fathers spend even less. Educators warn that our children are arriving at school linguistically impoverished, unable to handle dense concepts. Studies also show the average person spends 6 hours per day watching TV. With about half of us having access to computers, between home and work we log several more hours in front of a screen. There is a chat room for any demographic subset, or any topic. We see more people in a day than we once saw in a lifetime. Yet despite all this access, in many ways we are more isolated from others than ever before in history. Surrounded by communication wonders, we connect less than ever.

The Bubble of Individuality

Western culture has increasingly moved in the direction of personal isolation. We keep the places we live far from the places we work. We keep increasingly separate from anyone who is different, living in communities of people with the same income and aesthetic sensibilities. We can work with someone for years without knowing anything about them and make life-changing deals with people we know even less. And now with the Web, we can even fall in love before we ever meet in person. Such effortless access to easy connections also makes it easy to remain untouched.

Madison Avenue encourages us to stay focused on defining what it is we need, what we want, what will serve us. Yet the increasing capacity to completely design our personal space according to our individual preferences does not necessarily lead to individualization, or even greater comfort and peace of mind.

For thousands of years, monks have gone into caves, retreating from external distractions, focusing entirely on their own thoughts. Some got it, but most didn't. Entering a digital cave is not a guarantee of enlightenment. If we are going to start entering caves en masse, we should at least study those few monks who did get it right. If not, we will have a lot of digital ascetics wandering around with emotional begging bowls.

The direction of information technology is to allow us to mold our surroundings, and that makes individual taste more significant. We will be able to endlessly describe and choose what we want to see, discarding and avoiding anything irrelevant to our tastes. As self-aware as this may at first seem, it is not true individualization. In fact, becoming more individualistic is often the opposite.

It is only by abandoning our endless stream of personal preferences that we begin to discover a higher order of what truly defines us.

Paul didn't write "woke up, fell out of bed, dragged a comb across my head," because he liked combs. In fact, sublimating all that kind of stuff is what allows true creativity to flow. Matisse said that his prayer was to be able to sit in front of a flower and see it for the first time. Artists know you have to stop thinking, wanting, knowing, desiring, indulging, or preferring in order to truly create.

The hidden cost of this hyperinvolvement with ourselves may be that we find it harder to relate to differences. It can breed a control mentality that is the death of any relationship, be it personal, creative, or economic. The proponents of the information wave proudly proclaim that geography will become a thing of the past; we can join with people anywhere, linked by common interests and collaboration on projects. Although this will open many exciting doors, one problem is that you never have to deal with anyone who has dramatically different opinions. We can scan the Web for people like us. Perhaps the digerati and the truly adventurous are using the information wave to become more tolerant and broaden their sense of self.[2] But many people are using virtual communities to connect with ever narrower segments of the population.

The Call of the Collective

The good news is that the forces demanding the ability to share and collaborate are also more powerful than ever. More than 20 years ago, John Naisbitt used the expression "high-tech, high-touch" to suggest that the more digital we become, the more relational we must also become. Another way to say this is that with each new degree of connectivity we gain, we also need to develop the next degree of depth.

And the new networking in business is doing just this; it is demanding more profound relationship skills than ever before.

> ➤ People now have to talk who were once buffered by chains of intermediaries.

> ➤ The less time you have to develop a product, the faster you need to collaborate. The faster you need to collaborate, the more interpersonal skills you need.

> ➤ As hierarchies collapse, the rules that once defined hierarchial relationships will also collapse, offering more interpersonal freedom.

> ➤ Customers have windows into your design and planning so you have to talk to them in ways you could once avoid. Suppliers now have windows into your inventory, so they have become new communication partners too.

> ➤ Business functions have become fuzzier and more intertwined, and so have the people in these roles. We are rubbing elbows with people we never even knew about.

> ➤ More and more businesses will be managed by teams and shifting work groups.

> ➤ Ideas about leadership have been turned upside-down. It is no longer about bringing people along in your direction, but rather about serving and following where they need to go, and therefore communicating more.

> ➤ To develop new markets, you must cultivate new communities. Building communities requires a bit more relationship savvy than just having a Web site that follows the ten how-to rules—large type, changing content frequently, etc.

As you can see, the myriad shifts in our work environment are requiring that we connect in far more meaningful ways. There are tons of resources available to teach you the technological side of connectivity, yet the personal skills for dealing with connectivity are often assumed. The high-touch world is definitely calling. Now we have to figure how to pick up the line.

Bursting the Bubble

I grew up in an apartment in Florida without air conditioning. I remember being mortified when my parents argued, because the windows were open and all the other kids could hear. Many years later, Philip and I began spending summers in a small village on a Greek island. It was a revelation to hear people arguing for all to hear, proudly displaying their personal lives for public view.

I now know that the future hinges on our ability to "get down and dirty," to be different, get angry and keep talking, to not feel ashamed when the windows are open. It hinges on the kind of intimacy I see in this Greek village. If we are going to work intimately on creative projects with people we barely know or let customers or suppliers have windows into our daily operations, then we better know how to *get real*. If we are going to rely on typed words on a screen as a way of getting to know someone, we better have very finely tuned skills for sensing who this person really is.

Recently, I saw an extraordinary documentary called *The Color of Fear*. It was a record of a racially mixed group of men spending several days together, eating, sleeping, and talking without direction. They start off being fairly polite. In the ensuing days, the tension builds with the men either screaming at each other or being overly reasonable in their attempts at understanding. At some point the wall of defensiveness finally breaks and a true vulnerability enters. In a moving scene the most militant black man and the most soft-spoken, self-proclaimed liberal white man finally start sharing their real fears of each other. It conveyed the hope that maybe we do have it within us to talk about our problems in a real way.

If this group was a political entity or business board, this would have been the point at which they could *first* begin communicating about issues in a fruitful way. Any talk before this point, which is when 99.9 percent of our decisions take place, would produce no in-depth, reality-based understanding. The kind of relationship depth that these men found is critical to our future. It is when the real power of relationship is revealed.

Emptying the Space/Getting Real

We have allowed relationships to become disposable. If it doesn't work, we throw it away. Someone new will always come along. As a result of this pattern, we often become more psychologically rigid, leaving whenever we reach a critical personal threshold. We check out when we get to the space in the song and the emptiness gets a little too uncomfortable.

The real power of long-term intimate relationships, either personal or professional, is that they offer a context for crossing thresholds. It is a place where we can bump up against old wounds, such as not being valued or not getting what we wanted, and pioneer new patterns of being seen and heard. Every time we cross such a threshold, we dissolve a projection from the past, and the space between us and another person becomes a bit more empty, making more room for new possibilities.

Projections from the past, predetermined opinions of the way people are, or encoded expectations of how a relationship will turn out are what most of use to fill up the space between ourselves and another. We can barely see the person who stands across from us, because there are so many filters between us and them. That is why emptying the space is the process for getting real. It is the only way to begin seeing someone as something other than a projected image from our past.

Down and Dirty

The future will demand knowing others far beyond the intimacy of our past. Relationships were once nurtured by proximity, lots of time together, by being able to hear our neighbors' conversations, and because we needed them to raise the barn and help with the harvest. We knew each other because there was no choice.

Since we don't need people in the way we once did, it becomes more imperative to discover why we do need them. This is an important point. The future will require that we find the impetus to go past the increasing potential we have to isolate, to only connect with people who seem like us, to move on when they are no longer a reflection of us, acting or thinking the way we would. A relationship doesn't even begin until you reach the point where there really is someone out there, not just a fantasy projection of who you think you deserve or what you think you want. *A relationship doesn't even begin until that person emerges as someone we can't control.*

In every case of personal and organizational breakthrough that I have witnessed, the quality of exchange has had to go to this deeper level. Ironically, a highly networked business sometimes offers more ways to avoid connecting. In the spin of perpetual communication, you can sometimes forget to check if all the connecting is yielding any real growth.

> *A senior partner in a large law firm with offices in four different cities and 50-plus staff in each office told us that when they became networked, face-to-face encounters declined radically. Somehow, the illusion of distance and objectivity afforded by digital communication unleashed a barrage of angry exchanges that were never addressed in person. The office became a nest of Jekyll and Hydes, and relationships seriously deteriorated.*

I do not know what happened for this firm in the long run, but initially the information world offered an escape from real encounters. Any breakthroughs we envision for the future will depend on our ability to defy such illusions of connectivity and to discern when exchanges are more real.

All traditional therapy is based on a process that allows patients to project images of their mother and father onto the therapist. The therapist is trained to not take these projections personally and to allow the client to work out these unresolved past issues in present time. Projecting a past story into a present time situation this way is called *transference.* It is equivalent to Narcissus pulling some unsuspecting bystander to the bottom of the pond with him to share his story. Yet we do it all the time. We make our boss into our parent or a peer into a sibling and revive all manner of unresolved issues from the past. *We make everyone into our therapist, and they do the same to us. We gladly take roles in each other's plays; it seems like a fair exchange.*

Cramming the empty space between us and them with all these "movies" from the past leaves little room for present issues. I am sure you have dealt with people who seem somewhat removed, as if the person they are talking to is not you. It's because this past movie is invisibly running. They are really looking at a tape loop, not you.

The only way to bridge this threshold is to open the windows and take it to the square, like in the Greek village we visit. It means moving past the easy stage, calling people on their "stuff," and letting them call you on yours. It means hanging tough, when it hurts, and having the courage to venture into a scary space where you don't know what will happen.

Getting down and dirty requires relentlessly releasing the characteristic ways you set people up to play roles from the past. It requires not being satisfied until you get something back that feels alive, authentic, and real. If your past projections persist, all your encounters will be so filled with history, you'll stay stuck with all your past incompletions. Although you may literally have many people in your life, you will have only *one* relationship, a frozen pattern from the past that you repeat with everyone.

The mostly polite, interpersonal dance we all participate in is incapable of dealing with any real conflict. Lies make any exchange unreal. If you don't like something, say so. Describe why.[3] The result is not chaos but more satisfying relationships.

Until we can traverse a stretch of healthy conflict and survive, then real community, real relationship does not exist. It's a hard bridge to cross though.

We will not be able to access increased creativity, heightened motivation, or more profound vision until our interpersonal culture is freed up. Ultimately, individuals and organizations that don't evolve their interpersonal styles will find that their evolution becomes stuck in every other way as well.

We must commit to emptying the space between us that is usually filled with projections, politeness, fear, and fantasy.

We know two women who created comparable levels of financial success and recognition.

The first one, Sally, noticed that people were talking to her differently because of her new promotion. She developed and practiced a way of responding that diffused the distancing that had begun to take place with her staff. She dove right in, clearly and directly, and emptied the space. Beyond that, she specified a more intense level of relationship that her new position would require—people telling her higher levels of truth, caring more deeply about her projects, digging deeper to find more subtle ways of supporting her. She worked systematically to deepen all these dynamics so that her advance in the organization was paralleled by advances in her relationships.

The second woman, Linda, unconsciously relished the distance that her promotion had triggered and allowed it, mistaking it for a form of power. When people felt intimidated by her, she did nothing, but chalked it up to their insecurities and her increasing brilliance.

One year later, Sally is having a much easier time implementing her projects and finds her promotion has led to a more meaningful connection with her staff. Linda has become cynical and complains about the weakness and jealousy of others who can't handle her success and being around powerful women.

Most of us reflexively back away when we hit an interpersonal threshold. We surround ourselves with people who think like us. We choose people who not only share our values but also share our interpersonal comfort level. This way we rarely have to go past a level of intimacy that is familiar. Yet despite our best efforts at avoidance, occasionally our unconscious contract breaks down. We hit a wall of difficulty or get too close for comfort. Then we have three options:

1. Drift further apart and solidify our own opinions.
2. Diminish the conflict; make up; forget it happened, but be much more vigilant not to go near that emotional territory again; and surround the issue with a few protective layers of numbness.
3. Meet the interpersonal shadow: find the primal thread that was exposed and look at it; trust the power of the conflict; and become changed by the process.

This moment is much like the wall that athletes face just before entering the zone, or the edge where the spider woman lives, or finding the alchemy to penetrate the shadow. Powerful interpersonal breakthrough has the same capacity to thrust us into a new realm of being and creativity.

New Social Images

Would you believe that just a couple of hundred years ago, the concept of childhood as we know it did not even exist? This is why early paintings portrayed children as short people with adult features. We now take childhood for granted.

Some sociologists have suggested that when we lived in tribes, we did not experience individuality as we do now. The experience of self was inseparable from the experience of the group. The thoughts in our minds were often the thoughts of the group. We did not ponder a personal vision or path separate from the tribe.

Social concepts are always a function of our historical context. Therefore, a new cultural domain requires new images. Over the last 40,000 years the cultural pendulum has slowly swung from an almost completely tribal and collective consciousness to the hyperindividuality that now prevails. And now a wired world, a collaborative workplace, an environment in trouble, and a society in crisis are providing the necessary gravity for the pendulum to begin swinging back. There is a relationship renaissance afoot.

➤ Some estimate that there is a 12-step program for every 250 people in the U.S. The language of personal responsibility has entered the mainstream culture.

➤ Even NPR's hit show *Car Talk* cites *Men Are from Mars; Women Are from Venus* and how sexuality affects our relationship to cars. Hardly any domain is exempt from relationship talk.

➤ Co-dependence, conscious relationship, and healthy communication are the fodder of talk shows, best-sellers, and popular magazines.

➤ More and more individuals have the means for economic independence, so they are freer to ask for heightened quality in their relationships.

In the same way our new organizational culture demands heightened relationship skills, so does our social environment. The average person has at least a first year of psychology training under his belt, courtesy of the mass media. There is increased freedom to say what you're feeling, and an expectation that we each have a certain capacity for self-analysis is now the norm. So when we go out into the interpersonal arena, odds are the person we are dealing with is psychologically sophisticated. *It raises the relationship curve for all of us.*

Many writers have also begun talking about something called *neotribalism,* the need to have people around who feel like members of your tribe. Several years ago, *Utne Reader* featured a segment on salons, based on the European tradition of gathering together a cross-section of creative people whose exposure to each other would spark new ideas. Salons were once the most efficient way to put your finger on the cultural pulse. *Utne* was besieged with requests from individuals who wanted to participate and many hundreds of groups were formed.

Most of us want the pendulum to start swinging back. We want a tribelike feeling. We want our communities back. We want to know our neighbors and have face-to-face experiences with people we find provocative and interesting. We want relationships that last. We want encounters that have substance. We know that only true intimacy will tear down the mounting isolation so many of us feel.

An insidious, mechanistic view of interpersonal exchange has made it's way into our relationship vocabulary. We speak of needing to "fix" a relationship, "tune it up," "keep it running," etc. We think if we provide *it* with the right lubricants, then *it* should go well. If it's just not working and can't be easily fixed, then we junk it and get a new one. We all toss around these notions without recognizing that it is a set of social values ushered in with factories and the philosophies of the industrial revolution. This mechanistic view permeates all levels of our culture, so it's into our private lives as well.

The big evolution/revolution in business, management, science, economic theory, and the like is to move from this mechanistic view into a new one informed by complexity or chaos theory. In this new world view information is accessed from every part of the system and systems are in constant motion, with order dissolving into chaos and strange attractors forming to bring about new layers of order. Our private lives are also being touched by these new conceptual models. The spirit of the information wave changes how we think about relationships. We are beginning to understand that relationships are never fixed. They never stabilize, but are in continual flux, breakdown, and breakthrough. Rather than trying to get our relationships to work, we should be trying to discover where they are going.

If we need each other more than in the past, if we need increased interpersonal literacy, if new world views are beginning to creep into our private lives, then what concepts will allow us to create relationships that will invite new possibilities? What images will propel our interpersonal world into the future?

We are the first generation that has collectively entertained the possibility of breaking free from the emotional patterns that have been handed down from father to son and mother to daughter.

We are the first generation that has collectively considered the possibility of emotional freedom. Enlightenment is no longer an esoteric, elite practice, it is publicly discussed. We no longer want companionship, we want conscious relationships. These concepts are all a function of our unique moment in history. They are social concepts that suit a culture in the thick of creative breakthrough. But the main clue I want to offer about new social images comes from a process that we stumbled upon in a couples seminar.

> *We had about 30 couples in the room, most of whom did not know each other. Without telling the group, we preselected four couples who had been with each other for 1, 5, 10, and 15 years. We tried not to let age be a clue. The two people in the 15-year relationship were younger than the couple who had been together only one year. We then asked the larger group to identify which couple belonged to each time period—1, 5, 10, or 15 years—merely by looking at them as they stood up together. The group identified each relationship perfectly with no additional information.*

We then asked the group what allowed them to make this evaluation. What did they see? The answers at this point were more vague and varied. Finally, we suggested that what they were seeing was intimacy. We suggested that intimacy was a real energy, a frequency that could be perceived by the ordinary eye. We "see" it when we walk into someone's home, enter a group, or go into a store. We "see" it when we meet someone new. We sense the threads of connection.

> *Once Philip and I checked into a resort in Aspen and our experience in the first two hours was so positive that we asked to meet the manager. He turned out to be an exceptional individual. Their staff meetings and company retreats focused on building real relationships. He shared with us that his biggest problem was that he had virtually no turnover of staff. He was constantly plagued by how to promote people, since no openings were ever available. (Keep in mind that the hotel industry is notorious for high turnover.)*
>
> *The feeling in this place was more wonderful than anything we had ever experienced. It was like checking into a resort owned by your best friend. The experience was far beyond great service, and can only be described as an intangible fabric of intimacy that permeated every interaction. He was not teaching about service in their staff meetings. He was developing people who felt smart. The result was an intelligence that flavored the entire facility. Even though people held different responsibilities, everyone acted with depth. We all have our own wisdom. If we are given the space, we can all express capacities far beyond what you might ordinarily see.*

Intimacy does not mean that you know lots of details about someone's life or continually talk about feelings. Intimacy is a *quality of intelligence* that allows every conversation to be somehow right. It knows and respects boundaries; it honors and respects individuality.

True intimacy allows any relationship to become more exceptional and meaningful, whether it is someone checking you in at the desk of a hotel or a conversation with a colleague. It feels very different to have someone say "Can I help you?" because that is how they have been trained versus someone who says the same words because they mean it. I am also willing to bet that this resort experienced far fewer ornery customers or frustrated delivery people. Just by walking in, you were brought to a higher level. *This is why intimacy will always be superior to ordinary training in service, and superior to learning communication skills.*

There are now many terms for businesses that continually evolve the quality of exchange between participants. Best known is Senge's "learning organization." You also have the "relational" or "adaptive" organization. These are based on the assumption that organizations are composed not only of individuals and resources, but arise out of relationships. It is not so much the talent of each individual, but the nature of their exchanges that determines the true creative potential of the group.

The Stutter and the Social Construction of Reality

Many years ago I was taking Tai Chi lessons. Our class met every Sunday morning in a public park. I usually came early and often would notice the same man sitting there. One day we got to talking; I can't remember about what. Soon this chat became part of my weekly ritual. It was extremely relaxed and quiet, and every week I would talk with this guy for 10 minutes or so before class started.

One day, as he and I were chatting, a friend of his walked by and said hello. My friend began talking, but something was very different. Within moments, he had developed a severe stutter. There was no evidence of a stutter when we had talked before. But from that day on, whenever he and I talked, he spoke with a stutter.

When he and I first started talking, there was a clean slate. It was relaxed and quiet. Maybe because I had no expectations and maybe because I was in a more meditative state anticipating my class, he was also able to forget his memory of himself. But once I heard the stutter, there was no turning back. I knew he stuttered, he knew that I knew, and I knew that he knew. A new mirror was in place. *We were both trapped in a cycle of reflections that neither of us could forget.*

In those first weeks, I was empty; there was more space. There was a more natural intimacy. Once I had a picture of who he was, the box started to form. We both had to be loyal to what we both now knew.

Reality is socially constructed. Who I think you are and who you think I think you are are powerful thought forms. This is the kind of material the manager of that Aspen resort was beginning to break down. He was pushing people to dissolve limiting opinions of each other, so their natural intelligence was freed up. In effect, a space was being developed so everyone could speak without their personal version of stuttering.

I believe when most long-term relationships end, it's because both people become more opinionated about who the other person is. Eventually the box becomes so limiting, we have to break out. The true cycle of intimacy should be that the better you know someone, the less you know and the more they surprise you. True intimacy is a process of releasing one's expectations and supporting the other person in becoming more emotionally free. It is a process not so much of getting closer, but of deepening and widening the space between you, noticing the unexpected, so that greater levels of personal creativity unfold.

> *Here's a story from a soldier in Vietnam, passed on by Daniel Goleman in his extraordinary book,* Emotional Intelligence.[4] *The soldier was on enemy turf, engaged in a fierce firefight. Suddenly, a dozen Buddhist priests, dressed in orange robes, walked directly into the line of fire.*
>
> *The firing stopped and for the rest of the day neither side could pick up their weapons. These priests possessed an emotional energy that was conveyed to others and was powerful enough to completely reorganize possibilites around them.*

The quality of peace that monks' held in their emotional field was more powerful than the emotions that allowed the soldiers to fight. When faced with this superior force, the soldiers were also brought to a higher level. That is the power of intimacy. As you learn to hold a space of true, down and dirty, out of the box, intimacy with more and more people, you too will begin to reorganize possibilities just by walking through the door.

I'm sure if there was such a thing as an intimacy meter, the quality of exchange between Lennon and McCartney would go off the charts. They stretched each other in ways that music rarely sees, yet according to most accounts, their partnership was often stressful, combative, and competitive. I believe it was the dynamic tension between them, the energy that filled the space when they both entered the room, that was responsible for their creative vision. I believe it was the intelligence you could feel when they were interviewed together.

Extending the depth of our relationships can only come from investigating what really happens in the spaces, between us, spaces like the one in the Lennon-McCartney song. This "inter-space" promises to become one of the hottest areas of inquiry in upcoming decades. It is where the real spirit of business lives. It is widely agreed that the real future of sustainable development in any field—business, politics, you name it—rests in the possibility of social innovation. And social innovations ultimately begin out of new dimensions in one-to-one exchange.

Out of learning to move through interpersonal thresholds, we gradually eliminate our projections from the space between us and other people. Our seventh tool shows us how we will for the first time in human history, collectively step out of the emotional world we have each inherited from our past. And in doing so we have the potential for a quantum leap, a new order of intelligence that can reshape our interpersonal world.

Practicing the Power of Intimacy

Interactional Synchrony

Whenever two people talk, an interactional dance develops. One person nods his head in time with the other's eye blinks. Cultures that are more emotionally volatile, like Mediterranean countries, are characterized by high interactional synchrony. They match each other's beat more frequently. More emotionally reserved cultures, such as many Asian countries, have a looser synchrony, fewer head nods and eye blinks. This has led anthropologists to deduce that when you are being more confrontational, it needs to be balanced by a more intense physical rapport. When our words are less charged, the dance can be looser. This underlying dance creates the fabric of intimacy.

An anthropologist named Eliott Chappelle found that adolescents who were considered popular had a greater ability to adapt their interactional rhythm to match others. Adolescents who had little ability to adjust their interactional dance were not only more socially isolated, they showed more displays of violence, as if they just couldn't connect, and literally they couldn't. (See suggested readings for Chapter 10 listed in the References section.) Early in my career, I supervised a project which worked with mothers who had severely abused their children. By coaching the mothers with videotape on how to get into an interactional dance with their children, the children cried far less and the incidents of violence went way down. Chappelle also found that when he coached these "interactionally" challenged teens on how to create synchrony, their violence decreased. So obviously, this dance is vital.

> To start this exercise, try spending a week just observing. When you are in a public setting, such as a restaurant or party, observe the dance. Notice pairs of people who seemed very keyed in to each other and those who don't. Notice how people display boredom or the desire to get out of a conversation by breaking the dance. Notice people who easily pick up on the cues and those who don't. You'll see that people who have a hard time with social exchange often seem to have great difficulty keying into the head nods and eye blinks. In your work setting, observe meetings and social exchanges. Look for the dance, for when it is effective, and for when it is discordant.
>
> In the second week experiment with your own rhythms. For a week, whenever you are speaking with someone, pay extra attention to matching their beat. Experiment with becoming very flexible, invisibly (I stress invisibly) matching their pauses and pace of talking. After a week of this, notice if your relationships feel different.

Effective speakers seem to have a beat that *many* people can relate to. We have all experienced speakers who are so uptight in their patterns or so controlled in their pacing that you literally find it hard to hear them.

> In the third week, focus on varying your own patterns. Whenever you speak, notice when people really seem to listen and when they tune out. Try shifting only the beat, not the content, in order to reclaim their interest.

In the fourth week, you can get even fancier. If you are presenting more confrontational information, trying moving in with a tighter synchrony. If the information is emotionally cool, loosen up on the head nods.

You can get away with confrontational statements if you are tight with your synchrony. The other person feels like you are with them, so they can take more. Many people do this naturally, but you would be surprised how many people pull away at the critical moment, just when they are getting to the heart of what they want to say. Unconsciously, the other person feels you distancing at precisely the moment you are saying what is most important. They don't hear you and you don't feel heard. It is valuable to perfect and fine-tune this capacity to match your rhythms with the intent of what you are saying.

Verbal Push Hands/Uncovering Blocks

In the martial arts, there is a wonderful warm up process called "push hands." You stand opposite your partner and with one hand, or two for those more advanced, you make continuous circles. One person pushes until her arm is fully extended, which flows into an invisible transition to the other person pushing.

The key is becoming very tuned to the other person. Whenever you detect a resistance, that is your moment of power. You push into the heart of their resistance. If pushed fully, they will fall to the ground, because their rigidity makes them stiff. If when you push into their resistance, they can find a way to soften, then the circling will continue. After 20 minutes or so, both people begin to really let go as their resistances are literally pushed out. It is an extremely energizing process.

In the same way, whenever a block appears in a relationship, one person energetically becomes stronger than the other. They can use this moment to metaphorically push the other person down, by being right, harming the other person in some way, or diminishing the other person's self-esteem. Or you can also use a block to awaken energy. The purpose of push hands is to press into each others energy, mutually discovering and releasing resistances. Rather than being pushed over, you are given space to learn and release. As a result the energy of "chi" starts buzzing all through your body. This is exactly what can happen in a relationship or project that has been "pushed" in this way.

If your partner is willing, the easiest way is to move out of content-based talk into "process" talk. For example, content talk might go something like, "You said you would pick up the paper and you forgot." The other person would respond something like, "Well I didn't know you really wanted it."

Process talk would assume that on some level I knew you weren't going to pick up the paper and on some level you also knew that I wanted it. We were both tolerating a dead space in our relationship. We would both press into that space and discover what it represented for each of us. We would discover a habit of not allowing ourselves to respond to information we each knew. We would both become more aware of when this "dead space" occurs and talk about it immediately.

There are layers and layers that you can explore with this kind of exchange. It's the kind of work that is best done with a coach, but hopefully it is enough to get you started so you can try it with someone in your life in relation to a real situation. The point is to move out of content, analyze why a dynamic is occurring or where it came from in your past, and focus on how things are happening.

Getting Out of Control

All relationships require that we continually clear the space. This means releasing our past projections. There are so many good books about this I won't really get into it here, except to recommend any of Harville Hendrix's books. He works with identifying and releasing what he calls the *imago*, the unconscious composite of incompletions we project on to others. We've got to get this image out of the space for any present time relationship to grow.

The next step is to pay more attention to the quality of energy between you and another person. It is this "between space" that shapes the quality of content that can occur. We often have partners talk about this space in terms of blocks and flows, tentativeness and boldness, dead spaces and live spaces. Sometimes we ask outside observers to offer similar impressions of the exchange between these two people. It wakes them up to an entirely different way of talking. We find individuals stop saying "You did this or that," or even the more appropriate "I felt this way when you did this or that." Instead, they look at the space in between and talk about how they could both shift it, how they could wake it up or calm it down. I have witnessed many individuals effortlessly flow into this new way of talking.

By focusing on the "interspace," we support people in "pressing into" our energy or trying to follow the "chi." Each person watches when the exchange is fresh, and for when it gets tired and repetitive. By working with someone in this way, you begin to understand the rhythms and habits of their energy flow and you learn to wake it up, challenge it, play with it, dance with it. Invariably, people who begin working in this way report feeling much more creative in their exchanges.

Metamessages

Another great process to wake you up to the energy underlying your speech is a process called metamessages.

> It requires four people, so you have to drag three friends into this. Two act as the main communicators and the other two serve as the alter egos. The first person says something. The first alter ego rephrases what he thinks the person is really saying, acting almost as a translator describing something that is underlying what the first person said. It takes a little patience, because before the second person responds, she must wait for both versions of the statement.
>
> After both the person and the alter ego have gone, then the second person responds. Then the second alter ego reinterprets that message. When they are done, the first person responds again. You keep going back and forth. The alter egos can pass and not say anything if they feel that what was said was clear. Two things usually happen in this process. First, the conversation tends to go deeper faster. Second, as the conversation progresses, the alter egos tend to have less to say, because the two principals' speech becomes more precise. It is an incredible process for learning to detect other people's hidden messages and for learning to integrate your own covert meanings.

Relationship work is probably the hardest to describe. It is best done with a coach you trust who can help you work with ordinary, everyday exchanges and bring them to a deeper level. So these few exercises are only intended to get you started.

For almost 20 years, an archeologist friend of Philip's, had been systematically searching for a lost city in a particular valley in northern Greece, where ancient texts indicated it was located. On a recent trip to Greece, Philip ran into her and she told him the following story.

> *One day, exhausted, frustrated, and about to call it quits, she decided to take a day off. She walked toward a nearby hill that had always attracted her, but which in the 20 years she had been in the area, she had never taken the time to explore.*
>
> *When she arrived at the hill, her foot struck a piece of pottery. She dug around and found the beginnings of her lost city!*

Her natural attraction to that particular hill had been with her from the first day she came to the valley. Why did it take 20 years to tap into knowledge that was with her from the start?" And there is something else she could have gained by **accelerating results.**

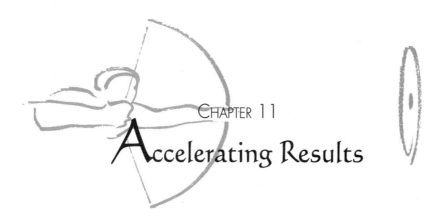

CHAPTER 11

Accelerating Results

The tempo of modern life makes our problems more immediate; we need solutions faster. Most of the research on peak performance states, such as the zone, shows that individuals who can access these states at will really do seem to get more done, more easily, and at a higher level.

In some ways this is a companion chapter to "The Future Zone." It shows how these heightened states can be translated into a strategy for action. Our last navigational tool focuses on accelerating results, decreasing the time it takes to move from an idea stage to its manifestation. The new context for action it offers allows us to deal more effectively with the main features of the coming decades: speed, pressure, and the unknown.

Let me reiterate briefly. Our feedback loops are collapsing. Once we have an idea, it moves into action faster. We collaborate with others sooner. We receive responses earlier in the delivery process and have far more capacity to shift direction. This means that the "energy" underlying an idea or project is more dominant. The blocks, the unclarity, the numbness, the powerplays all come to the surface much faster. There is no honeymoon. If we know how to identify the energetic anatomy underlying any event, we can adjust the chemistry earlier on.

Popular futurist and consultant Faith Popcorn says that our present culture increasingly demands that we know how to "click."[1] This "being in the right place, doing the right thing, that somehow is more in synch" allows us to sail through the fluctuations of markets and events with a little more grease on our wheels.

What Do Frequent Peakers See?

Abraham Maslow was the father of transpersonal psychology and much of the personal growth movement. He felt that peak performance states like the zone were a natural human need, that the urge to enter expanded states of consciousness was an instinctual drive. In his attempt to define what allowed people to enter this state, he found that some people reported having these experiences quite easily and regularly, while others rarely did. He referred to them as "frequent peakers" and "nonpeakers."

One of his main findings was that frequent peakers had a world view that allowed them to understand how these events could happen and why they were significant, whereas nonpeakers did not. He concluded that a person's belief system is key to whether that person can harness the power of these states. Following are six principles that will help build such a world view.

1. Time Is Emotional Distance

We tend to keep things we are not ready for out in the future—3 months, 6 months, a year, often longer. When this emotional distance is eliminated, the results we envision—an important deal, a new job, a relationship—transpire readily, i.e., time collapses. If the emotional distance is not addressed, then the result stays perpetually 6 months or a year away. We never quite get there. Thus time can be viewed as a function of how ready we are for a particular result to appear in our lives.

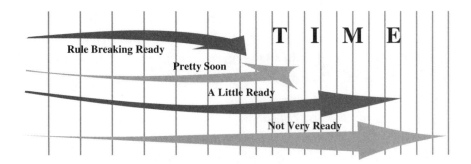

After Philip and I met, we discovered that in the 2 prior years, there were three occasions where we almost met. Once, he registered for a seminar I was organizing in Florida, and he canceled at the last minute. Once, I registered for a seminar in New York and canceled, discovering later that he had attended that very seminar. The last "near meeting" was more amazing. I was supposed to go on vacation with two friends to California and at the last minute had to finish a project at work. These friends were camping and Philip had the campsite next to theirs! They ended up hanging out with him for a few days, which we only discovered when I brought Philip to meet them and they all recognized each other from the trip.

Both of us now feel that had we met any of the previous three times, we would not even have noticed each other! We were both coming to terms with unresolved feelings from past relationships and getting clear on what we really wanted, the emotional distance thing. Once these personal entanglements were neutralized, the way was literally cleared for us to physically meet. Which is exactly what happened. We met while vacationing in Greece 15 years ago.

Let me give another example of a result entering someone's life almost immediately after they released an emotional block.

The founder of a small, but growing clothing company said her main goal was to create more publicity for her company. Yet every time she described this goal, no one in the seminar could "get it;" it just didn't ring true. As she looked at this clue a little more closely, she uncovered fears about losing her privacy. In effect, she was giving us two conflicting messages: "I want to be out there with my company." and "I don't want anything interfering with my privacy, I don't want to be too noticed."

This conflicting "metamessage" had a push-pull effect on the listeners in the seminar. It was coded in her body language, how she spoke, and in all the invisible ways we have of communicating what really is going on. There is no formula for resolving internal conflicts such as these, it is much more of an art form. After some emotional work, she was able to talk about publicity for her company so that all levels of her communication were aligned. Although she had been working on publicity for over a year, within days of having this emotional breakthrough, she was contacted by two national magazines wanting to do stories on her clothing line.

Coincidence? Perhaps if it were an isolated example. But we have many similar stories where people manifested very tangible results the moment they released an emotional block. So does every seminar leader and therapist. In the same way we all have untapped skills for problem solving, we also have powerful skills for unconsciously delaying results.

The key is to begin thinking about time differently. The time that stands between you and a specific result is not a fixed measure. It is elastic. Results can approach very closely and then inexplicably recede into the distance as our awareness fluctuates. **Ultimately, time is a function of your psychological readiness to literally see that result in your life.**

2. Coherence

Coherence is an internal state in which all our various messages—internal, external, verbal, nonverbal, overt, covert, etc.—become aligned and produce a complimentary energy rather than conflicting directions. Part of what allows time to collapse is that our resistance to a result is decreased.

The light from a laser can travel to the moon with virtually no loss of intensity, whereas the light from an ordinary bulb diminishes in a few hundred feet. Both emanate light. The difference is that a laser is composed of coherent light; all the photons are aligned in the same direction, rather than being scattered. In the same way our speech, our presence, our intentions all have the capacity to become more laser-like, able to have a more sustained and far-reaching impact. Whenever this state of coherence is created within an individual, relationship, project, or organization, time begins to collapse. Since we don't need to deal with conflicting energy, action happens more quickly and results arrive unexpectedly.

It's also interesting that when we are in the zone, our bodies take on a greater physiological coherence: brain wave patterns align and various rhythms, such as pulse and blood pressure, enter into a more ideal relationship with each other. Psychologically, people report that they "feel" more coherent.

Entrainment is the word biologists use to describe what happens when biological systems connect with each others' rhythms. For example, if a group of fireflies alights on a tree, at first they will all flicker at random. Slowly, they will begin to subtly alter their rhythms until they almost appear to be flickering in unison. Perhaps when internal alignment occurs, it increases the odds that external events will entrain and match our rhythms. This is exactly how it feels. When you are in the flow, it feels like people are in synch. When you are having one of those off days, somehow everything seems to just miss.

Much of our seminar work deals with uncovering conflicting issues and unconscious directions that are at odds with our stated goals and allowing people to experience what it feels like to be in synch.

> Once a woman came to a seminar who was working as a secretary for a medium-size company. Over a series of processes, she worked on her stated goal of managing a restaurant, releasing all sorts of extraneous agendas that were hidden in her posture, patterns of speech, etc. In the final process, we had her talk about managing the restaurant in the past tense as if it had already happened. She was so convincing that everyone completely entered the fantasy. There was something very electric about her presentation. It was quite extraordinary to watch, although at the time we didn't know what it meant.

> She called us the next day and told us she went into work the day after the seminar and her boss invited her into his office. He explained that he had just finalized the purchase of a large restaurant and wanted to know if she was interested in managing it! Less then 24 hours later, she realized her dream. She had no knowledge of any of this during the weekend. What happened?

Frequent peakers would say she unconsciously "tuned in" to what was happening with her boss, allowing her to feel more charged when she did the process. "True believers" and "heavy peakers" would say the quality of how she did the process somehow affected the course of destiny. Nonpeakers would probably say it was just coincidence.

I have noticed that "an electricity" seems to surround many cases where people qualitatively shifted their level of results. It leads me to believe that a tangible energy may flow from us into the events in our lives, reorganizing them in new ways.

Unfortunately, there is not enough hard research on the relationship between psychological states and physical reality to scientifically confirm the existence of synchronicities. Michael Talbot provides a plausible model, using the new physics, to support how psychological events could alter external reality.[2]

Believing you can influence the course of destiny with your mind is still a bit of a leap of faith. But if you are willing to leap a bit, the next few pages will show how fun it can be, and if Maslow is right, it may also provide a framework that will allow you to have many more peak experiences.

3. Synchronicity

The shortest distance between two points is synchronicity. Of course, how else could all those lucky breaks and unexpected opportunities enter our lives so quickly. *Synchronicity,* or the collapse of cause-and-effect connections, occurs whenever resolutions occur at a faster or higher level than can be explained by the actual actions we have taken. For example, we might make one phone call to get some information on a product, and in this seemingly simple act, set into motion a chain of events that leads to a new job.

There is a principle in physics called Bell's Theorem. It established the physical possibility for simultaneity. In this experiment, the turn of one subatomic particle occurs at the exact moment a different particle turns. In other words, information is nonlocal; it exists outside of space and time and was accessed by two different events simultaneously. If consciousness has the same capacities as subatomic particles, then I can conceive of a result at the same time that result is experiencing the information to enter my life. Desire and fulfillment merge, i.e., there is no emotional distance. If you will reflect back to the Zen archer, this is what he was doing, allowing his internal experience to become one with his outer expression.

This what Jung called synchronicity, which in later life he hypothesized might be the organizing field of our entire universe. Jung felt that synchronicity is what allows human minds to connect outside of space and time and forms a collective unconscious where the knowledge of past, present and future is held. In his view, archetypes are huge organizing fields that cause vast amounts of information to form into timeless patterns. That is why a myth like that of the spider woman can be as relevant to a culture 10,000 years ago as it is now, with virtually the same meaning and power.

Synchronicity is the moment when we touch that realm of the collective unconsciousness, or to use Hindu terms, the "field of all possibilities." In this moment the normal laws of cause and effect break down and the same information can be received and acted upon by two different people simultaneously.

We all experience synchronicity. A lot of the good stuff that happens in our lives just can't be explained otherwise. *The main thing is that when connections occur like this, whether they involve quantum realities or the poetry in our souls, we begin to hang out in that chaotic, self-organizing river that gives our intentions added power.* We think something and almost magically it appears in our life. We need to meet someone and there they are. We need a solution and the next book we pick up has the answer. We call a new customer and they exclaim, "I was just going to look for someone with your product." In those moments, we drop down in a deeper, more intelligent level of organization of the events in our life.

4. Signature

One of the personal qualities that seems to heighten synchronicities is what might be called the strength of one's "signature." A well-known musicologist named Clymes asked individuals across cultures to listen to musical pieces composed by such greats as Beethoven, Handel, Mozart, etc. The listeners had a device attached to their armchairs which registered pressure and duration. They were asked to press this button in a rhythm that they felt described the piece. Clymes found that listeners came up with very comparable patterns and that when they heard different pieces by the same composer, their pattern remained the same.

It led him to conclude that every artist has a *signature,* a clear note of individuality that is recognizable no matter what they do. One of the characteristics of creative genius would seem to be that the person's signature is highly developed; you can recognize their essence in almost every action they take. Look at Picasso's scribble on a piece of paper and then look at Guernica; the essence is the same. Developing your signature is a key path to improving the quality of your work.

When this note of individuality is developed, it allows your intentions to be more powerful and accurate. When you strike a C note on a tuning fork while in a room with other instruments, all the instruments will vibrate to the C note. In the same way, someone who can hit a clearer note, or even a louder one, will more easily cause events and people to *resonate* to what they want. *Strengthening your note is like hanging out in the part of the river where the current is strongest. Therefore your thoughts reach far-*

ther, have more impact, and connect with those invisible threads of synchronicity more often. Thus, it is yet another key to attracting support at a higher level, once again allowing the time between a goal and its manifestation to collapse.

5. Ecology of Action/Holographic Change

The movie *Bull Durham* tells the story of a minor league baseball player who breaks out and makes it to the big leagues, "The Show." Susan Sarandon plays the local team supporter who every year chooses one lucky minor league player to be her "project" for the season. Tim Robbins is her lucky choice. He has an extraordinarily powerful arm but absolutely no control. Kevin Costner, the team manager, begins focusing on his character. At the same time, Sarandon coaches him on the romantic end of things. No one is working with him on his pitching. As he changes as a person—talking, listening, carrying himself differently—his pitching magically undergoes the same transformation, enough to take him to the majors.

This is the *ecology of action;* everything we do is tied to everything else we do. Taking cooking class may improve your golf game, which may lead you to a breakthrough on a creative project and a better relationship with your kids. Usually when one area is blocked, in small, often subtle ways, everything is blocked. People will often say to us something like, "Work is awful, but my relationship is great." or vice versa. Statements like this are rarely completely true. When someone describes a problem to us we always look for a small way it may be showing up in another area, even in their conversation, so they can begin to confront a habit of energy. Often "the presenting problem" is not the most efficient place to begin.

6. Microanalysis/Small Shifts that Create Big Changes

A computer programmer named Tim told us he had three major projects going and he couldn't find the willpower or solutions to finish any of them, which he also admitted was a common problem for him. Rather than directly addressing issues having to do with this project, his dislike of his boss (and before that his dominating father) or his lifelong pattern of incompletion, we looked for a small indication of the pattern. We noticed that he had a curious habit of not really finishing sentences. They would either trail off at the end, or he would switch direction, or he would imply the end without specifically saying it.

In the seminar we merely had him focus on completing his sentences and pointed out whenever he didn't. We then asked him to practice this on his own as much a possible. When we saw him again about seven weeks later, he reported that one of the projects was done and that he had incredible enthusiasm and ideas for finishing the others.

Completing sentences helped him address the same energy source that was affecting his projects. It was far easier to make these small changes, and it paved the way for the much larger pattern to shift almost effortlessly.

Every communication reveals volumes about the result we want. We frequently offer video work in our seminars, taping small segments of communication. We have found that with as little as 60 seconds of tape, we can often decode patterns about work, money, love, etc. This holographic property allows small shifts in behavior to generate far larger repercussions in our lives.

A New Context for Action

Action is the deepest affirmation. When you act from a new context, you anchor an expanded view of reality. The most powerful reason to consciously have experiences of accelerating results and collapsing time is that you begin to rewrite your beliefs about causation. It is mythmaking at it's core. Not only do the six principles just covered offer an expanded view of reality, they are patterns of thought which are much more suited to our current economic and cultural climate.

> ➤ *Time is emotional distance.* In an economic environment that increasingly relies on imagination and the capacity for innovation, emotional resistance is one of the key factors that will slow us down. Learning to examine projects through this lens is a valuable asset.

> ➤ *Coherence heightens efficiency.* The massive exchange of information and cooperation now required to get a project off the ground demands an organizational flow that does not impede this

exchange. Alignment within a group or an individual allows information to flow the fastest, with the least distortion.

➤ *Synchronicity is an attitude.* Believers in synchronicity hold higher expectations for how things can happen and have an implicit faith in the benevolence of chance. This spirit of optimism and expansiveness allows their imaginations to soar more easily than people who subscribe to a strictly rational model.

➤ *Our personal signature accelerates a direction.* You can choose any style of leadership—laissez-faire, centralized/top-down, technology-reliant, back to basics—and find someone who has defied all expectations to make this style an inspirational model for how to do business. Thus exceptional success does not rest in an ideology. Success arises out of a very developed personal style. Since the style rings true, it promotes results far beyond what might be normally expected.

➤ *All action is holographic and ecological.* There is a rigor that accompanies this belief. An organization that does not view things holographically might say, "It's OK to publicly declare that the customer is our first priority, but we can cut corners on the product if we need the profits in a given month." A business that knows that *everything reflects everything* will persist in finding new ways to put the customer first and never consider cutting corners. And somehow, the customer will feel this integrity in every exchange, often without knowing why.

➤ *Small shifts create big changes.* We must respond to such a massive volume of demands, small shifts are usually all we can handle. In a complex and overwhelming environment, this is a powerful strategy for implementing changes that will stick.

It is natural to assume that psychological shifts, say, becoming more coherent in your speaking style, will make results happen more easily. The real point of this chapter is that the impact of such shifts is "discontinuous." It is greater than what can be rationally explained.

Naturally, a more coherent speaking style will make others respond more positively, but it will also have an impact far greater than just the people who hear you speak. This seemingly small shift transmits a message that reverberates in ways that can't be predicted or measured.

It's as if we have a topographical map of reality coded in our being, a representation of how we believe things will happen. The events in our lives get placed on top of that map. If the patterns of our personal reality stay the same, then the events also repeat. The river of life just flows over this map, forming the same eddies and currents over and over again.

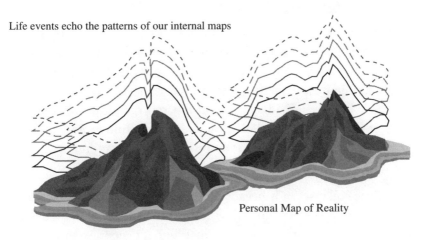

Life events echo the patterns of our internal maps

Personal Map of Reality

Accelerating results involves beginning to play with your map of reality. This why the impacts are discontinuous and allow you to make unexpected leaps or collapse time in seemingly impossible ways. It's not just getting results, but a form of "metamanifestation." You have altered not just your experience of a particular result, but your patterns surrounding all results.

The point of accelerating results is not so that everyone can squeeze more "stuff" into their lives at a faster rate. The purpose is to understand the state of consciousness that allows any and all results to accelerate, to understand the nature of how consciousness works and how these discontinuous impacts can begin to reshape your world. This is the eighth tool.

Accelerating results is actually a way of slowing down. Learning to consciously speed up results requires hanging out in this space and becoming more familiar with it. It is a state of consciousness that allows the mad pace of contemporary life to somehow feel more effortless, possibly even relaxing. When an individual, relationship, or organization is accelerating results, it produces the psychological sensation of things moving slower. It is a centered, relaxed feeling that accomplishes much more than our more typical state of hyperactivity.

When time collapses, it is because you have dropped into a deeper order of organization. Actions that flow from this awareness allow us to personally experience and become familiar with a deeper order of reality. It is not the specific results we attain, but rather the state of awareness we are entering that is most interesting and ultimately most useful. Resources, support, information, and action become more unified, as if they were part of one experience. The linear sequence of action that is so familiar to the ordinary mind begins to collapse, and unexpected coincidences and linkages appear. The more we learn about how to hang out in this place, the greater the volume of challenges of all descriptions we will be able to manage.

Practicing Accelerating Results

Emotional Distance

Select a specific, somewhat challenging result you wish to attain and that you think will take a certain amount of time, at least six months to a year, or even two. I'll use one year for this example.

Imagine that some invisible force is assuring you that one year from now, this result will definitely happen. Notice how that makes you feel.

Next, imagine that you are again reassured that this result will occur, the only change being that it will happen in nine months. How do you feel now?

Then you are assured it will happen in six months. Pause again; check the feeling. Next, reduce it to three months, one week, and then tomorrow.

Finally, imagine this result has already taken place; you just forgot.

Try this visualization a few times. You are looking for the cut-off point. Up to a certain point, say six months, your rational mind can still figure out how it could happen. Then at three months, you might say, "No way, impossible." The moment you are looking for is a threshold, when your rational mind cuts off and says this is impossible. Some people become exhilarated at the cut-off point and think, "Great I don't have to do anything. " Other people disconnect and think, "This is crazy. " It doesn't matter which happens, the important point is the threshold. That is where the emotional resistance lives. You want to dig around in there to see what thoughts, feelings, and beliefs are keeping your result "out there in time."

Speaking the Vision

Speaking your vision out loud is one of the fastest ways to detect conflicting messages.

Ask a friend to listen to your plans or intentions while trying not to listen for content. Ask them to listen for points when the energy seems to go down, when their attention seems to wander, when they feel drawn in, when they feel pushed away. They are looking for anything that doesn't match your words. After you receive their feedback, replay the process.

Before you replay, it is sometimes helpful to discuss what you are afraid of or denying, or anything that is triggered by the feedback. Remember the point is not to defend yourself, but to explore what made this person feel disconnected from what you were saying. Sometimes people replay it many, many times until they can state their vision without any discrepancies between their words and the energy. If you want to do a videotaped version, you'll find this analysis can be even more rigorous. The main purpose of getting your presentation more coherent is so you begin to recognize what this feels like. It then becomes easier to discover this coherence in other actions. The second benefit is that when we become more coherent in how we speak about something, results do tend to speed up.

Strengthening Your Signature

Sometimes people don't realize how important they are. Very often someone will have to miss part of a seminar for logistical reasons. In my opinion 75 percent of these situations could have been worked out so the person didn't have to miss it. Most of the time they figure it will make no difference to the group if they are not there. But it always does. You can sometimes pinpoint a person's unique contribution by what happens when they are *not* there. I always have this fantasy that if that person could only see what happens to the group when they are not there, they would have a far greater awareness of what it is they do offer.

> We built a process around this experience. We break the group into groups of four. After about ten minutes of sharing, one person leaves the group. When he has left, that person reflects on what impact it may have had. The remainder of the group also reflects on what they sensed when the person left. The person then returns and everyone describes what they felt the impact was. Repeat the process with a second person, and so on. Figuring about 30 minutes per person, this exercise will take about two hours.

In the movie *Cocoon*, there is a scene where the alien takes off her skin, which is a replica of human form, and underneath is a light being. If you didn't have your skin on, how would somebody describe your energy pattern? That is the kind of description you are trying to sense in this exercise. As you gain a handle on the unique ways you affect a project or group, reflect on what would happen if you increased this signature, and raised the volume on the characteristics that are closest to who you are.

Finding Key Shifts in the Holographic Field

Choose a project or relationship that you wish to understand more completely.

> Try to determine the key pattern that you feel describes the project or relationship. For example, you might feel that the beginning is explosive and the middle phase never lives up to your initial impression. Then look at this same pattern and see if it is reflected in and of your everyday actions.

> Perhaps you give people a big hello with lots of warmth and then find yourself tuning out and wanting to leave after a few minutes. Experiment with changing the pattern. For example, try a greeting that warms up more slowly and be conscious of allowing your interest in this other person to deepen from there. When you go to a movie or eat a meal, focus on increasing your attention in the middle phase of the picture or meal. Don't worry about your project. Just spend a few weeks entering conversations slowly and building steadily and consciously. I guarantee this new pattern will start showing up in everything you do.

Riding Time Collapse

We have had the good fortune to be able to watch quite a few people undergo time collapse, usually when their career catches a bigger wave than before. The main thing to do in such moments is to slow down, consider options very carefully, to focus on taking all your relationships deeper, and let yourself relax even more. It is the opposite of your instinct. When things speed up, your pulse naturally starts to rise, and you will feel like glancing around at a faster pace. You tend to be cursory and more superficial in your relationships. If you can somehow consciously breathe more deeply and allow yourself to relax, the speed becomes pleasurable rather than challenging.

When time collapses or synchronicities occur at a higher level, you have tapped into a deeper order of experience. Relaxing allows you to stay focused on what is really allowing this speed-up to happen. Therefore the experience sustains itself longer and results expand. When external results are speeding up, it is because something within you has become more coherent, more individualized, more tuned in. It is only by slowing down in the face of an accelerating result that you can stay connected with the true nature of the experience.

The Eight Navigational Tools

Navigating is a way of perceiving events and determining a direction. The very same situation can be seen through each of these eight filters, each yielding a different set of possibilities.
The power of these strategies is not revealed through mere intellectual understanding, it requires an ongoing commitment to practicing the particular realm of knowledge that each one makes available. Through continued work with each tool you will discover its unique power to usher you into the future.

Navigational Tool 1: The Future Zone

We have the ability to access heightened states of awareness where the mind/body relationship is more integrated. These experiences are a form of metaintelligence brining all our our faculties to a higher level.

Navigational Tool 2: A New Sense

When you perceive information that was not previously available to you, you experience prophecy, the ability to see through the invisible barrier of time. You see further ahead in a way that goes far beyond the obvious images our culture flashes us.

Navigational Tool 3: The Emotions of Change

We are surrounded by a culture in rapid transition. The art of shamanic change allows these external shifts to also change us internally. The emotions associated with this transformation are equivalent to a psychological death and rebirth.

Navigational Tool 4: Mythmaking

We have the power to redesign the world by constructing new stories about ourselves, our culture, and reality itself. We are witnessing a rapid collapse of our shared myths— to survive we must each reclaim our skills as mythmakers.

Navigational Tool 5: Shadow Dancing

A natural alchemy occurs when we bring submerged aspects of our conciousness into full view and transform this encounter into new possibilities. Locked in the shadow—in the lost, denied, and projected parts of our personality—is always a missing piece of our power.

Navigational Tool 6: Why We Need to Sweat

We must release the dream we have absorbed from our culture, discover a path of our own making, and assume the responsibility of a vision. Such a discovery can only be found by transcending your mundane goals and objectives and touching the realm of the sacred.

Navigational Tool 7: The Power of Intimacy

For the first time in human history, we have the tools for stepping out of the emotional world we have inherited from our past. This will allow us to be more fully present, thus allowing us to tap into the true power and intelligence of relationship.

Navigational Tool 8: Accelerating Results

We can collapse time, drawing results to us almost magically. Sychronicity is the shortest distance between our desires and their fulfillment. The real purpose of learning to accelerate a particular result is to discover a state of conciousness that will allow all results to manifest more easily.

PART 3
WHAT WILL WE FIND?
The Other Side of the Portal

One Sunday about twenty years ago I was reading The New York Times. *When I came to the magazine section, I saw on the cover one of the first photos taken from space of the earth rising over the moon.*

I was deeply moved by its beauty. You may recall how dramatic it was when you first saw this image. Something inside all of us was forever changed.

The accompanying article was by the late Joseph Campbell, the great mythologist. He said that the image of *earthrise* would provide a new myth for our culture, guiding our psyches to the next step in our evolution. The image of the earth rising continues to be a powerful cultural icon, used widely by individuals and organizations for their logos and ad campaigns. They know that aside from its natural beauty, there is a deeper meaning to this image that is virtually irresistible.

The "myth of earthrise" is not so much a myth of global unity. That idea has been available for some time. It is a myth about the power of self-reflection. The earthrise showed us for the first time that we could look back at ourselves. We could hold up a mirror and reflect on who we are. The new myth says that by looking at the earth as a whole, we can gain self-awareness. Like the space ship that gave us those first photos of the earth, by reflecting on our collective reality we can gain **a new angle of vision.**

Chapter 12

A New Angle of Vision

If the eyes are a mirror to the soul, then how we collectively look at the world is a mirror to our collective soul.

Never before has a culture looked at itself so deeply. The moment an event takes place, a team of analysts descends to examine why it happened, what it means, how we need to respond. We are reflecting, reflecting, reflecting endlessly, and almost everyone has a take on what our problems really are and what's up with the spirit of our time. As a society, we publicly ask: What is consciousness? What is a healthy organization? What is real community about? We are desperately trying to figure out the big picture. But what are we really sensing? What's fluttering at the edges of our collective unconscious?

The Fifth Solution

Memory is a complex Gestalt intertwined with emotions, motives, and passions. Yet our conscious images of the future are usually much less rich. They usually are based on a few plans we place on our calendars and our expectations about what these events might bring. We might have some loosely based intentions that we may or may not follow through on. We tint these vague premonitions with some mixture of fear, dread, optimism, and excitement. Our sense of the future seems to stop there. But is it possible that we sense things in a more sophisticated and developed way than we realize?

In his book *Holographic Universe,* Michael Talbot describes a fascinating study of how people conceptualize what lies ahead. Subjects in the study were hypnotized and travelled into the future. They were asked what the world looked like in the near future. In their hypnotic state, they expressed extraordinarily clear and developed ideas about what the future held, often including what countries would participate in which events and even on what dates. It was as if they were reading a script to a play, complete with characters and plot.

We may discover that our sense of what lies ahead is as complex and powerful as our memory; it's just locked in our subconscious.

The most remarkable feature of these hypnotic progressions is that only four main scenarios emerged:

> After the disaster—nuclear, environmental, earth changes, social breakdown, or financial collapse. Like Tina Turner in the *Mad Max* movies, we are wandering survivors left to pick up the pieces.

> Big brother, high-tech cybersociety. We live underground, where we are surrounded by mechanical solutions to human problems.

> Back to nature; craft-based society. Either the cities have crumbled or we have realized the dangers of modern life and have voluntarily chosen to live more tribally, closer to nature, again pursuing spiritual goals and personal growth.

> Living outside the body or in orbiting space stations eating synthetic food. This image is reminiscent of sci-fi fantasies and tales of alien encounters.

It's an insightful study, but these are the same four choices Hollywood and the mass media have been entertaining us with for years. And you can comb the Net for sites that will feed you abundant evidence for each of the above scenarios, where previously undisclosed "facts" are offered as to why this or that direction is inevitable and imminent. And our political scientists and public commentators continually add fuel to these fires. It would appear that locked in our collective unconscious are some pretty clear images of the other side of the Stargate.

None of these four scenarios fills the bill for me. In fact, if our collective unconscious is only serving up these four choices, we had better put in a worldwide visioning curriculum starting in nursery school right away.

But maybe we can't envision any new scenarios until we release our unconscious attraction to these first four. I've had my share of gloom and doom conversations, where I put forth strong evidence about how bad things are, how disaster or breakdown of some sort is probably unavoidable. I've also given my fair share of big-brother/global-monopoly/down-with-technology speeches. And I've had my share of idealizing a back-to-nature scenario. And sometimes space stations in the sky, perhaps with alien support, seem like the only solution. Like Jodie Foster in *First Contact,* we sometimes feel pretty alone and could use someone out there who knows more than we do.

There are definitely pieces of our culture that appear to be heading in each of these directions. We need to investigate not only our unconscious attraction to each scenario but the part of us that can't see any other way out. These four scripts are more powerful than we realize. Like the story about the man with the stutter, they may be invisibly compelling us to act within the outlines of the story. What we expect lies ahead will cause us to unwittingly move in that direction.

Philip and I have led discussions where each person in the group talks about the part of them that is unconsciously drawn to each of these four plots. There are always pieces of your personal history—feelings of helplessness, unvented rage, revenge, terror, jealousy, self-hatred, judgments of others, etc.—that cause us to be unconsciously predisposed to a particular scenario. So each scenario is also a statement about us. The back-to-nature scenario might reveal fears that we will not be smarter than our machines. The savior scenario works well when we feel especially helpless and tired. Like with shadow work, we need to explore the part of our own power that is locked in to these stories.

But even more important, there has to be a fifth solution taking shape somewhere in our collective heart.

Like the dots in the Magic Eye, the details may still be a bit too sketchy to allow a clear glimpse. Like the wall before entering the zone, there can be an overwhelming feeling that the forces against us and our fatigue are just too great. It is hard to get past all the evidence that real breakthrough is impossible and the die has already been cast.

The thesis of this book is that a fifth solution rests in advancing our own being, expanding states of awareness we can touch, building more profound relationships, or letting our imaginations soar. **It is in the alchemy** of producing a personal response to a very complex and wild game that a fifth solution is slowly being pieced together.

I believe the portal to a different future has been slowly forming just outside our ordinary awareness. The outlines of this new domain are described by the edges of our very own psyche.

One Degree of Difference

When a rocket is launched into space, the trajectories are on such a scale that a single degree of difference can send the rocket to a completely different galaxy. In the same way we might find that seemingly small shifts in how we relate to our bodies or communicate with or relate to others, these one degrees of difference, may lead to an entirely different cultural destination.

> When we consciously access the zone, we automatically tap into a larger view of reality and feel a heightened vitality and creativity as a result.

> When we see with a new sense, we glean far more information from the flow of everyday events, and the true direction of experiences becomes more obvious.

> When we use change shamanically, then we awaken deeper sources of personal freedom and self-knowledge.

> When we learn to weave new stories about ourselves, then we learn how to also begin telling new myths about our organizations, reality, and the culture-at-large.

> When we have encountered our own shadows and wrestled with their underlying power, we see our larger difficulties through a much different lens.

> When we build a strong sense of our own purpose, we more effortlessly maneuver through the ebb and flow of a culture in trouble.

> When we have broken through our relationship thresholds, we more easily see through the fears that shape so many social encounters and know how to evoke more powerful collaboration.

> When we understand the invisible dynamics underlying all action, then we have a different view of how we can solve our collective problems and in what time frame.

Each chapter in turn has offered a more profound way of being in the world, a way of seeing that reveals different possibilities for the future, a new angle of vision.

If you have been sitting for a while discussing a particular topic, you will find that something as simple as getting up and changing chairs can allow you to see the discussion from a different vantage point and most likely lead to somewhat different opinions. This book is designed to give you an experience of "changing chairs" and clear steps for recognizing the perceptions you will gain as a result. By using the vantage points provided by these navigational tools, you gain the potential for a very different take on the future. These relatively small shifts will head you to a new destination.

We can't think ourselves into the future, we must feel our way in. If we really want to enter expanded domains, then we must inch our way forward in a way that truly leaves our past experience behind. This is how the fifth solution will arise. The other side of the Stargate is not yet completely in view. But the one degree of difference that we each learn to make will most certainly bring about an entirely different destination.

How Far Can We Leap?

Some historians see this era as an echo of past cultural upheavals. An excellent book called *The Fourth Turning* offers a thorough analysis of the tides of social change beginning in the 1500s.[1] It describes our current cultural milieu as a very predictable phase in the regular turnings of societal change. Every 20 years or so, we enter a new phase of social organization. The main feature of the next 10 to 20 years will be increasing chaos and breakdown, and out of that a new era of hope and trust will arise. This cycle has happened before, and it will happen again.

The historian Arthur Schlesinger has put forth a similar view in his description of a social pendulum that swings back and forth from conformity and order to rebellion and breakdown. The sixties were a reaction to the denial of the fifties; the nineties had to break down the high-flying eighties. Over and over, periods of questioning and upheaval inevitably lead to periods of stability and calm; periods of social irresponsibility flow into times where compassion is held more dear.

Although these cyclical features certainly explain parts of the current cultural era, there are elements to our current predicament that defy past patterns, that are unprecedented. There are *progressive* features of our time, dimensions of change that cannot be compared to past instances of upheaval.

In part because this moment builds on past cultural transformations, and in part because stresses have reached a new order of magnitude, this period of breakdown and reorganization will be different than any that has gone before. For 5,000 years we have been building the conceptual underpinnings of modern life, and the price of our choices is becoming painfully clear. We cannot go back to the past; the wave of technological progress has too much momentum and is too compelling. We must find a way to go forward that retains the essence of what ancient cultures also knew, that resettles our bodies and deepens our relationships. A unique convergence of factors will make this a turning point like no other.

There are many events in the womb of time, yet to be delivered.

Shakespeare

Authors like Peter Russell, Willis Harmon, Barbara Marx Hubbard, Jean Houston, Fritjof Capra, Jose Arguilles, Marilyn Ferguson, Terrence McKenna, and others have been the first to describe the even greater magnitude of transformation we now face. Extensive upheavals in the social, political, technological, and economic realms are only the beginning. We are approaching an all-encompassing transformation of consciousness itself.

Physicist Fritjof Capra describes this shift as a conceptual reorganization.[2] In order to negotiate this time of paradigm collapse and rebirth, we need to structure our thinking in fresh ways. The call is to look at systems ecologically and holographically, every event not only revealing information about the whole but being connected to every other event. We need to approach problems with the understanding that systems, people, organizations, the planet cannot be understood by reduction. They are always greater than the sum of their parts. This new conceptual angle will allow us to experience our world differently and locate a new order of solutions.

Terrence McKenna goes a step further, calling this historical moment "timewave zero."[3] He feels we are approaching a moment when not only will we think differently, not only will culture break down, but we will escape our current notions of reality. Out of this theoretical collapse will come the discovery of how to live from a more "magical" dimension, in which we reclaim the skills of our ancestors and blend them with contemporary approaches for understanding how personal and objective reality are intertwined. A post-modern shamanism will begin to emerge.

Peter Russell's vision is more radical still.[4] Taking off on ideas from physics and eastern thought, he postulates that a time will arrive when our current level of consciousness will no longer be adequate for the challenges we face. We must expose another layer of self-awareness, a deepening of self-reflection and how we organize self-knowledge. In this moment of deepening complexity, our unique moment in history will be transformed by human consciousness, thus creating a white hole in time.

Curiously, these radical descriptions aren't too far from what economists like Paul Romer and Hazel Henderson are defining as the next dimension of economic evolution. As we move from an era in which natural resources and other finite resources cease to be the main focus of business into the infinite realm of ideas and imagination, the world economy will be increasingly designed and driven by personal creativity. The effect will be comparable to McKenna's timewave zero or Russell's white hole in time, in that the quality of human consciousness will dictate the quality of economic activity. Intellectual capital and the ability to imagine new dimensions of exchange will become drivers in the new economy.

Many social commentators are exploring a more personal side of this new frontier. Poet Robert Bly offers an example in his exploration of modern culture, *The Sibling Society.*[5] Culture is getting flatter, he contends. We are losing our depth. The history of our past has always provided dimension and that is being discarded as no longer relevant. Relationships used to encompass more shadows and mystery, but now we want everything easily digestible, so intimacy has become one-dimensional. The culture at large is spewing out more and more of the same, so we no longer have time for excellence. Bly goes beyond the familiar argument that TV culture is obliterating diversity and promoting mediocrity. He claims it is playing with the way the brain works by destroying our ability to produce our own images.

So increasingly we only look side to side, envying each other, wanting only what our neighbor has, letting go of the ability to look for ourselves and find our own depth. This flatness renders us less compassionate, tolerant and authentic. It's a tight analysis. We should be grieving for what we have lost. Yet in this deplorable flatness, lies an embryonic hope.

We're stretching our culture thinner and thinner. Language and critical thought are fading into a subsistence diet of one-liners and soundbites. When our tolerance diminishes to the point that we want the answer before we have to ask the question, we'll crack, and a hunger for a new center may arise. Out of our rampant mindless pursuit of new directions and our insatiable lust for profit without responsibility, something inside us may finally snap in favor of a new inner dimension. Out of the vacancy we will be driven to seek out a new vision.

This urge for a deeper dimension is exactly what is sweeping the planet. The secret teachings of every major world tradition are not only available, they have been translated for the layperson and updated for the modern mind. We are witnessing the rapid growth of many spiritual traditions. Profound principles of ecology are entering the mainstream. We are seeing an astronomical rise in reports of paranormal experiences and the emerging acceptance of consciousness as a factor in healing, business, and as a shaping force of the future. **As these new beliefs cross the bridge from ideology to practice, it will lead to what could be described as the "shamanization" of our culture.** The following story is based on a Hopi legend.

> In the beginning of this world, all knowledge was held in one place. Eventually, because of growing forces of imbalance, this became too dangerous. So the father gave each of his sons a tablet and told them to go to a different part of the world and keep their piece of the truth safe and pure. One day, when the time was right, the sons would be called back. When they returned home carrying their tablets, the world's knowledge would once again be reunited. When this occurred, it would be the sign that we are about to enter a new world.

Perhaps this is our sign. The entire world's knowledge is about to be reassembled and placed at our fingertips.

The Means Are the End/The Question Is the Answer

Back to the problem posed in the introduction: How do we envision ourselves in the future as being somehow more conceptually, perceptively, emotionally, and kinesthetically advanced than we are now? How do we give substance to an image in which we become more honest, kinder, and wiser in the years ahead?

The solution I offer throughout this book is that the only way to do this with any certainty is through a thorough and committed exploration of our psychological future. A psychological futurism allows us to consider the personal shifts that must accompany cultural chaos. It allows us to explore how to catch up with our technology, how our bodies can begin catching up with our minds, how our relationships can catch up with our culture. A psychological futurism brings our focus to bear on how the individual can evolve in fast-moving and turbulent contexts.

The eight tools are only a beginning. I hope volumes of articles and books arise agreeing, disagreeing, and advancing the public debate on how we can more effectively participate in a world that is simultaneously digital and spiritual, wired and ecological, fracturing at the same time it is spinning new tales.

First, I used these eight domains to describe a portal, features that would delineate a new psychological world. Then I used these same eight domains to describe a path, a way to travel through an increasingly turbulent terrain and hold your center.

Finally, they also represent the other side of the Stargate; they describe an expanded concept of ourselves. We will feel differently about ourselves with new sensory faculties, being able to enter the zone at will, shapeshifting as we spin ever more amazing myths that arise out of a deeper knowledge of the shadow, a truer purpose, extraordinary intimacy, and a growing ability to allow it all to accelerate. It is not any one skill that will make the difference, but in the convergence of all eight paths that our true direction is revealed. That is how we will come to understand new dimensions of our own consciousness. In other words, the portal we choose determines the path we take which shapes the outcome we find. Where you begin is the most powerful way to determine where you end.

The definition I offered in the preface read as follows: the future does not exist out there in time *but as the moment you transcend habitual patterns and touch something that is truly beyond what you already know.* Each of the eight navigational tools are a way of transcending our habitual relationship with our bodies, senses, emotions, thoughts, relationships, and actions; thus they are a way of beginning to reshape the future.

Regardless of what we do, we will find ourselves on the other side of the Stargate. What we find there depends on what door we walk through.

➤ If we *only* walk through technological doors, we will find ourselves more mechanistic on the other side.

➤ If we *only* walk through economic doors, we will become more calculating.

➤ If we *only* walk through doors of paranoia and fear, we won't even recognize ourselves on the other side.

➤ If we insist on walking through doors that allow us to remain in denial, we will reach the other side in a deep sleep.

On the other hand, if we walk through doors that are more playful, humane, visionary, and gentle; then on the other side we may find that we like ourselves—a lot.

Becoming a Navigator

These tools do not comprise a solution, they are more like a compass or polestar. They offer a reference point.

With a reference point you can negotiate a direction. You can decide. Do I need to open my perceptions? Do I need to become more emotionally fluid? Do I need to become a mythmaker and tell a new story? Or do I need to tell a deeper truth? A navigator is just somebody who has a destination in mind and is able to adjust course as needed. With improved navigational tools you can fly even if the weather is stormy or fog has settled in. Since we don't really know what lies ahead, navigation is really all we have.

Navigation is the psychological metaphor that suits our time. In the past, we focused on techniques and solutions. We have focused on healing and coping. A fast-paced world requires that we pronounce ourselves healed enough, and that we redirect our energies toward learning to move ahead in the most effective and brilliant way possible. Navigating allows us to focus on flow and following opportunities as they arise rather than on fixing and analyzing.

Ariadne's Thread

Greek legend said it was impossible to find your way out of the famed Cretan labyrinth. Ariadne offered Theseus an elegant solution. She gave him a thread to unwind as he went in search of the Minotaur hidden in the depth of this maze. The path out of our current confusions may rest on an idea almost as simple.

Joseph Campbell made an interesting point in an interview with Bill Moyers. For much of his early life, Campbell wondered if he had made mistakes or was headed the right way. One day he had a spontaneous realization in which he understood why everything that had happened to him in his life, even if it was painful at the time, was necessary in order for him to fulfill his personal destiny. He no longer had a perception of good or bad, right or wrong. Suddenly, all the events in his life made sense, as if an invisible thread linked them all together.

Perhaps at some point in the future we will also look back at this time in human history and see our current directions not as good or bad, but as necessary to fulfill our collective destiny.

➤ Perhaps our shadow needs to become huge, so that when we finally encounter it, the power we gain is proportionately magnificent.
➤ Perhaps our physical stress needs to become so painful that we have no choice but to live in the zone.
➤ Maybe we will become so bored with what we see on our collective screens, we will begin mythmaking again.
➤ Perhaps our demands need to become so unmanageable that we commit to collapsing time.
➤ Maybe the information ahead will become so dense that we can only permeate it with a radical new sense.

Perhaps we will begin to see the invisible thread that is linking together all the seemingly disparate directions of our world.

This is the other side of the Stargate. We will all become smarter because we will have no other choice. As the myth of earthrise counsels us, we merely need to continually look at ourselves personally and collectively for evidence that we are heading into a place of greatness. This is the key to the way out. It is this reflection that will change the course of our shared destiny. Each of us in our own way must seek the invisible thread that is leading us out of this cultural labyrinth.

A passenger ship was cruising along on holiday, when it suddenly began taking on water. It was sinking rapidly. The captain and his head officers quickly assessed the situation and determined that it was hopeless.

Then they did the unthinkable: they jumped ship. They saved themselves, thinking that no one would be left alive to tell the tale. As water lapped over the side of the ship, the passengers saw the captain and officers floating by in a life raft.

Moments later, an authoritative voice began to issue orders. In the midst of the chaos, this mysterious voice directed people where to go and how to lower the rafts. It orchestrated the successful rescue of everyone on board.

Was it an Angel? No. What is a Captain from another ship? No.

This mysterious voice of authority was a man who had been hired to provide entertainment on the boat. How fitting that, in fact, this entertainer was hired as a magician.

This is my myth for the new millennium. The raw facts look pretty bad; it may be hopeless. A lot of leaders have jumped ship.

But on the other side of the Stargate, the passage to safety will be negotiated by ordinary people who can harness **future flow.**

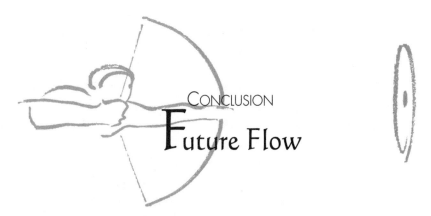

CONCLUSION

Future Flow

Many years ago, NASA asked James Lovelock, a British biochemist, to determine which planets might be more likely to have life. He had already done a spectrographic analysis of earth, and he had found that the readings of planets without life were predictable and stable. There were ups and downs, but they could be anticipated.

When he looked at the earth, there was a different tune, unstable, chaotic, wild. It led him to conclude that life is revealed in relentless instability, innate creativity, and connected intelligence. It also led him to conclude that the ancient myths were right: the only force that could hold this seething mass together was a massive intelligence.

If this is so, then the main feature of our current cultural climate is that it is becoming more alive—greater turbulence, heightened creativity, a more connected wisdom. Therefore, as individuals we must also become more alive. That's what's so magnificent about the story of the ship's magician. He stepped out in the most unpredictable way, defied all rules and expectations, and tapped into a heightened level of personal freedom and social artistry.

The contemporary future moved into pop culture with *Future Shock*, by Alvin Toffler. He described future shock as the feeling that occurs with the premature arrival of the future. It feels like too much, too fast.

Although feelings of future shock still persist and are a big part of what we are all learning to cope with, there is an equally strong dynamic taking hold. We are slowly making the transition from future shock to *future flow;* feeling expanded because of new developments in our culture. Future flow is the sensation of getting smarter.

Perhaps you have noticed that at the deepest level, the eight navigational tools are the same. They each involve dropping down into a deeper level of organization.

Accelerating Results by moving around in the energy that underlies appearances.
Intimacy and designing a fabric of intelligence between you and another.
Sweating and entering into a more dynamic relationship with problems we face.
Shadow Dancing, becoming an alchemist and turning feelings into power.
Mythmaking, weaving, and reweaving new realities.
Change as a shamanic journey to the source of personal freedom.
A New Sense and the ability to see things through time.
Zone and new level of performance.
A more profound sense of self.
Greater complexity.
Intelligence.

Dropping down into a vortex of solutions; that's where we seem to be headed. It's not any one skill that will make the difference, but in the convergence of an array of skills that a new direction and greater life is going to be revealed. This new individual depth—creativity—intelligence—is what will shape our lives, the nature of business, and the culture at large. Who we are becoming is what will change the direction of the world.

That is the reflection that the myth of earthrise suggests. That is also the message of the ship's magician. He left his habits behind. For a moment, he walked around on the other side of the Stargate.

> *The almost incalculable challenges of our time are about to go head-to-head with the human soul. Out of this clash, a new level of possibility will emerge. This evolution of the human spirit and the power of our time will co-create the next dimension of our collective future.*

A Guide for Group Study

If you want to take the ideas in this book a step further, I highly recommend working with them in a small group. Groups are an extremely powerful learning environment because they work on so many levels simultaneously. There is the value of the explicit content, the relationship dynamics, and the qualities of leadership that naturally happen.

Philip and I have led group experiences for 15 years and have watched many people continue to meet on their own after a seminar, sometimes for years. One thing I know about groups is that no two are alike. *Like snowflakes, every group has it's own character and intelligence that is unique.* If you do decide to form a group to continue exploring the material in this book, allow the specific direction and flavor of your group to become the guiding force. Simply coming together with a common purpose creates a kind of magic. You will see that the group energy quickly becomes greater than the sum of its parts.

Getting a Group Together

You can form a group where you work, by gathering a group of friends, or even by placing an advertisement. Occasionally people like to make these groups all women or all men. One group we know set up separate women's and men's meetings and then met all together every two months.

Before you get started, decide the following—how large a group, who, when, where, how long for each session, and how frequently. Decide if new people will be allowed to join and at what points. Decide if it is to be leaderless or whether to have a facilitator. Each member of the group can take a turn facilitating the group and keeping the discussion on track. Be careful not to take yourself too seriously. Often an apparent breakdown in the group can preface a subsequent breakthrough into a new level of creativity.

Following is a guide for a group lasting 11 sessions. You could easily lengthen or shorten the time period by spending more time on each chapter or doubling up on the chapters. It is nice to have a journal for each person to use during the course of the series, so you might want to bring this for the first meeting. You also might want to select a time keeper and designate how long each section or process should take.

Part I: Finding the Portal/Meetings 1–2

Meeting I: Everyone should have read the Preface, Introduction, and Chapter 1.

a. Have everyone introduce themselves and briefly (2–3 minutes) describe what they would like to get out of this study.

b. *What Is the Future?* The preface offered the following definition: "The future is the moment we transcend habitual patterns and touch something that is truly beyond what we already know." For 10–15 minutes, discuss this definition and its relevance to your daily life. How does this definition change you relationship to goals and visions? How does it make you think differently about time? Go around the circle and have each person share the main way in the last few weeks that they have been sensing the future, or spontaneous openings in their habitual patterns.

c. *The Stargate Dilemma and Psychological Futurism.* Discuss the premise of the introduction, that much of what lies ahead will be shaped by the soft side of the future; the evolution of how we perceive, think, feel, and act. Have each person give an example of one psychological skill that could dramatically reshape the direction of their career or business.

d. *The Spirit of Our Time.* Have one person lead a short visualization where each person tries to personally connect with an image that represents the spirit of our time. Visualize a spirit or a personification of this particular moment in human history. What does it look like? What does it want to do? How is it affecting us? After the visualization let each person describe what they sensed.

e.   Practice assignment. In the period between now and the next meeting pay even more attention than normal to moments when your present time experience expands and "the future" enters. At the end of each day make a note in your journal of key moments when you went beyond the familiar.

(For the next session you will need to bring large sheets of paper and crayons or colored pens. Ask if anyone would volunteer to take care of this.)

Meeting 2: Each person should have read Chapters 2 and 3.

a.   Begin by having each person share ideas about the assignment from last session. What did they notice?

b.   *Global Alchemy.* We all have a sensitivity to certain social issues more than others. For example, we might be more affected by youth issues, or the environment, or human rights, etc. Have each person share the three issues that seem to affect them the most. Is there any theme to what seems to affect you?

c.   *Co-evolution and the Participation Mystique.* Choose one issue or theme from the previous sharing that you will work with in this next process. For example, you might choose an issue such as the environment or a theme like developing leadership. Divide into pairs, or you can do this one by one in the whole group. One person at a time will do a role-play with the issue they chose. The other person will play the role of the social issue. Talk directly to this issue *as if it were a person.* This is a very important point. Some people will have a tendency to talk *about* this issue rather than to it. You may have to occasionally remind them to go back to talking *to* the issue, using *I* and *you* statements. Tell this issue why you are so moved. What does it touch in you? Why does it attract you? How could you go further in your relationship with this issue? What might it look like? The person playing the role of the social issue can occasionally respond or ask questions. After each person has had a turn, let everyone share how the process affected them. It is an interesting way to explore your feelings about an issue of an idea. It leads to different kinds of insights than just talking about an idea.

d. *A Psychological Map of the Future.* You will need paper for this next process and crayons or colored markers. Have each person spend a half hour creating a personal map of what lies ahead for them in the next year. Try not to think too much about this and to do it very freely, almost stream of consciousness. First, place on this map the critical personal issues you will face in the next year. Create shapes and patterns that represent these personal thresholds. Next, put in representations of the ideas that seem to be pulling you forward. Finally, put in key pieces of your vision, things that you would like to see happen. Unconsciously, you will find that you have placed things in certain relationships that are very revealing.

e. Have each person present the map to the entire group. If you want, when each person is finished with their own interpretation, they can ask others to add what they see that might be different.

f. Assignment: Have each person draw their map again and bring it to the next meeting. It is valuable to see how your relationship to these elements can change and deepen with each revision.

Part 2: Eight Navigational Tools/Meetings 3–10

Ideally, you should cover one tool per meeting. In each case everyone should have read the chapter or chapters relating to that meeting. Use the practice session at the close of each chapter as the basis for the next eight meetings. Some practice sections are too long for one meeting, and you will have to select the processes that interest you most or spend two sessions.

You will notice several kinds of processes:

> Visualizations can be led by one person, and afterward everyone can share their experience.

> Some of the processes are best done in pairs, such as resetting your internal clock from the Zone chapter or the first three observation processes from the New Sense chapter. Have each person take a turn guiding their partner through the experience.

> Other processes are dialogues or role-plays and require two to four people. Split up the group accordingly.

➤ Still other processes require self-observation and need to be done on your own. These could be assignments for the time between groups. You can open the following session with everyone sharing what happened for them with the assigned processes.

Part 3: The Other Side of the Portal/Meeting 11

Meeting 11: Everyone should have read the final chapter and the conclusion.

You might want a tape recorder for this session.

    a.   *The Four Solutions.* Have each person talk about the four scenarios introduced in the last chapter—big brother, after the disaster, back to nature, and out of the body/alien savior. What part of you resonates to each of these four scenarios? What part of you thinks these are likely to happen? Is there anything in your own personal history, emotional, intellectual, or spiritual, that makes you more partial to a particular scenario? Close this section with a short visualization in which each person releases their unconscious attractions and limiting beliefs about each of these scenarios.

    b.   *The Fifth Solution.* This is the part that could be interesting to tape. As a group, you will be creating a group story, a collective fantasy about what the future could look like 10–20 years from now. One person begins by giving a 1–3 minute statement of this future scenario. Then the next person picks up where the previous story left off. You keep going around the circle with each person adding a piece. You will find that one person's idea triggers another. The story should include a new fantasy about how we work, play, and relate. It should include ideas for how we got from where we are now into this new story. It should be a story based on the idea of a fifth solution, something different than the previous four scenarios. Wind it up when the story seems developed enough, after you have gone around the circle a few times.

    c.   *The Magician.* Go straight into this next process. Staying in the fantasy space about the future, have each person in turn share what their personal role was in making the new fantasy take place. Don't worry if what you say seems impossible or very different from what you now do. Let yourself stretch, let your subconscious be free to say what it wants.

d. If you have taped this, it is nice to give a copy to each person. Often these final visions are a nice meditation tape or memory of the group.

e. *Future Flow.* Close the session with acknowledgments. One person begins and shares how she feels she has become more open to the future, how she has grown during her time with the group. When this person has finished acknowledging herself, let other people in the group add their acknowledgments of the growth they have seen. Continue until each person has had a turn.

f. Finally, as a group decide if you feel complete and want to end the group here or if you still have a purpose together. If you still have a purpose for staying together, decide what that is and where you want to go next.

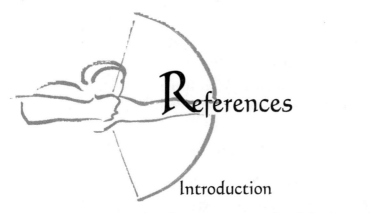

References

Introduction

1. John Hagel III and Arthur Armstrong, *Net Gain: Expanding Markets Through Virtual Communities*, Boston: Harvard Business School Press, 1997.

Chapter 1

1. David Shenk, *Data Smog: Surviving the Information Glut*, San Francisco: Harper, 1997.
2. Joseph Chilton Pierce, NPR radio interview.
3. James Hillman, *Kinds of Power: A Guide to Its Intelligent Uses*, New York: Doubleday, 1995.
4. John Briggs and David Peat, *The Turbulent Mirror: An Illustrated Guide to Chaos Theory and the Science of Wholeness*, New York: HarperCollins, 1990.
5. Margaret Wheatley, *Leadership and the New Science: Learning About Organization from an Orderly Universe*, San Francisco: Berret-Koehler, 1994.
6. John Parker Barlow, Electronic Frontier Foundation.
7. Deepak Chopra, *Quantum Healing: Exploring the Frontiers of Body, Mind, Medicine*, New York: Bantam, 1990.

Chapter 2

1. Michael Dertouzos, *What Will Be: How the New World of Information Will Change Our Lives*, San Francisco: Harper, 1997.

2. William Greider, *One World, Ready or Not: The Manic Logic of Global Capitalism,* New York: Simon And Schuster Trade, 1997.

3. George Soros, *Soros on Soros: Staying Ahead of the Curve,* New York: Wiley and Sons, 1995.

4. Arlie Hochschild, *Time Bind: When Work Becomes Home and Home Becomes Work,* New York: Henry Holt & Co., 1997.

5. Alvin Toffler, *Power Shift: Knowledge, Wealth, and Violence at the Edge of the 21st Century,* New York: Bantam, 1991.

Chapter 4

1. Edward T. Hall, *Beyond Culture,* New York: Anchor Books, 1997.

2. Lyall Watson, *Beyond Supernature,* New York: Bantam, 1988.

3. Ibid.

4. Arthur Koestler, *The Act of Creation,* New York: Arkana, 1990.

5. Itzhak Bentov, *Stalking the World Pendulum: On the Mechanics of Consciousness,* Rochester, VT: Inner Traditions International, Ltd., 1988.

6. Mihaly Csikszentmihalyi, *Flow: The Psychology of Optimal Experience,* New York: HarperCollins, 1991.

7. Michael Murphy, *The Future of the Body: Explorations Into the Further Evolution of Human Nature,* New York: Tarcher, 1993.

8. *All of a Sudden* from Laraji tape. To order tape, call 212-316-5042.

There are many more useful books on each topic. I've limited myself to the top three in each area.

Additional books on the body/mind relationship:

Deepak Chopra, *Quantum Healing: Exploring the Frontiers of Body, Mind, Medicine,* New York: Bantam, 1990.

Michael Murphy and Rhea White, *The Psychic Side of Sports,* Reading, MA: Addison-Wesley, 1978.

Caroline Myss, *Anatomy of the Spirit: The Seven Stages of Power and Healing,* New York: Random House, 1997.

Chapter 5

1. Don Tapscott, *The Digital Economy: Promise and Peril in the Age of Networked Intelligence*, New York: McGraw-Hill, 1996.

2. Steven Birkers in Charlene Spretnak, *Resurgence of the Real*, Reading, MA: Addison-Wesley, 1997.

3. Chuck Martin, *Digital Estate: Strategies for Competing, Surviving, and Thriving in an Internetworked World*, New York: McGraw-Hill, 1997.

4. David Shenk, *Data Smog: Surviving the Information Glut*, San Francisco: Harper, 1997.

Additional books on new perception:

Kevin Kelly, *Out of Control: The New Biology of Machines, Social Systems, and the Economic World*, Reading, MA: Addison-Wesley, 1995.

Peter Schwartz, *Art of the Long View: Planning for the Future in an Uncertain World*, New York: Doubleday, 1996.

Margaret Wheatley, *Leadership and the New Science: Learning about Organization from an Orderly Universe*, San Francisco: Berrett-Koehler, 1994.

Chapter 6

1. Petru Popescu, *Amazon Beaming*, New York: Penguin, 1992.

Additional books on change:

Robert Gerzon, *Finding Serenity in the Age of Anxiety*, New York: Macmillan Publishing USA, 1997.

Daniel Goleman, *Emotional Intelligence*, New York: Bantam, 1995.

Sogyal Rinpoche, *Tibetan Book of Living and Dying*, San Francisco: Harper, 1994.

Chapter 7

1. William Taylor, "At Verifone It's a Dog's Life," *Fast Company*, Special Collector's Edition, vol. 1, 1996.

2. Robert Ornstein, *Psychology of Consciousness,* New York: Penguin, 1996.

3. David Sheff, "Levi's Changes Everything," *Fast Company,* Special Collector's Edition, vol. 1, 1996.

4. Peter Senge, *The Fifth Discipline: The Art and Practice of the Learning Organization,* New York: Bantam, 1994.

Additional books on mythmaking:

Robert Bly, *Iron John: A Book About Men,* New York: Random House, 1992.

Jean Houston, *A Mythic Life,* San Francisco: Harper, 1995.

Mary Bray Pipher, *Reviving Ophelia,* New York: Putnam Publishing Group, 1994.

Additional books about the new digital myth:

Esther Dyson, *Release 2.0: A Design for Living in the Digital Age,* New York: Broadway Books, 1997.

William Mitchell, *City of Bits: Space, Place and the Infobahn,* Cambridge, MA: MIT Press, 1996.

Nicholas Negroponte, *Being Digital,* New York: Knopf, 1995.

Chapter 8

1. Robert Bly, *The Sibling Society, Reading,* MA: Addison Wesley, 1996.

2. David Sheff, "Levi's Changes Everything," *Fast Company,* Special Collector's Edition, vol. 1, 1996.

3. Mort Myerson, "Everything I Thought I Knew About Leadership Is Wrong," *Fast Company,* Special Collector's Edition, vol. 1., 1996.

4. Paul Hawken, *The Ecology of Commerce: A Declaration of Sustainability,* New York: Harper Business, 1994.

Additional books about the shadow:

Anything by Carl G. Jung.

M. Scot Peck, *People of the Lie: The Hope for Healing Human Evil,* New York: Touchstone, 1985.

Connie Zweig and Jeremiah Abrams (eds.), *Meeting the Shadow: The Hidden Power of the Dark Side of Human Nature*, New York: Tatcher Putnam, 1991.

Chapter 9

1. Frances Lappe and Paul Du Bois, *The Quickening of America: Rebuilding Our Nation, Remaking Our Lives*, San Francisco: Jossey-Bass, 1994.

2. Marianne Williamson, *The Healing of America*, New York: Simon and Schuster, 1997.

3. *Newsweek.*

Additional books about purpose:

Duane Elgin, *Voluntary Simplicity: Toward a Way of Life That Is Outwardly Simple, Inwardly Rich*, rev. ed., New York: Quill Paperbacks, 1993.

Paul Hawken, *Growing Business*, New York: Simon and Schuster Trade, 1988.

Marsha Sinetar, *Do What You Love, The Money Will Follow: Choosing Your Right Livelihood*, New York: Dell, 1989.

Chapter 10

1. George Martin and William Pearson, *With a Little Help from My Friends: The Making of Sgt. Pepper*, Boston: Little Brown, 1995.

2. Kevin Kelly, *Out of Control: The New Biology of Machines, Social Systems, and the Economic World*, Reading, MA: Addison-Wesley, 1995.

3. Brad Blanton, *Radical Honesty: How to Transform Your Life by Telling the Truth*, New York: Dell Trade Paperbacks, 1996.

4. Daniel Goleman, *Emotional Intelligence*, New York: Bantam, 1995.

Additional books about relationships:

Anything by Harville Hendrix, especially *Keeping the Love You Find*, New York: Simon and Schuster, 1993.

Anything by M. Scott Peck, especially *A World Waiting to Be Born*, New York: Bantam, 1994.

Peter Senge, *The Fifth Discipline: The Art and Practice of the Learning Organization*, New York: Bantam, 1994.

Chapter 11

1. Faith Popcorn, *Clicking: 17 Trends That Drive America*, New York: Harper Business, 1997.

2. Michael Talbot, *Holographic Universe*, New York: Harper Perennial, 1992.

Additional books about accelerating results:

Any book by Wayne Dyer.

Stephan Rechtschaffen, *Time Shifting: Creating More Time to Enjoy Your Life*, New York: Doubleday, 1997.

Chapter 12

1. William Strauss and Neil Howe, *The Fourth Turning: An American Prophecy*, New York: Broadway, 1997.

2. Fritjof Capra, *The Turning Point: Science, Society, and the Rising Culture*, New York: Doubleday, 1988; and *The Web of Life: A New Scientific Understanding of Living Systems*, New York: Doubleday, 1997.

3. Terrence McKenna, lectures and conversations.

4. Peter Russell, *A White Hole in Time: Our Future Evolution and the Meaning of Now*, San Francisco: Harper, 1993.

5. Robert Bly, *The Sibling Society*, New York: Addison-Wesley, 1996.

Additional books about a sociological view of the future:

Marilyn Ferguson, *Aquarian Conspiracy: Personal and Social Transformation in Our Time*, rev. ed., New York: Putnam Publishing Group, 1987.

Willis Harman, *Global Mind Change: The Promise of the Last Years of the Twentieth Century*, New York: Bantam, 1991.

Alvin Toffler, *Power Shift: Knowledge, Wealth, and Violence at the Edge of the 21st Century*, New York: Bantam, 1991.

About the Authors

For over 20 years, husband-and-wife team Mikela Tarlow and Philip Tarlow have led seminars around the world, including the popular "Accelerating Results" which has attracted thousands of people a year seeking new models for taking action in today's world. Mikela has a social science and organizational analysis background while Philip is an internationally recognized artist with works in major collections throughout the world. Together they bring a unique blend of the visionary and practical to their work.

The authors may be contacted as follows:

Phone: toll free 1-877-938-8873 (1-877-9FUTURE)
Fax: 719-256-4331
Mail: P.O. Box 353
Crestone, CO 81131
E-mail: tarlotym@fone.net
or visit our Web site at www.navigatingthefuture.com
We would love to hear comments, suggestions, and ideas on our material. We will also be happy to send information on our seminars, tapes, and additional materials. Just let us know what interests you.